"Paul Dini manages the impossible: a powerful tale of healing and redemption, an autobiographical story, using the cast of Batman characters to symbolize what happened inside his damaged psyche and injured body. It shouldn't work, and it does. Bravo!"

— Neil Gaiman

New York Times best-selling writer of THE SANDMAN and *American Gods*

"DARK NIGHT: A TRUE BATMAN STORY is riveting from start to finish: so revealing, so poignant, so insightful...a masterpiece."

— Mark Hamill

Actor in *Star Wars,* Voice actor in *Batman: The Animated Series* and *Batman: The Killing Joke*

"Dini's signature style of veracity and fun mixes with unprecedented courage in this powerfully crafted tale of triumph. While struggling to navigate a seemingly endless cycle of man's inhumanity to man, Dini brings us the most crucial, final frontier of true heroism: confronting the critical voices within."

— Chase Masterson

Founder of Pop Culture Hero Coalition

"Paul Dini's DARK NIGHT is breathtaking: fearless, searingly honest, heart-breaking, and, ultimately, inspiring. Combined with Eduardo Risso's gorgeous art and colors, this is a work that moves the soul and gives a naked look into the mind of an artist. An instant classic."

— Marc Andreyko

New York Times best-selling writer of FAIREST, *Manhunter* and *Wonder Woman '77*

"Moving, vulnerable and yet, somehow, often hilarious, Mr. Dini has the courage to confront his deepest fears and insecurities in a very public way. It's more brave than wearing underwear over your tights."

— Taran Killam

Writer/performer *Saturday Night Live*, creator/writer of *The Illegitimates*

"Dini takes the cliche 'write what you know' to a very dark and profound place in this extremely brave and revealing story that also uncovers Eduardo Risso at the very top of his game."

— Steven T. Seagle

Writer of IT'S A BIRD..., co-creator of *Big Hero 6*

dark night: a true batman story

dark night

a true batman story

WRITER: PAUL DINI | ARTIST AND COVER ART: EDUARDO RISSO
LETTERER: TODD KLEIN | LOGO DESIGN: CHIP KIDD
BATMAN CREATED BY BOB KANE WITH BILL FINGER

DEDICATIONS

This book is dedicated with all my heart to Misty Lee. Through her love and understanding I found the courage to throw open old doors and stand up to the lurking demons inside. I adore you.

Deepest gratitude to Kevin Smith, who prompted me to talk about the mugging on his podcast and for convincing me it was a story worth writing. You rock, Sir.

More bows than I can give to Shelly Bond, who believed in the project from the beginning, embarked with me on the journey, and made me cross the finish line when I had convinced myself I couldn't. You are the toughest coach and best friend this writer could have had.

My awe and esteem to Eduardo Risso, for the power of his images and the sensitivity of his storytelling. Your vision made the story everything I hoped it would be: terrifying, funny, sad and strong.

Thanks to Alan Burnett, who is much nicer in person than he may appear in this book. If you ever are lucky enough to work with him, you won't find a more inspiring collaborator or a kinder friend.

To Tom Ruegger, Jean MacCurdy, Steven Spielberg, Bruce Timm, Eric Radomski, Tom Minton, Sherri Stoner, Randy Rogel, Michael Reaves, Martin Pasko, Kevin Conroy, Mark Hamill and so many bright talents who made WB Animation a magical place to be way back when.

To Ruth and Rob Clampett and to Neil Gaiman for generously allowing their marvelous creations to appear in this story.

To Dan DiDio and Geoff Johns for encouraging and supporting the project, and to Jack Mahan for the year's worth of rights wrangling that made it possible.

To Stephen Langford, Barry Caldwell, Flint Dille, Eddie Gorodetsky, Mark Evanier, Alex Ross, David Mandel, Gordon Kent and Richard Howell, heroes all who got me through many a dark night over the last 23 years.

To Chip Kidd for his encouragement, friendship and stunning sense of design.

To David Alvarez for Ivan Ivorybill.

To Arleen Sorkin for Harley, and for the blender.

To Mom, Dad, Bruce, Steve and especially Jane. And of course, Worf, Deuce, Mugsy, Pixie and the Tank.

—Paul Dini

To all the editors who have trusted and supported me unconditionally in each project I have undertaken throughout my time at DC Comics.

To my beloved wife and children, because they've stayed with me through every single moment. To my dear family, mother, brothers, relatives, friends... because they give me the opportunity to appreciate and learn the meaning of life every day.

—Eduardo Risso

Shelly Bond Editor **Rowena Yow** Associate Editor
Steve Cook Design Director – Books **Louis Prandi** Publication Design

Shelly Bond VP & Executive Editor – Vertigo

Diane Nelson President **Dan DiDio** and **Jim Lee** Co-Publishers
Geoff Johns Chief Creative Officer **Amit Desai** Senior VP – Marketing & Global Franchise Management
Nairi Gardiner Senior VP – Finance **Sam Ades** VP – Digital Marketing
Bobbie Chase VP – Talent Development **Mark Chiarello** Senior VP – Art, Design & Collected Editions
John Cunningham VP – Content Strategy **Anne DePies** VP – Strategy Planning & Reporting
Don Falletti VP – Manufacturing Operations **Lawrence Ganem** VP – Editorial Administration & Talent Relations
Alison Gill Senior VP – Manufacturing & Operations **Hank Kanalz** Senior VP – Editorial Strategy & Administration
Jay Kogan VP – Legal Affairs **Derek Maddalena** Senior VP – Sales & Business Development
Jack Mahan VP – Business Affairs **Dan Miron** VP – Sales Planning & Trade Development
Nick Napolitano VP – Manufacturing Administration **Carol Roeder** VP – Marketing
Eddie Scannell VP – Mass Account & Digital Sales **Courtney Simmons** Senior VP – Publicity & Communications
Jim (Ski) Sokolowski VP – Comic Book Specialty & Newsstand Sales **Sandy Yi** Senior VP – Global Franchise Management

Library of Congress Cataloging-in-Publication Data is Available.

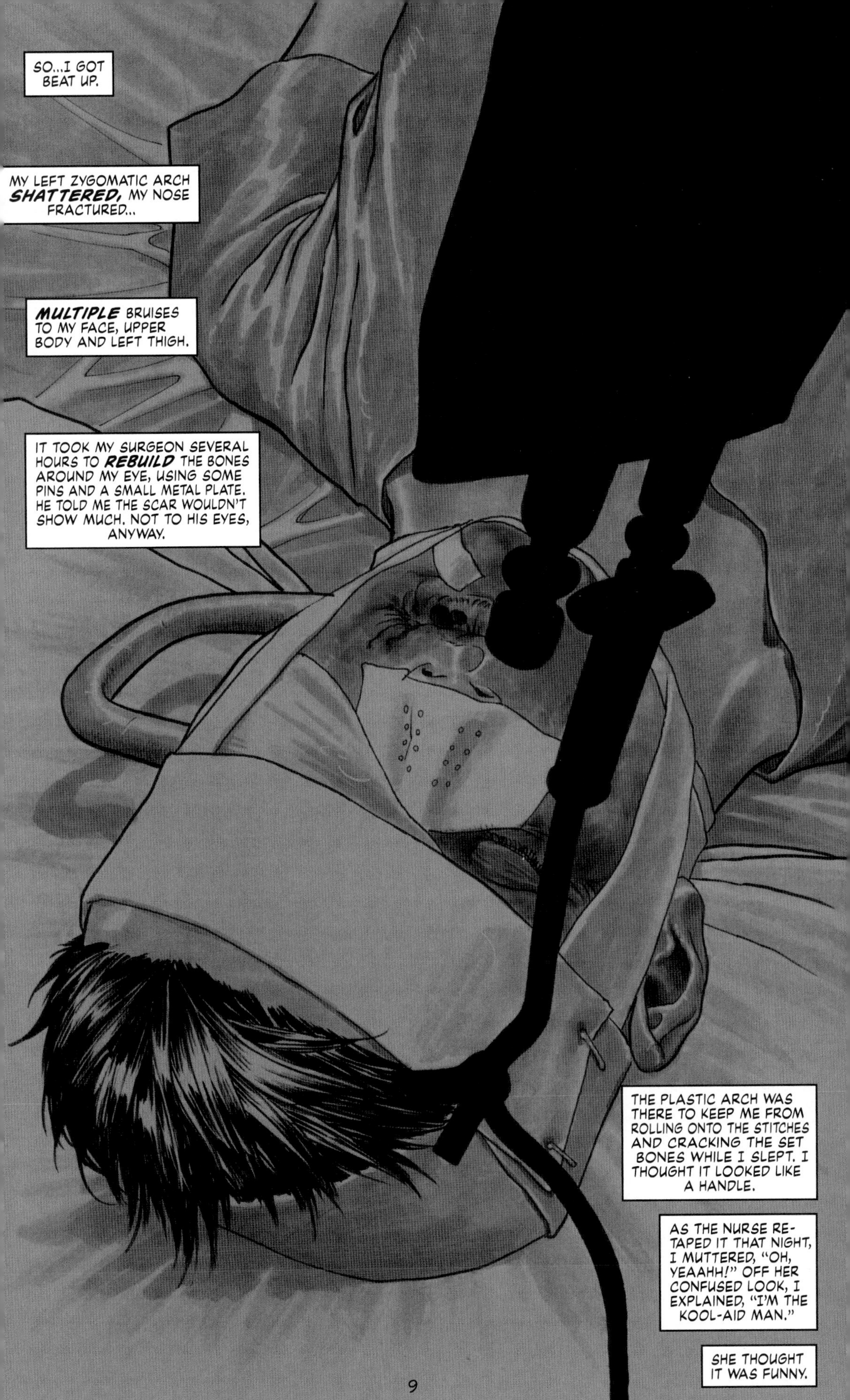
SO...I GOT BEAT UP.
MY LEFT ZYGOMATIC ARCH SHATTERED, MY NOSE FRACTURED...
MULTIPLE BRUISES TO MY FACE, UPPER BODY AND LEFT THIGH.
IT TOOK MY SURGEON SEVERAL HOURS TO REBUILD THE BONES AROUND MY EYE, USING SOME PINS AND A SMALL METAL PLATE. HE TOLD ME THE SCAR WOULDN'T SHOW MUCH. NOT TO HIS EYES, ANYWAY.
THE PLASTIC ARCH WAS THERE TO KEEP ME FROM ROLLING ONTO THE STITCHES AND CRACKING THE SET BONES WHILE I SLEPT. I THOUGHT IT LOOKED LIKE A HANDLE.
AS THE NURSE RE-TAPED IT THAT NIGHT, I MUTTERED, "OH, YEAAHH!" OFF HER CONFUSED LOOK, I EXPLAINED, "I'M THE KOOL-AID MAN."
SHE THOUGHT IT WAS FUNNY.

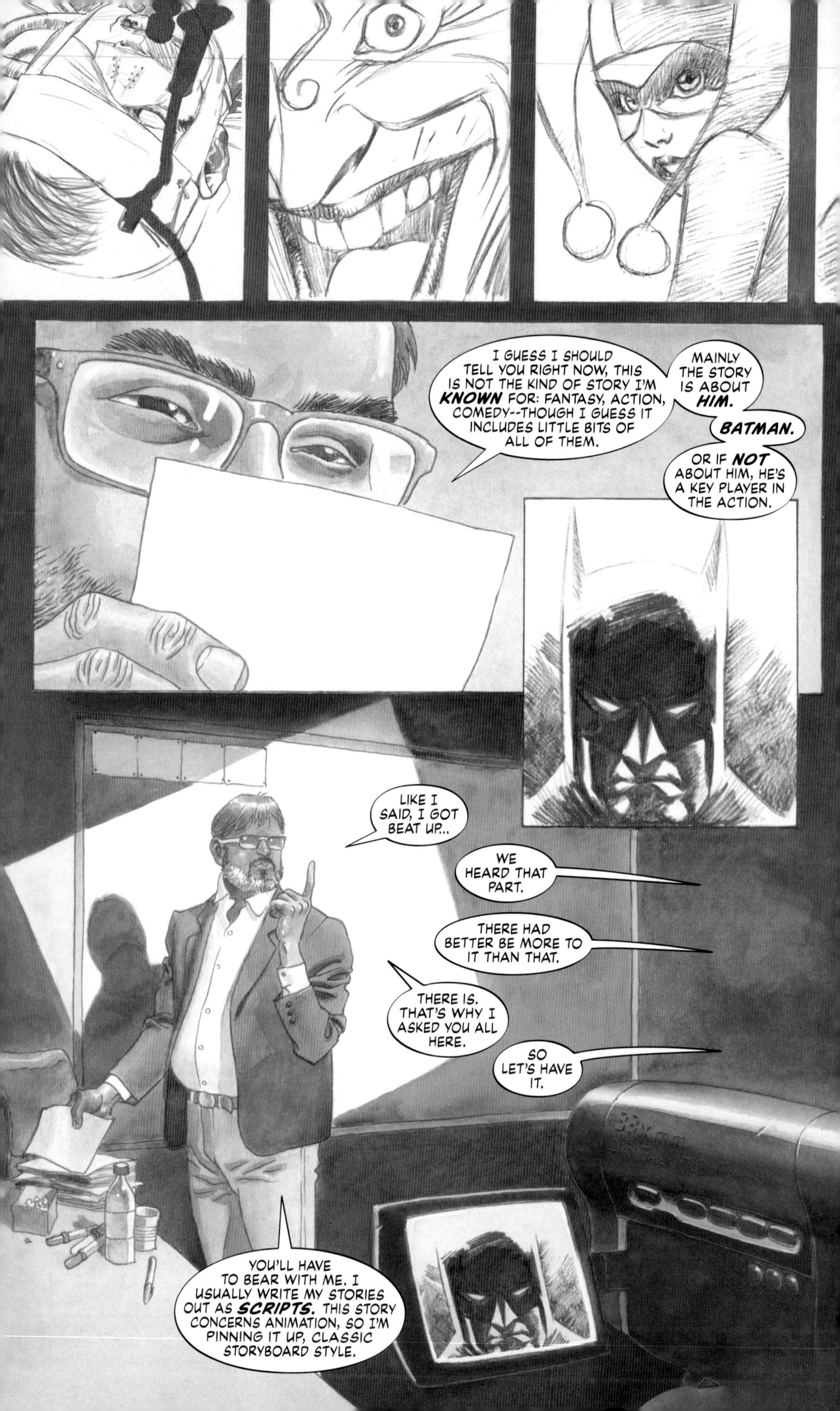
I GUESS I SHOULD TELL YOU RIGHT NOW, THIS IS NOT THE KIND OF STORY I'M **KNOWN** FOR: FANTASY, ACTION, COMEDY--THOUGH I GUESS IT INCLUDES LITTLE BITS OF ALL OF THEM.
MAINLY THE STORY IS ABOUT **HIM.**
BATMAN.
OR IF **NOT** ABOUT HIM, HE'S A KEY PLAYER IN THE ACTION.
LIKE I SAID, I GOT BEAT UP...
WE HEARD THAT PART.
THERE HAD BETTER BE MORE TO IT THAN THAT.
THERE IS. THAT'S WHY I ASKED YOU ALL HERE.
SO LET'S HAVE IT.
YOU'LL HAVE TO BEAR WITH ME. I USUALLY WRITE MY STORIES OUT AS **SCRIPTS.** THIS STORY CONCERNS ANIMATION, SO I'M PINNING IT UP, CLASSIC STORYBOARD STYLE.

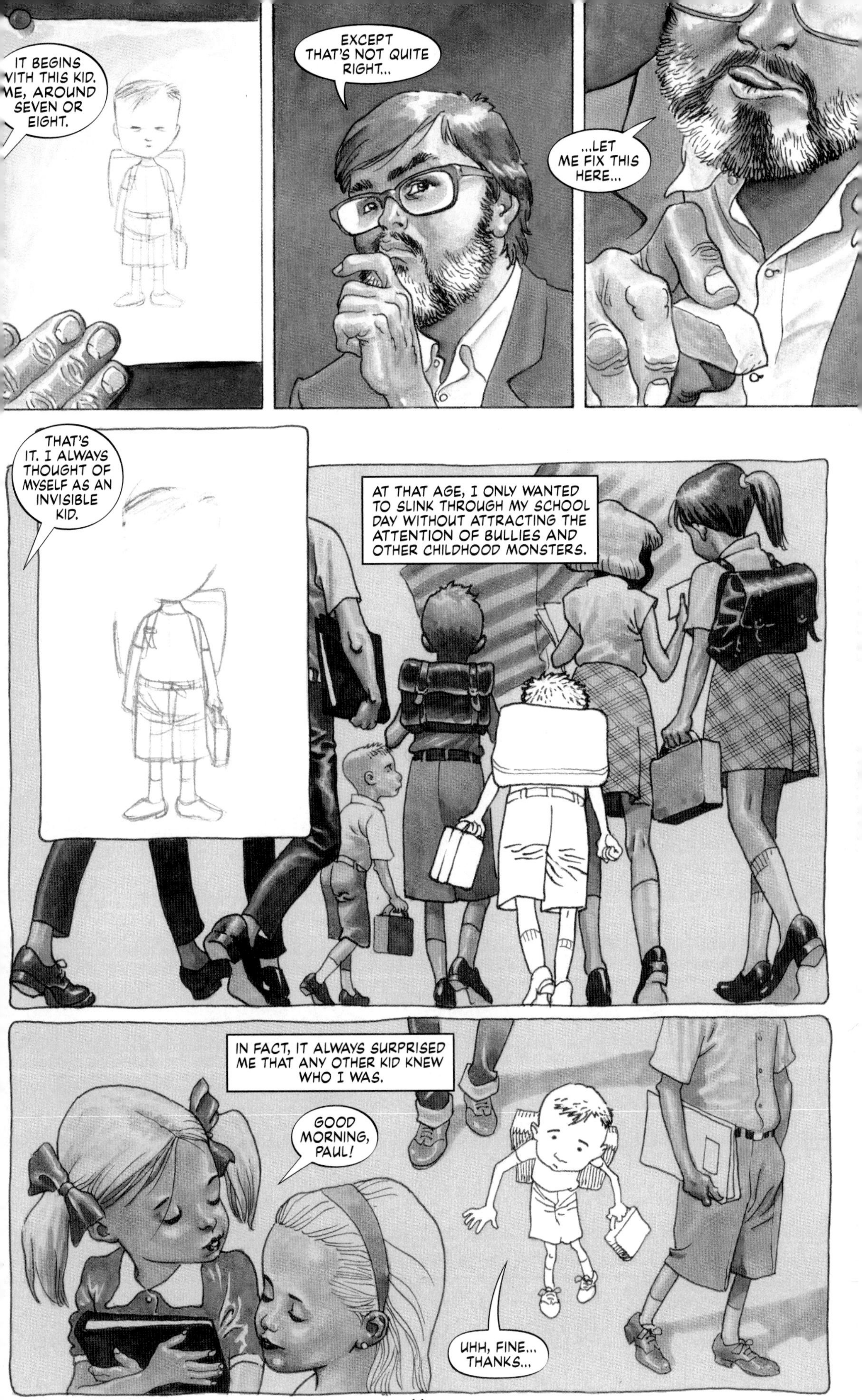

IT BEGINS VITH THIS KID. ME, AROUND SEVEN OR EIGHT.
EXCEPT THAT'S NOT QUITE RIGHT...
...LET ME FIX THIS HERE...
THAT'S IT. I ALWAYS THOUGHT OF MYSELF AS AN INVISIBLE KID.
AT THAT AGE, I ONLY WANTED TO SLINK THROUGH MY SCHOOL DAY WITHOUT ATTRACTING THE ATTENTION OF BULLIES AND OTHER CHILDHOOD MONSTERS.
IN FACT, IT ALWAYS SURPRISED ME THAT ANY OTHER KID KNEW WHO I WAS.
GOOD MORNING, PAUL!
UHH, FINE... THANKS...

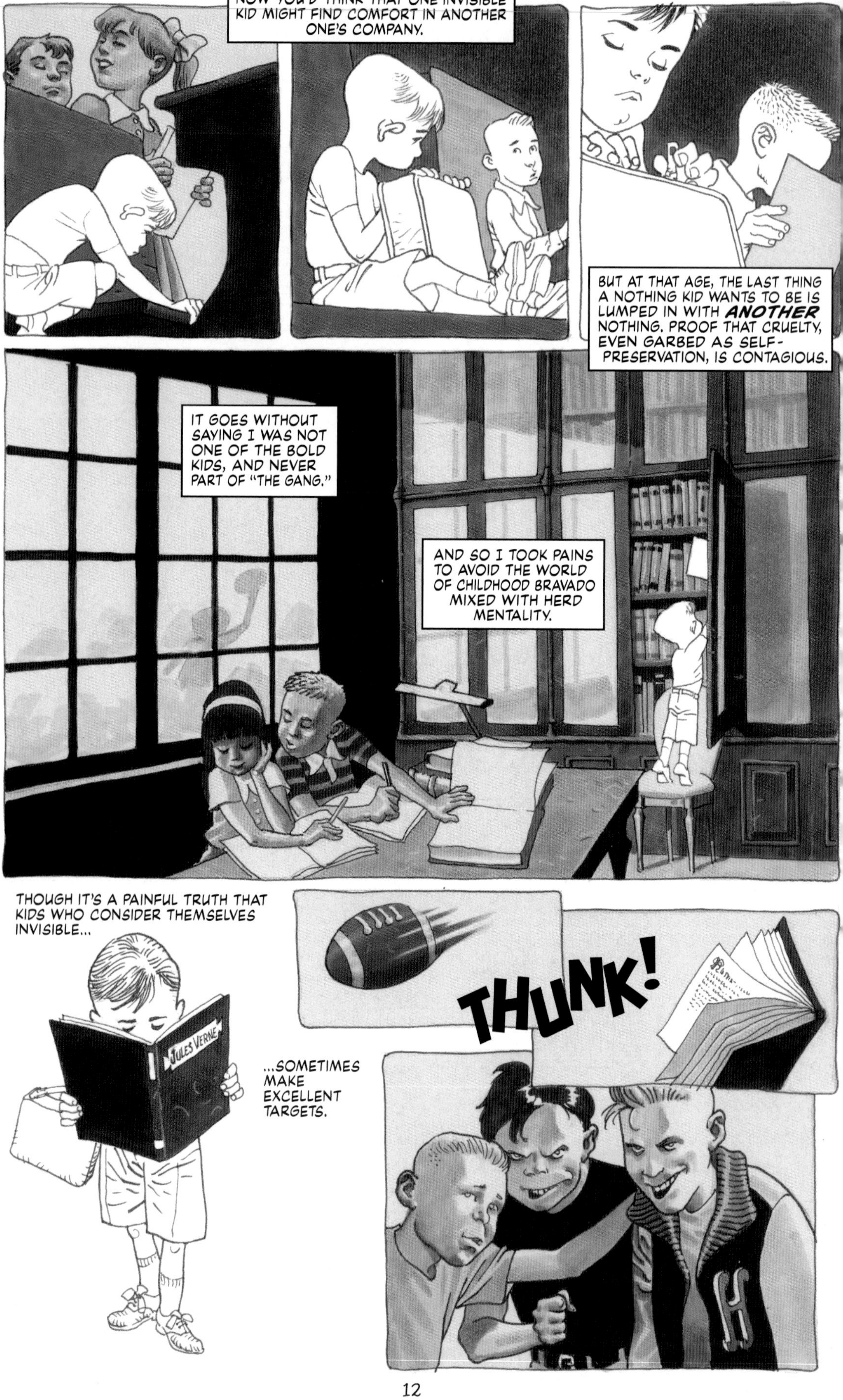
NOW YOU'D THINK THAT ONE INVISIBLE KID MIGHT FIND COMFORT IN ANOTHER ONE'S COMPANY.
BUT AT THAT AGE, THE LAST THING A NOTHING KID WANTS TO BE IS LUMPED IN WITH ANOTHER NOTHING. PROOF THAT CRUELTY, EVEN GARBED AS SELF-PRESERVATION, IS CONTAGIOUS.
IT GOES WITHOUT SAYING I WAS NOT ONE OF THE BOLD KIDS, AND NEVER PART OF "THE GANG."
AND SO I TOOK PAINS TO AVOID THE WORLD OF CHILDHOOD BRAVADO MIXED WITH HERD MENTALITY.
THOUGH IT'S A PAINFUL TRUTH THAT KIDS WHO CONSIDER THEMSELVES INVISIBLE...
JULES VERNE
...SOMETIMES MAKE EXCELLENT TARGETS.
THUNK!

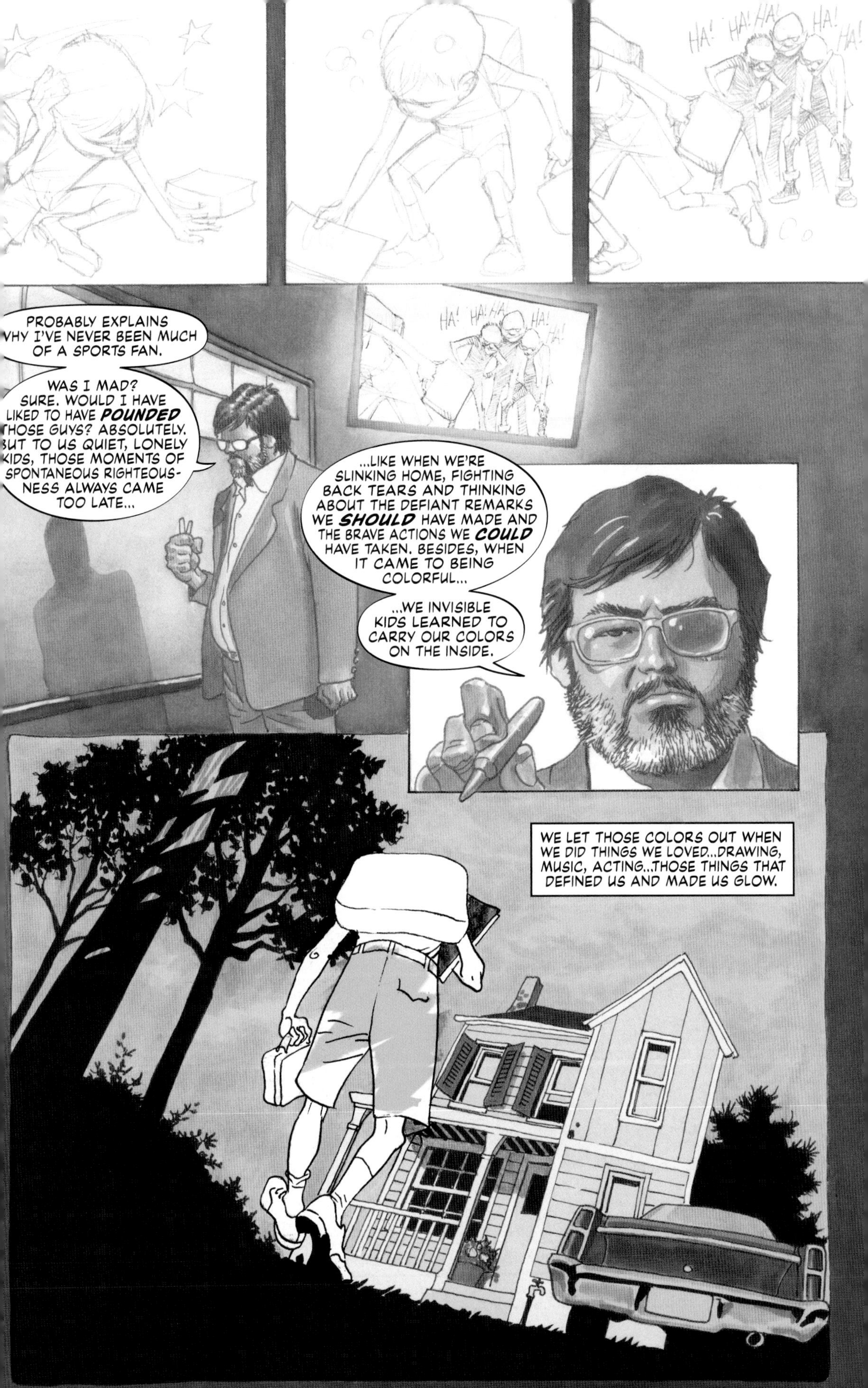
HA! HA! HA! HA! HA!
PROBABLY EXPLAINS WHY I'VE NEVER BEEN MUCH OF A SPORTS FAN.
WAS I MAD? SURE. WOULD I HAVE LIKED TO HAVE **POUNDED** THOSE GUYS? ABSOLUTELY. BUT TO US QUIET, LONELY KIDS, THOSE MOMENTS OF SPONTANEOUS RIGHTEOUS-NESS ALWAYS CAME TOO LATE...
...LIKE WHEN WE'RE SLINKING HOME, FIGHTING BACK TEARS AND THINKING ABOUT THE DEFIANT REMARKS WE **SHOULD** HAVE MADE AND THE BRAVE ACTIONS WE **COULD** HAVE TAKEN. BESIDES, WHEN IT CAME TO BEING COLORFUL...
...WE INVISIBLE KIDS LEARNED TO CARRY OUR COLORS ON THE INSIDE.
WE LET THOSE COLORS OUT WHEN WE DID THINGS WE LOVED...DRAWING, MUSIC, ACTING...THOSE THINGS THAT DEFINED US AND MADE US GLOW.

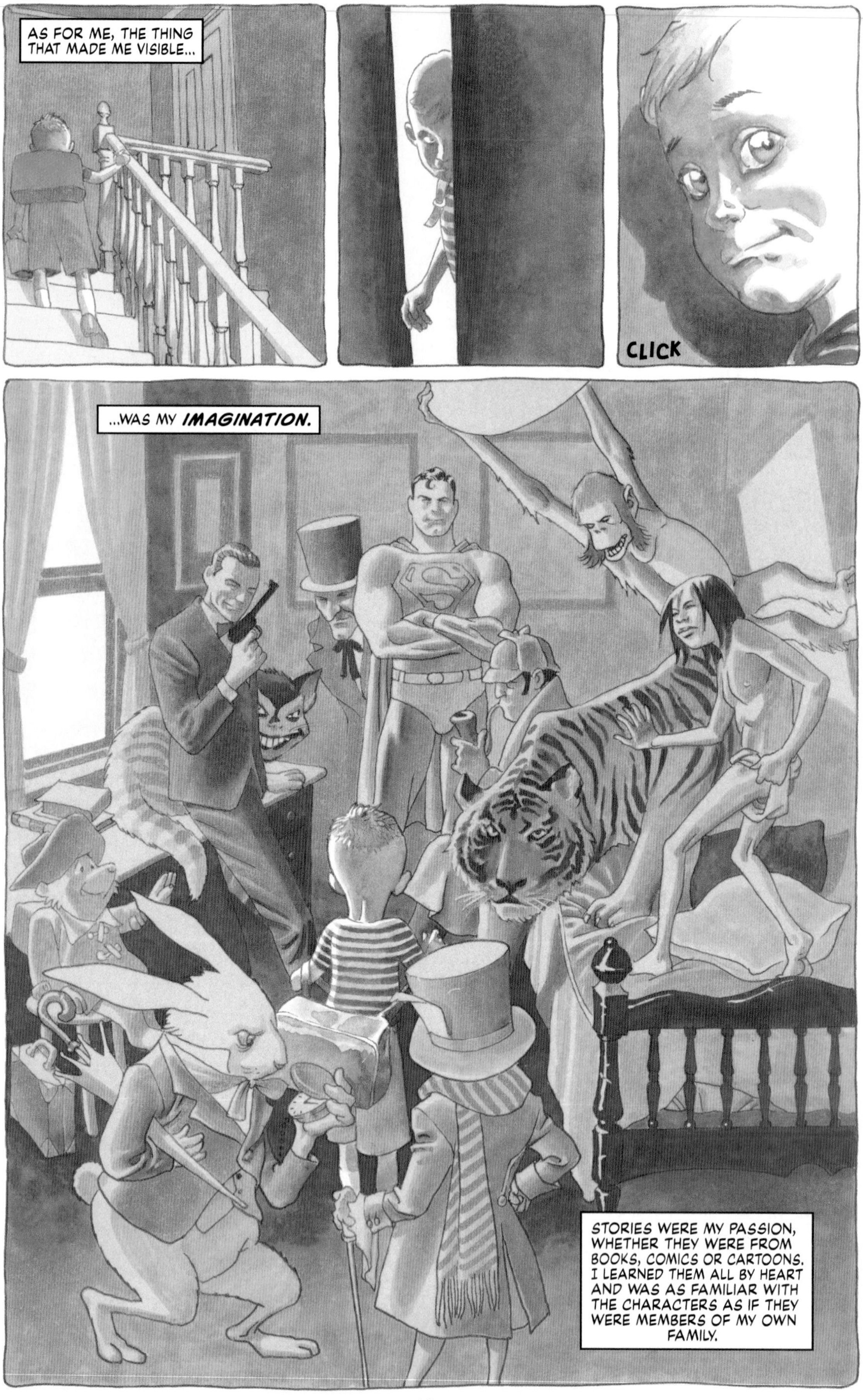
AS FOR ME, THE THING THAT MADE ME VISIBLE...
CLICK
...WAS MY IMAGINATION.
STORIES WERE MY PASSION, WHETHER THEY WERE FROM BOOKS, COMICS OR CARTOONS. I LEARNED THEM ALL BY HEART AND WAS AS FAMILIAR WITH THE CHARACTERS AS IF THEY WERE MEMBERS OF MY OWN FAMILY.

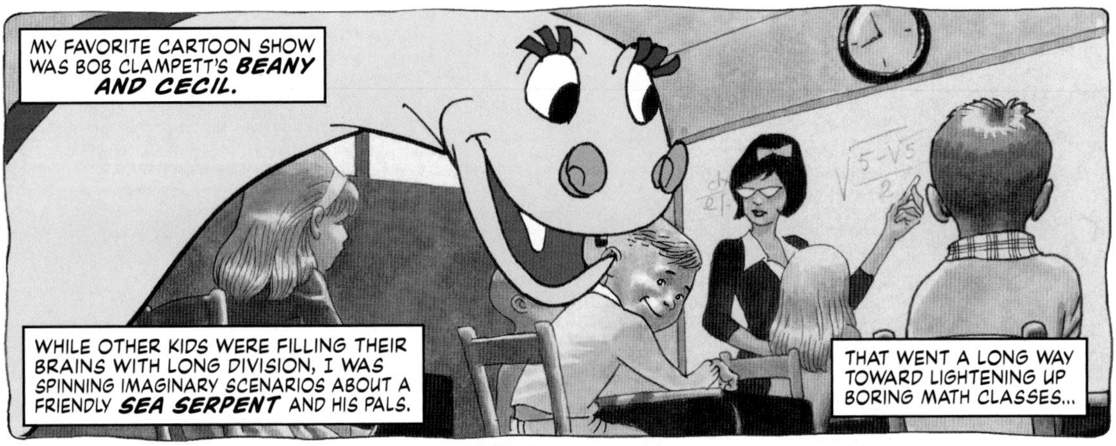
MY FAVORITE CARTOON SHOW WAS BOB CLAMPETT'S BEANY AND CECIL.
WHILE OTHER KIDS WERE FILLING THEIR BRAINS WITH LONG DIVISION, I WAS SPINNING IMAGINARY SCENARIOS ABOUT A FRIENDLY SEA SERPENT AND HIS PALS.
THAT WENT A LONG WAY TOWARD LIGHTENING UP BORING MATH CLASSES...

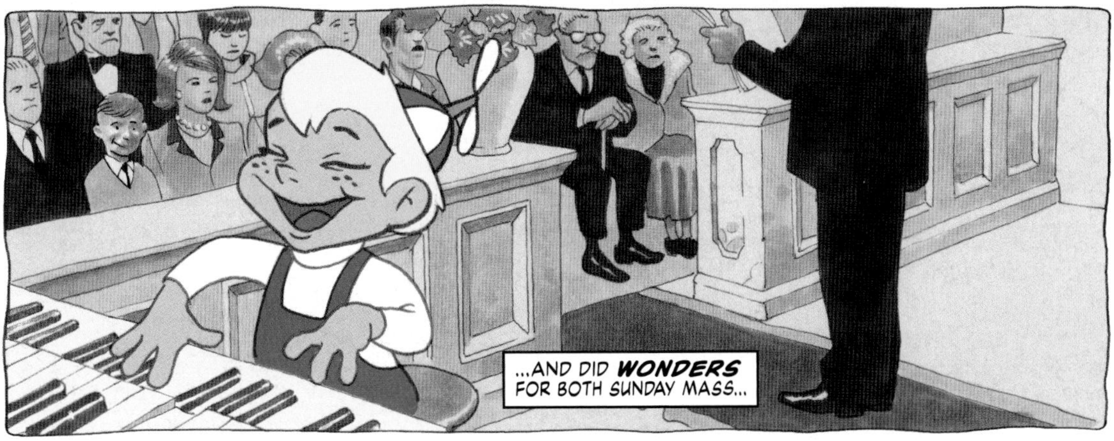
...AND DID WONDERS FOR BOTH SUNDAY MASS...

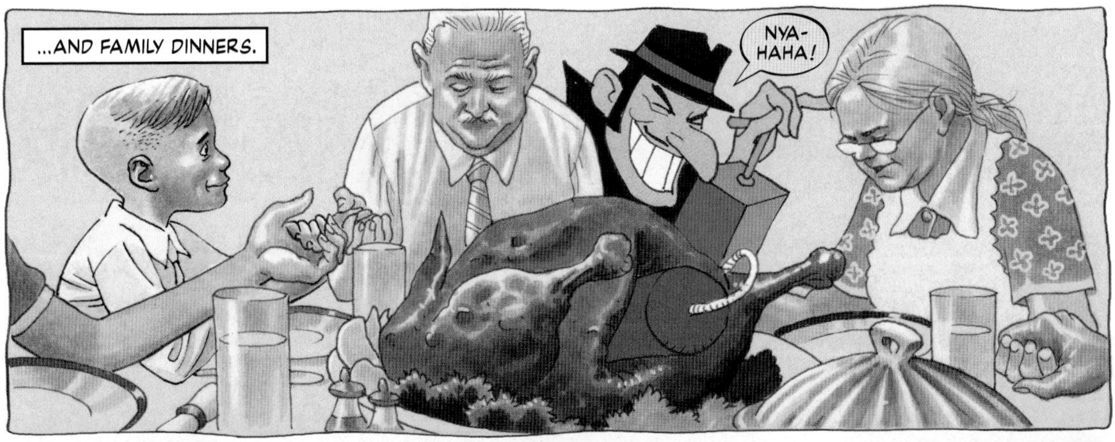
...AND FAMILY DINNERS.
NYA-HAHA!

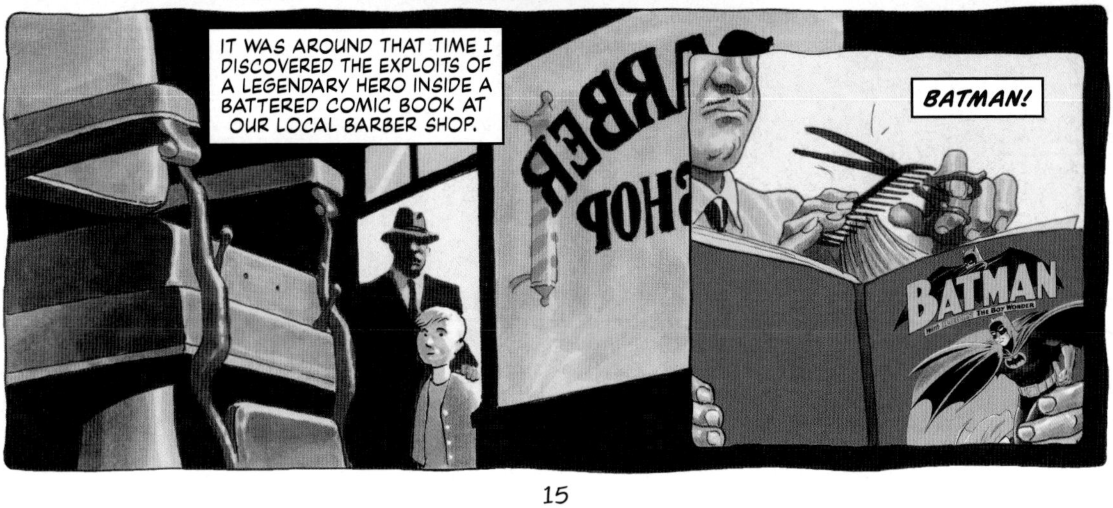
IT WAS AROUND THAT TIME I DISCOVERED THE EXPLOITS OF A LEGENDARY HERO INSIDE A BATTERED COMIC BOOK AT OUR LOCAL BARBER SHOP.
BATMAN!
BATMAN

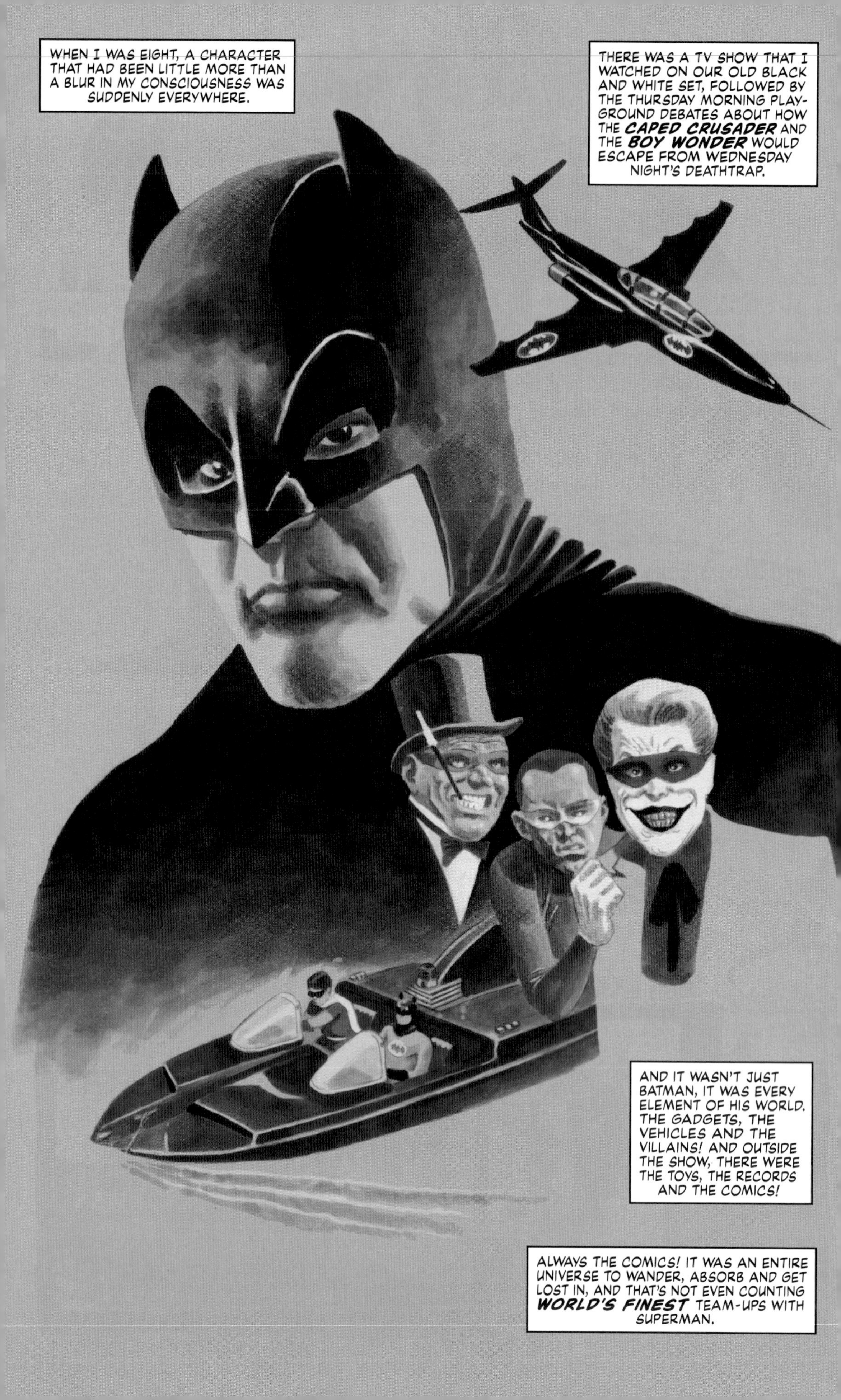

WHEN I WAS EIGHT, A CHARACTER THAT HAD BEEN LITTLE MORE THAN A BLUR IN MY CONSCIOUSNESS WAS SUDDENLY EVERYWHERE.
THERE WAS A TV SHOW THAT I WATCHED ON OUR OLD BLACK AND WHITE SET, FOLLOWED BY THE THURSDAY MORNING PLAY-GROUND DEBATES ABOUT HOW THE ***CAPED CRUSADER*** AND THE ***BOY WONDER*** WOULD ESCAPE FROM WEDNESDAY NIGHT'S DEATHTRAP.
AND IT WASN'T JUST BATMAN, IT WAS EVERY ELEMENT OF HIS WORLD. THE GADGETS, THE VEHICLES AND THE VILLAINS! AND OUTSIDE THE SHOW, THERE WERE THE TOYS, THE RECORDS AND THE COMICS!
ALWAYS THE COMICS! IT WAS AN ENTIRE UNIVERSE TO WANDER, ABSORB AND GET LOST IN, AND THAT'S NOT EVEN COUNTING ***WORLD'S FINEST*** TEAM-UPS WITH SUPERMAN.

BATMAN, ALONG WITH OTHER COMIC BOOKS AND COMIC STRIPS, INSPIRED ME TO CREATE MY OWN CHARACTERS. DERIVATIVE AND POORLY RENDERED, OF COURSE, BUT I HAD MADE THAT PROVERBIAL FIRST STEP TOWARD BECOMING A CREATOR.
I'LL ALWAYS BE GRATEFUL TO MOM AND DAD FOR THEIR ENCOURAGEMENT.
BUT ART WAS ONE THING, AND A NEAR-TOTAL DISCONNECT FROM THE REST OF MY SCHOOLWORK WAS ANOTHER.
SO AFTER A WHILE, PROFESSIONAL HELP WAS CONSULTED.
MY PSYCHOLOGIST GAVE ME MODELS TO BUILD WHILE WE DISCUSSED MY ANXIETIES AND GENERALLY POOR SCHOOL PERFORMANCE. IT KEPT MY MIND FOCUSED. MOSTLY.
DR. BENJAMIN
PSYCHOLOGIST
THIS REALLY MAKES NO SENSE. I MEAN, BATMAN LIVES IN THE CITY, NOT THE WOODS.
WHY WOULD THEY MAKE A MODEL KIT OF HIM AND HAVE HIM SWINGING THROUGH THE TREES LIKE TARZAN?

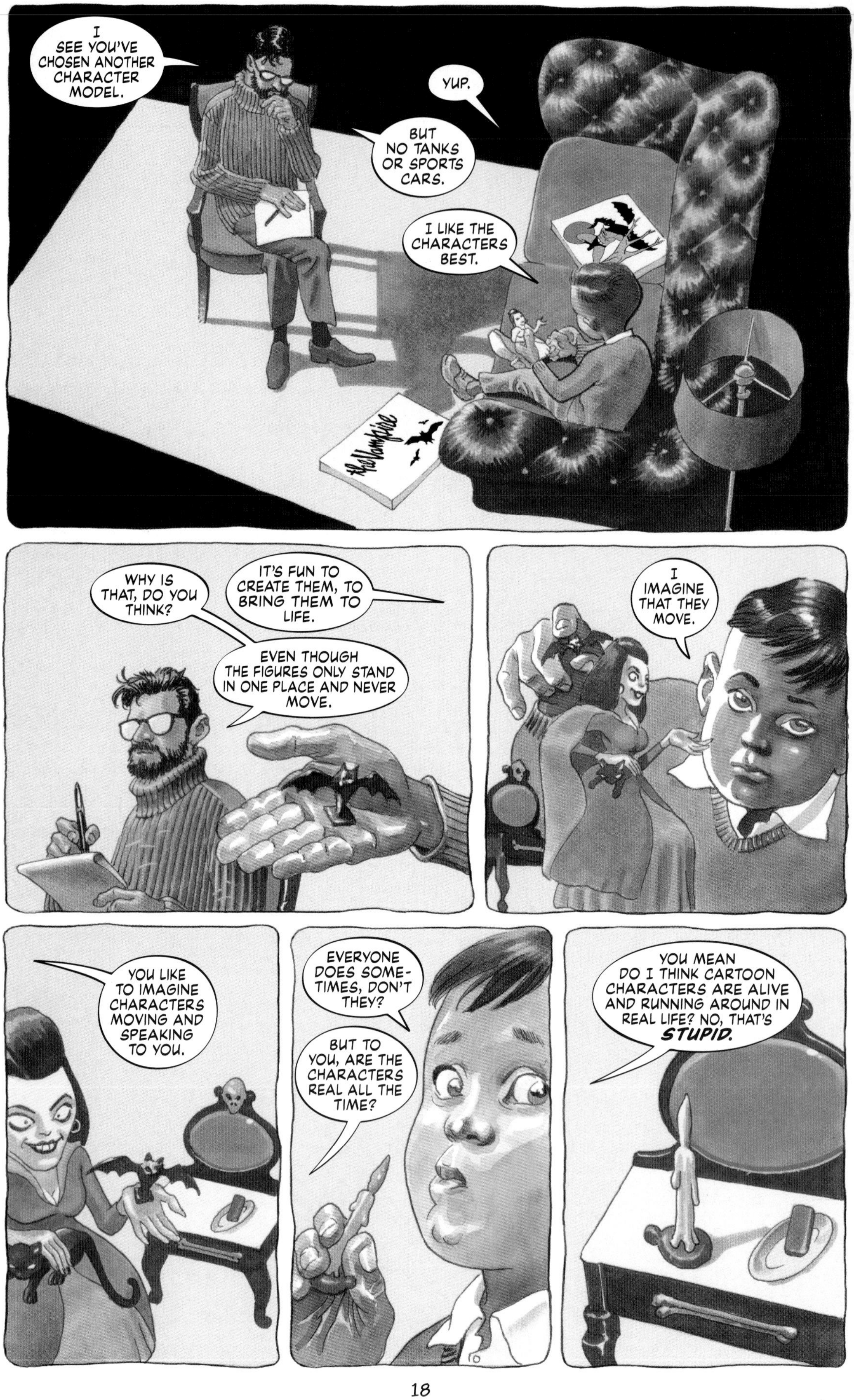
I SEE YOU'VE CHOSEN ANOTHER CHARACTER MODEL.
YUP.
BUT NO TANKS OR SPORTS CARS.
I LIKE THE CHARACTERS BEST.
WHY IS THAT, DO YOU THINK?
IT'S FUN TO CREATE THEM, TO BRING THEM TO LIFE.
EVEN THOUGH THE FIGURES ONLY STAND IN ONE PLACE AND NEVER MOVE.
I IMAGINE THAT THEY MOVE.
YOU LIKE TO IMAGINE CHARACTERS MOVING AND SPEAKING TO YOU.
EVERYONE DOES SOME-TIMES, DON'T THEY?
BUT TO YOU, ARE THE CHARACTERS REAL ALL THE TIME?
YOU MEAN DO I THINK CARTOON CHARACTERS ARE ALIVE AND RUNNING AROUND IN REAL LIFE? NO, THAT'S ***STUPID.***

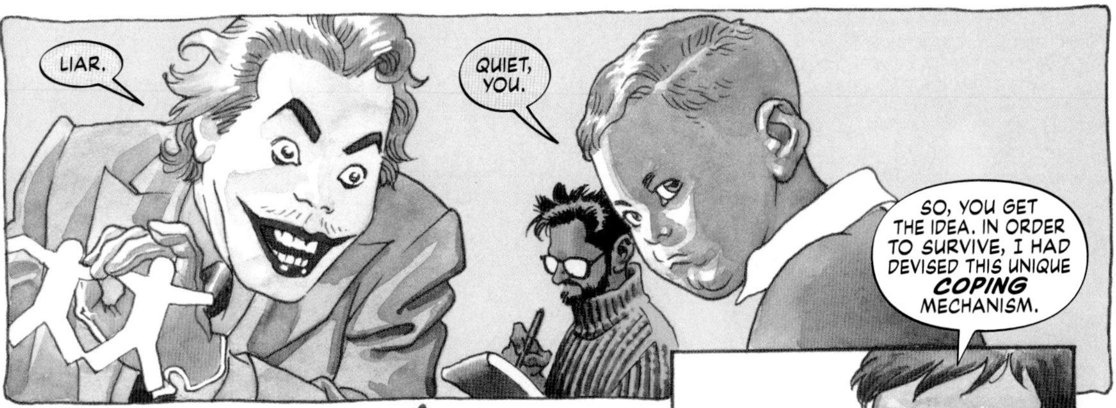
LIAR.
QUIET, YOU.
SO, YOU GET THE IDEA. IN ORDER TO SURVIVE, I HAD DEVISED THIS UNIQUE COPING MECHANISM.

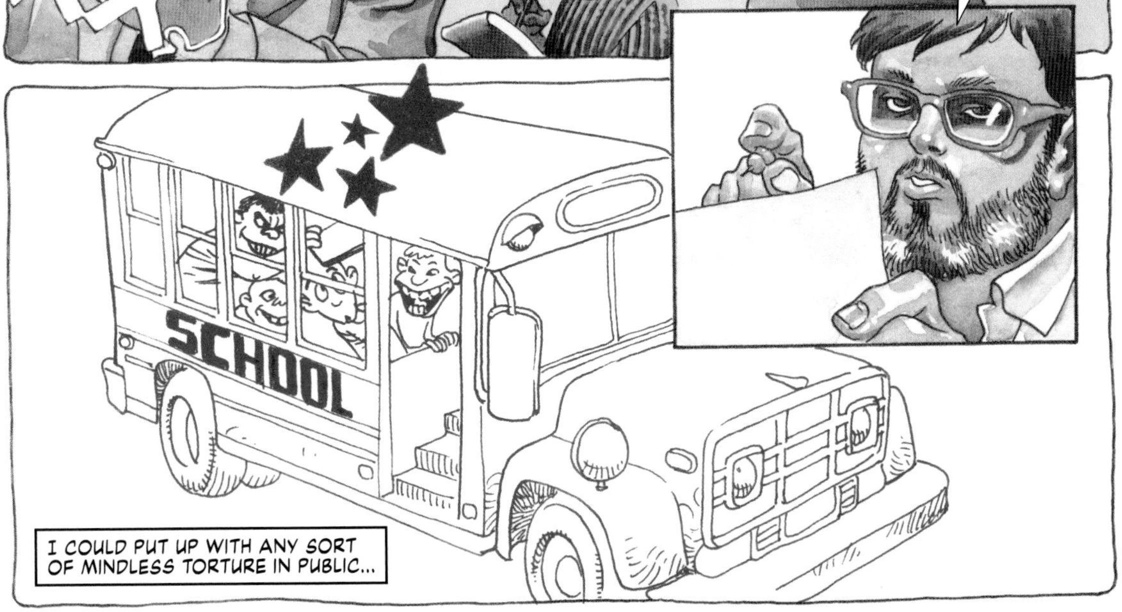
SCHOOL
I COULD PUT UP WITH ANY SORT OF MINDLESS TORTURE IN PUBLIC...

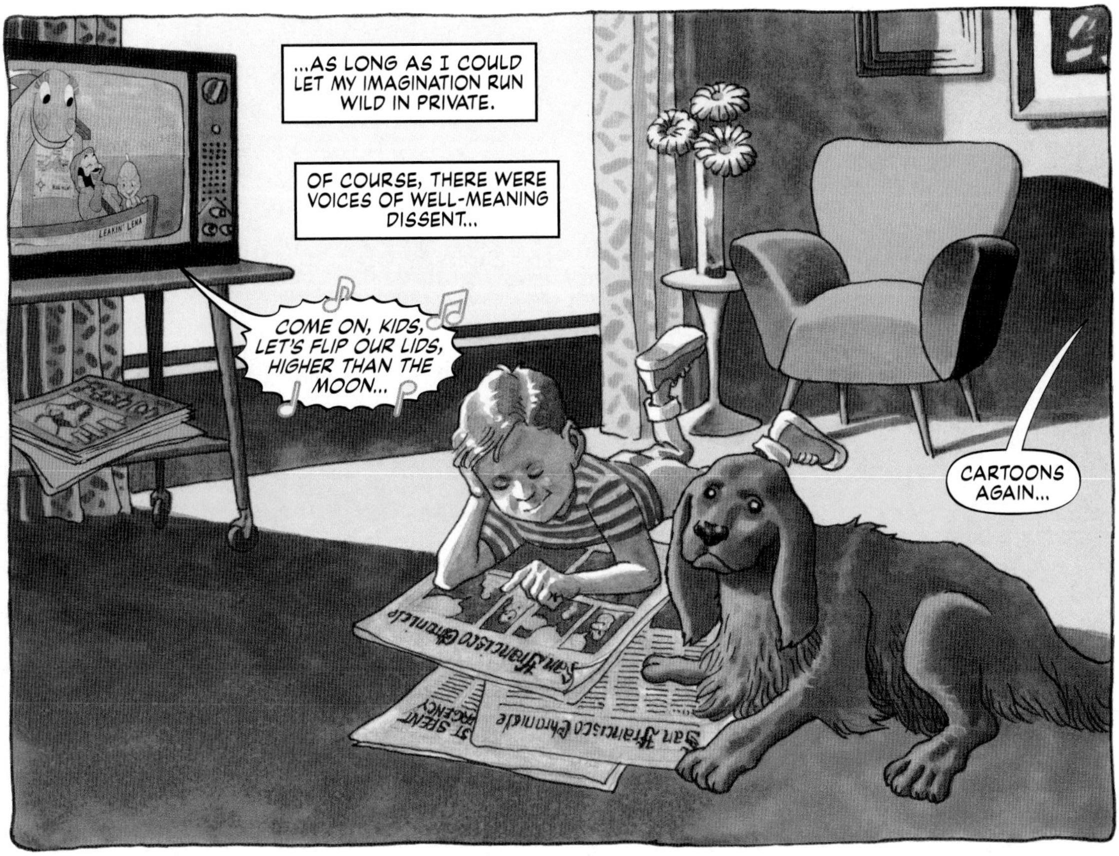
...AS LONG AS I COULD LET MY IMAGINATION RUN WILD IN PRIVATE.
OF COURSE, THERE WERE VOICES OF WELL-MEANING DISSENT...
LEAKIN' LENA
COME ON, KIDS, LET'S FLIP OUR LIDS, HIGHER THAN THE MOON...
CARTOONS AGAIN...
San Francisco Chronicle
San Francisco Chronicle

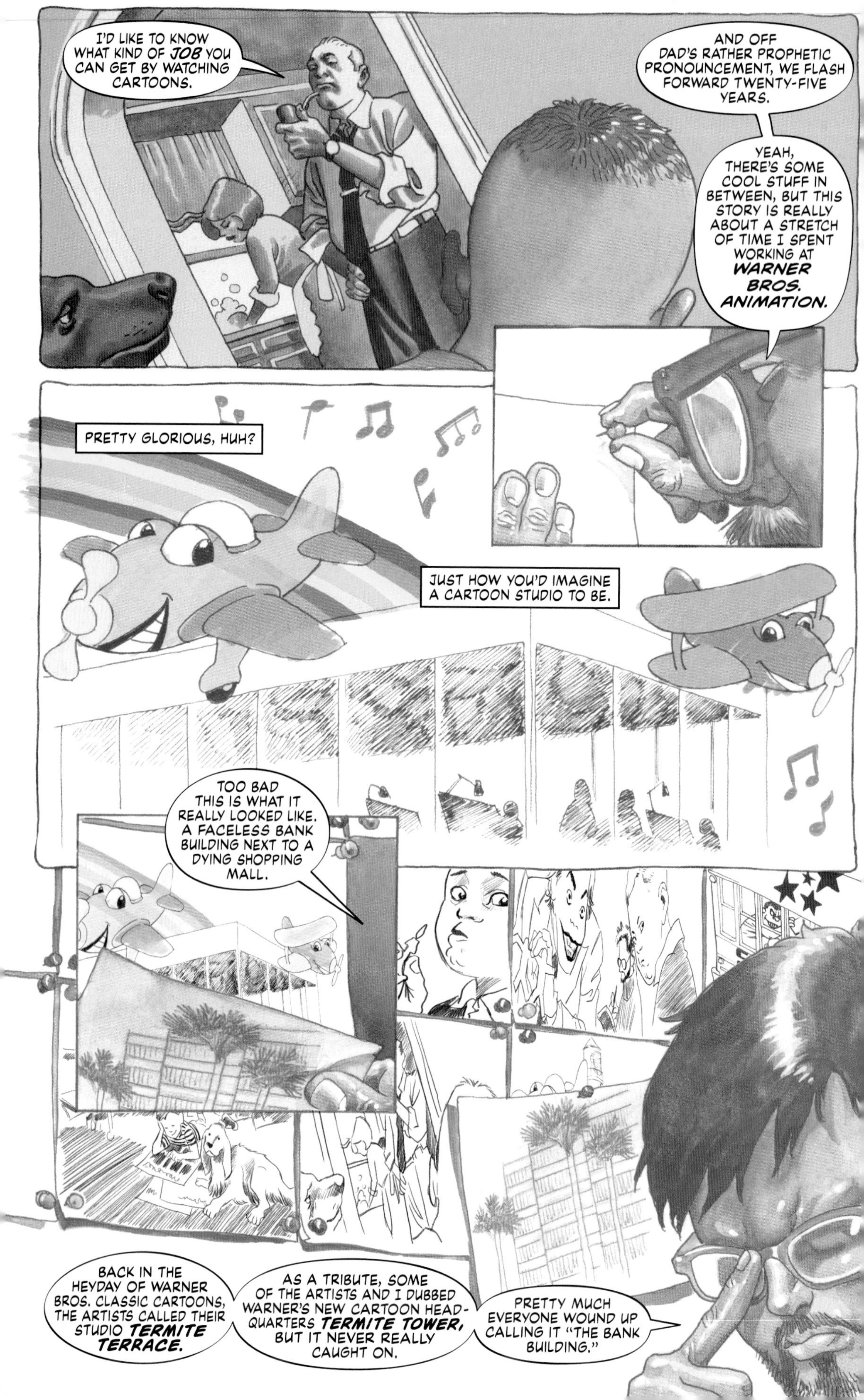

I'D LIKE TO KNOW WHAT KIND OF JOB YOU CAN GET BY WATCHING CARTOONS.
AND OFF DAD'S RATHER PROPHETIC PRONOUNCEMENT, WE FLASH FORWARD TWENTY-FIVE YEARS.
YEAH, THERE'S SOME COOL STUFF IN BETWEEN, BUT THIS STORY IS REALLY ABOUT A STRETCH OF TIME I SPENT WORKING AT WARNER BROS. ANIMATION.
PRETTY GLORIOUS, HUH?
JUST HOW YOU'D IMAGINE A CARTOON STUDIO TO BE.
TOO BAD THIS IS WHAT IT REALLY LOOKED LIKE. A FACELESS BANK BUILDING NEXT TO A DYING SHOPPING MALL.
BACK IN THE HEYDAY OF WARNER BROS. CLASSIC CARTOONS, THE ARTISTS CALLED THEIR STUDIO TERMITE TERRACE.
AS A TRIBUTE, SOME OF THE ARTISTS AND I DUBBED WARNER'S NEW CARTOON HEAD-QUARTERS TERMITE TOWER, BUT IT NEVER REALLY CAUGHT ON.
PRETTY MUCH EVERYONE WOUND UP CALLING IT "THE BANK BUILDING."

AND WHILE IT MAY HAVE BEEN DRAB ON THE **OUTSIDE,** INSIDE THE FLOORS WERE PULSING WITH THE ENTHUSIASM OF ARTISTS AND WRITERS ANXIOUS TO REVIVE THE WARNER ANIMATION LEGACY.

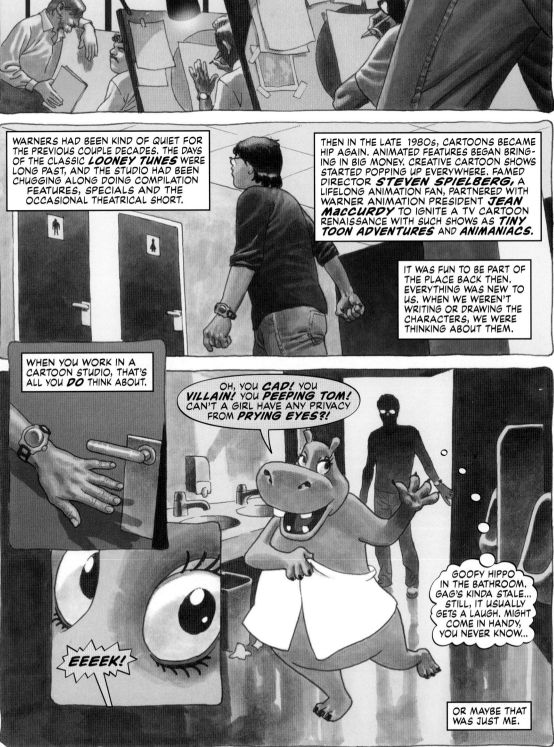

WARNERS HAD BEEN KIND OF QUIET FOR THE PREVIOUS COUPLE DECADES. THE DAYS OF THE CLASSIC **LOONEY TUNES** WERE LONG PAST, AND THE STUDIO HAD BEEN CHUGGING ALONG DOING COMPILATION FEATURES, SPECIALS AND THE OCCASIONAL THEATRICAL SHORT.

THEN IN THE LATE 1980s, CARTOONS BECAME HIP AGAIN. ANIMATED FEATURES BEGAN BRINGING IN BIG MONEY. CREATIVE CARTOON SHOWS STARTED POPPING UP EVERYWHERE. FAMED DIRECTOR **STEVEN SPIELBERG,** A LIFELONG ANIMATION FAN, PARTNERED WITH WARNER ANIMATION PRESIDENT **JEAN MacCURDY** TO IGNITE A TV CARTOON RENAISSANCE WITH SUCH SHOWS AS **TINY TOON ADVENTURES** AND **ANIMANIACS.**

IT WAS FUN TO BE PART OF THE PLACE BACK THEN. EVERYTHING WAS NEW TO US. WHEN WE WEREN'T WRITING OR DRAWING THE CHARACTERS, WE WERE THINKING ABOUT THEM.

WHEN YOU WORK IN A CARTOON STUDIO, THAT'S ALL YOU **DO** THINK ABOUT.

OH, YOU **CAD!** YOU **VILLAIN!** YOU **PEEPING TOM!** CAN'T A GIRL HAVE ANY PRIVACY FROM **PRYING EYES?!**

GOOFY HIPPO IN THE BATHROOM. GAG'S KINDA STALE... STILL, IT USUALLY GETS A LAUGH. MIGHT COME IN HANDY, YOU NEVER KNOW...

EEEEK!

OR MAYBE THAT WAS JUST ME.

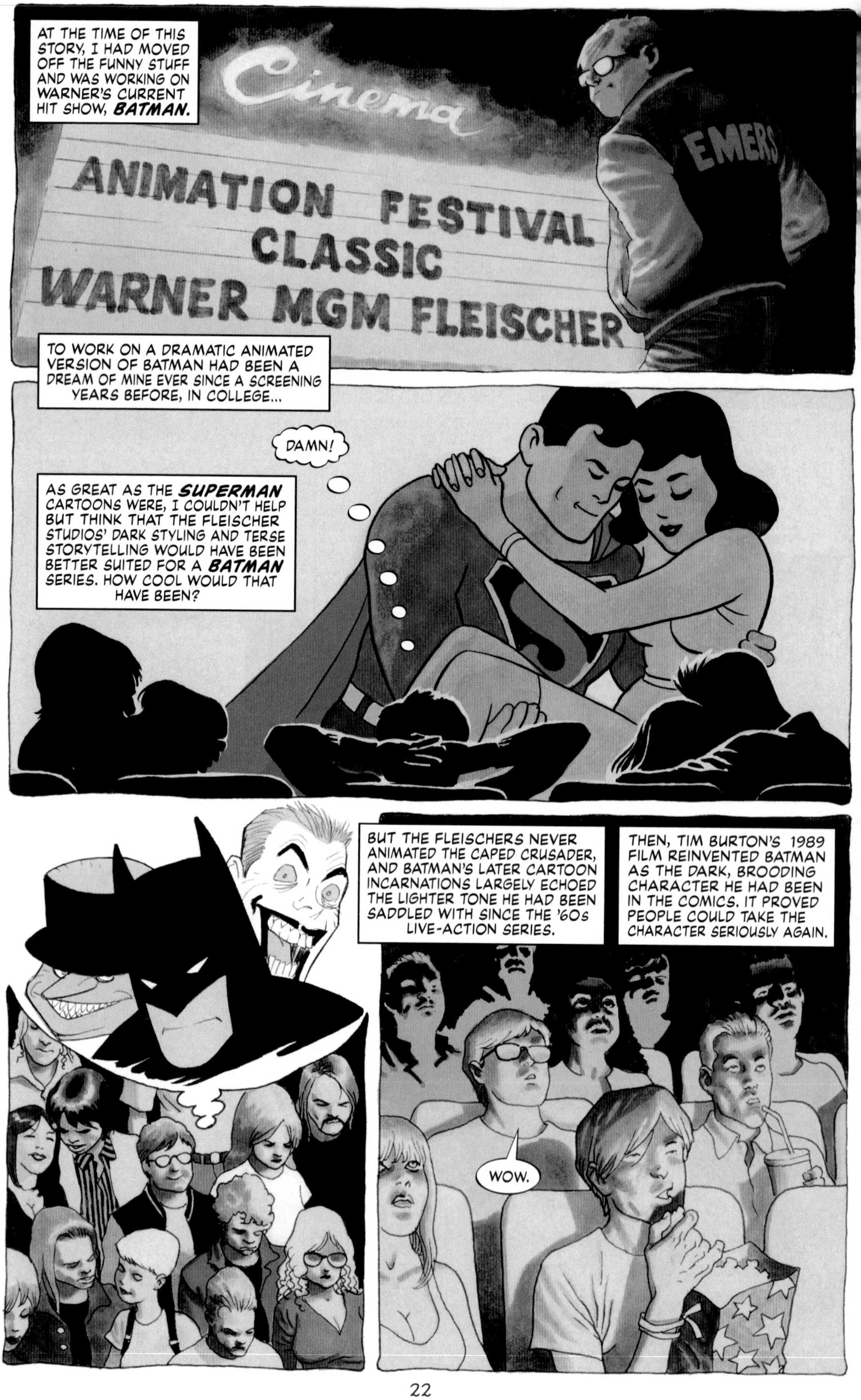
AT THE TIME OF THIS STORY, I HAD MOVED OFF THE FUNNY STUFF AND WAS WORKING ON WARNER'S CURRENT HIT SHOW, **BATMAN.**
Cinema
ANIMATION FESTIVAL
CLASSIC
WARNER MGM FLEISCHER
EMERS
TO WORK ON A DRAMATIC ANIMATED VERSION OF BATMAN HAD BEEN A DREAM OF MINE EVER SINCE A SCREENING YEARS BEFORE, IN COLLEGE...
DAMN!
AS GREAT AS THE ***SUPERMAN*** CARTOONS WERE, I COULDN'T HELP BUT THINK THAT THE FLEISCHER STUDIOS' DARK STYLING AND TERSE STORYTELLING WOULD HAVE BEEN BETTER SUITED FOR A ***BATMAN*** SERIES. HOW COOL WOULD THAT HAVE BEEN?
BUT THE FLEISCHERS NEVER ANIMATED THE CAPED CRUSADER, AND BATMAN'S LATER CARTOON INCARNATIONS LARGELY ECHOED THE LIGHTER TONE HE HAD BEEN SADDLED WITH SINCE THE '60s LIVE-ACTION SERIES.
THEN, TIM BURTON'S 1989 FILM REINVENTED BATMAN AS THE DARK, BROODING CHARACTER HE HAD BEEN IN THE COMICS. IT PROVED PEOPLE COULD TAKE THE CHARACTER SERIOUSLY AGAIN.
WOW.

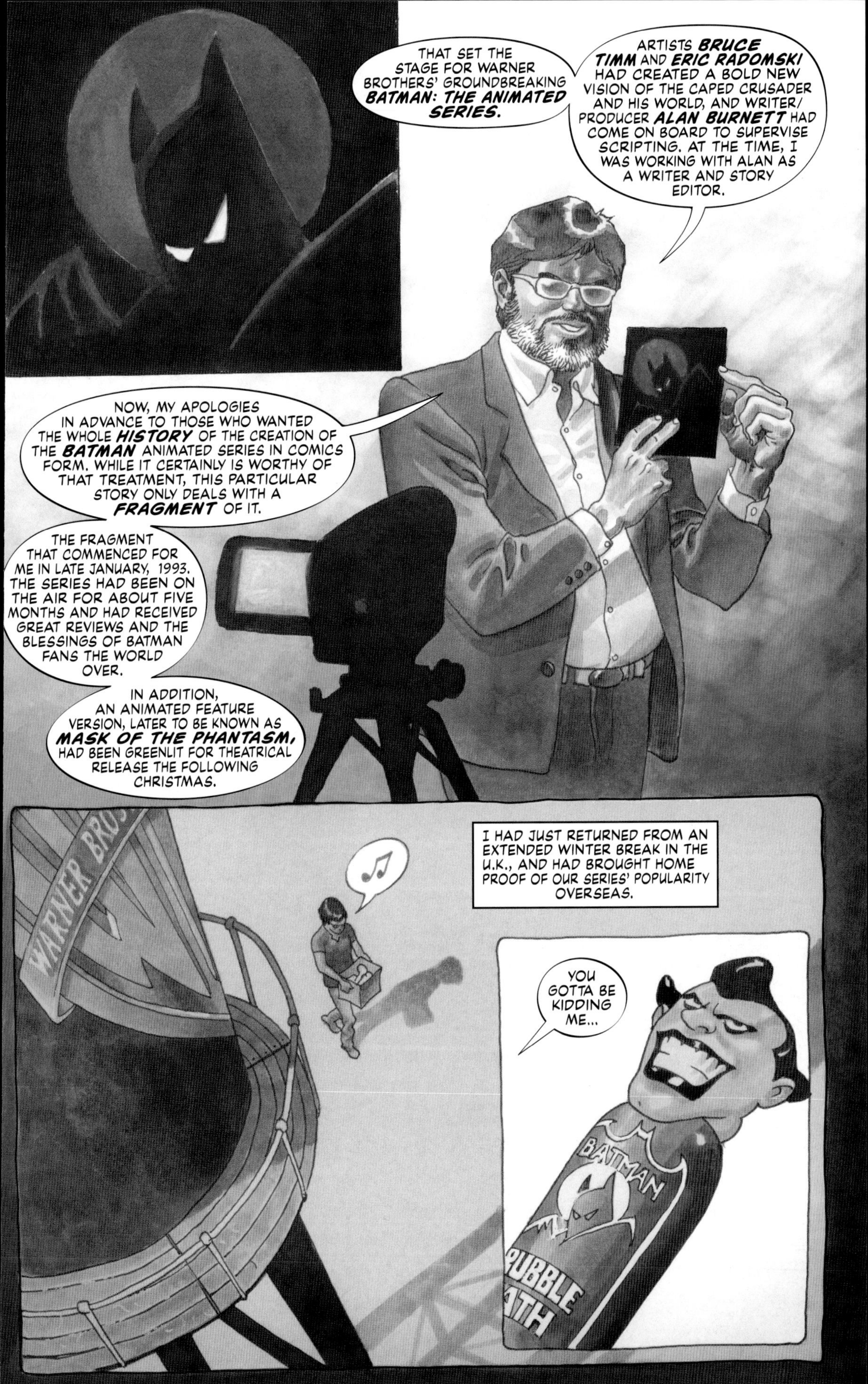
THAT SET THE STAGE FOR WARNER BROTHERS' GROUNDBREAKING BATMAN: THE ANIMATED SERIES.
ARTISTS BRUCE TIMM AND ERIC RADOMSKI HAD CREATED A BOLD NEW VISION OF THE CAPED CRUSADER AND HIS WORLD, AND WRITER/PRODUCER ALAN BURNETT HAD COME ON BOARD TO SUPERVISE SCRIPTING. AT THE TIME, I WAS WORKING WITH ALAN AS A WRITER AND STORY EDITOR.
NOW, MY APOLOGIES IN ADVANCE TO THOSE WHO WANTED THE WHOLE HISTORY OF THE CREATION OF THE BATMAN ANIMATED SERIES IN COMICS FORM. WHILE IT CERTAINLY IS WORTHY OF THAT TREATMENT, THIS PARTICULAR STORY ONLY DEALS WITH A FRAGMENT OF IT.
THE FRAGMENT THAT COMMENCED FOR ME IN LATE JANUARY, 1993. THE SERIES HAD BEEN ON THE AIR FOR ABOUT FIVE MONTHS AND HAD RECEIVED GREAT REVIEWS AND THE BLESSINGS OF BATMAN FANS THE WORLD OVER.
IN ADDITION, AN ANIMATED FEATURE VERSION, LATER TO BE KNOWN AS MASK OF THE PHANTASM, HAD BEEN GREENLIT FOR THEATRICAL RELEASE THE FOLLOWING CHRISTMAS.
WARNER BROS
I HAD JUST RETURNED FROM AN EXTENDED WINTER BREAK IN THE U.K., AND HAD BROUGHT HOME PROOF OF OUR SERIES' POPULARITY OVERSEAS.
YOU GOTTA BE KIDDING ME...
BATMAN
BUBBLE BATH

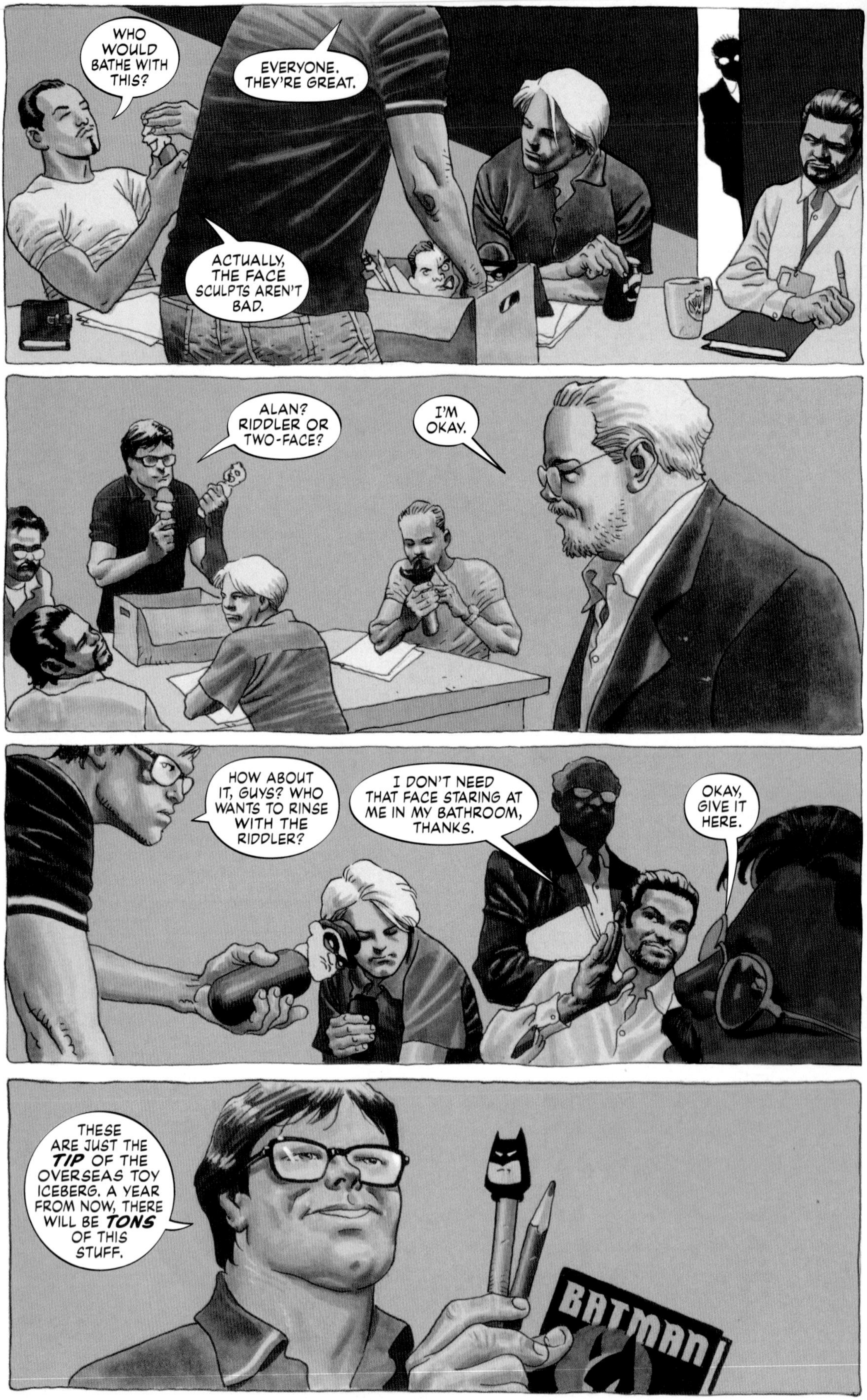
WHO WOULD BATHE WITH THIS?
EVERYONE. THEY'RE GREAT.
ACTUALLY, THE FACE SCULPTS AREN'T BAD.
ALAN? RIDDLER OR TWO-FACE?
I'M OKAY.
HOW ABOUT IT, GUYS? WHO WANTS TO RINSE WITH THE RIDDLER?
I DON'T NEED THAT FACE STARING AT ME IN MY BATHROOM, THANKS.
OKAY, GIVE IT HERE.
THESE ARE JUST THE ***TIP*** OF THE OVERSEAS TOY ICEBERG. A YEAR FROM NOW, THERE WILL BE ***TONS*** OF THIS STUFF.
BATMAN

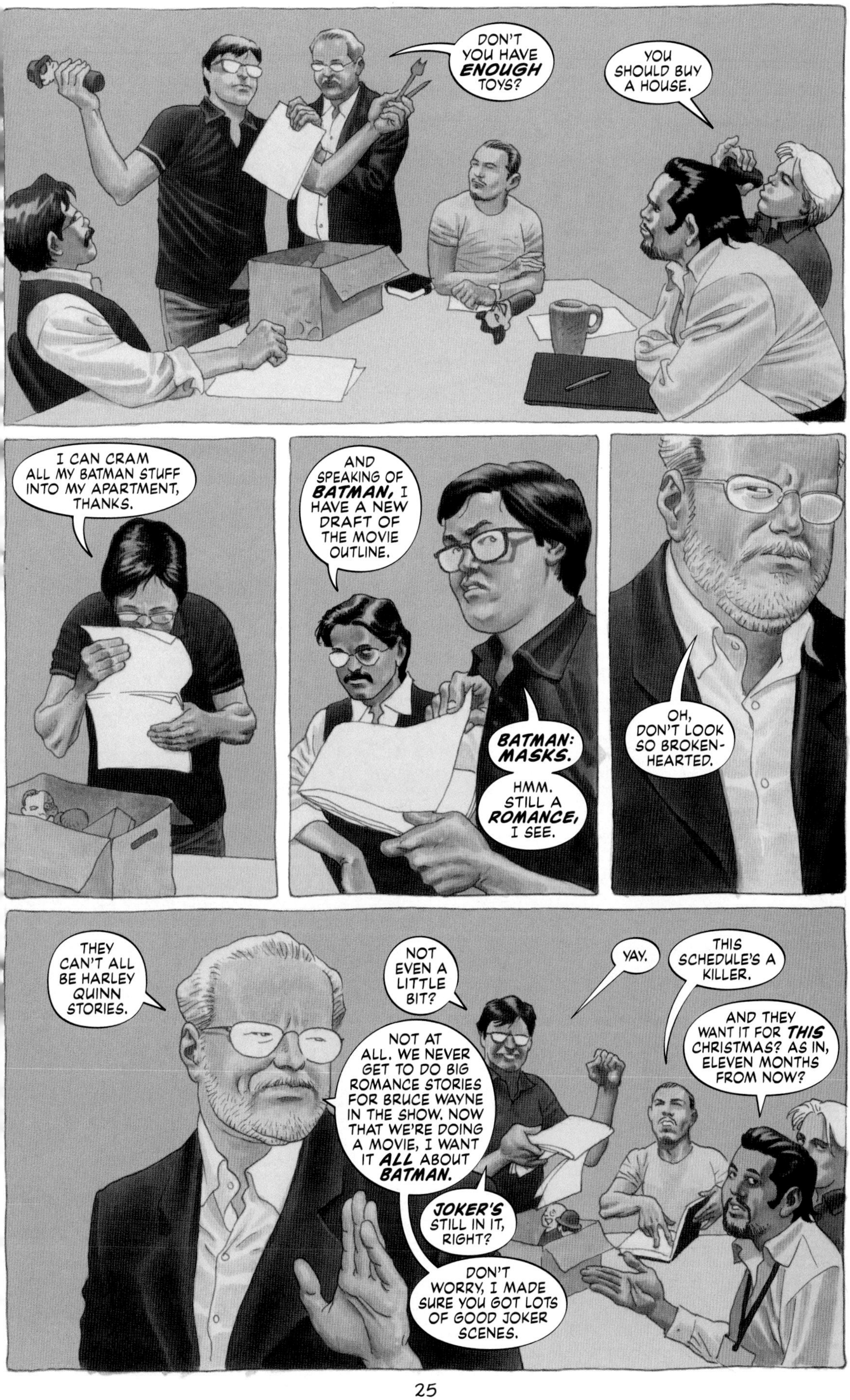
DON'T YOU HAVE **ENOUGH** TOYS?
YOU SHOULD BUY A HOUSE.
I CAN CRAM ALL MY BATMAN STUFF INTO MY APARTMENT, THANKS.
AND SPEAKING OF **BATMAN,** I HAVE A NEW DRAFT OF THE MOVIE OUTLINE.
BATMAN: MASKS.
HMM. STILL A **ROMANCE,** I SEE.
OH, DON'T LOOK SO BROKEN-HEARTED.
THEY CAN'T ALL BE HARLEY QUINN STORIES.
NOT EVEN A LITTLE BIT?
NOT AT ALL. WE NEVER GET TO DO BIG ROMANCE STORIES FOR BRUCE WAYNE IN THE SHOW. NOW THAT WE'RE DOING A MOVIE, I WANT IT **ALL** ABOUT **BATMAN.**
JOKER'S STILL IN IT, RIGHT?
DON'T WORRY, I MADE SURE YOU GOT LOTS OF GOOD JOKER SCENES.
YAY.
THIS SCHEDULE'S A KILLER.
AND THEY WANT IT FOR **THIS** CHRISTMAS? AS IN, ELEVEN MONTHS FROM NOW?

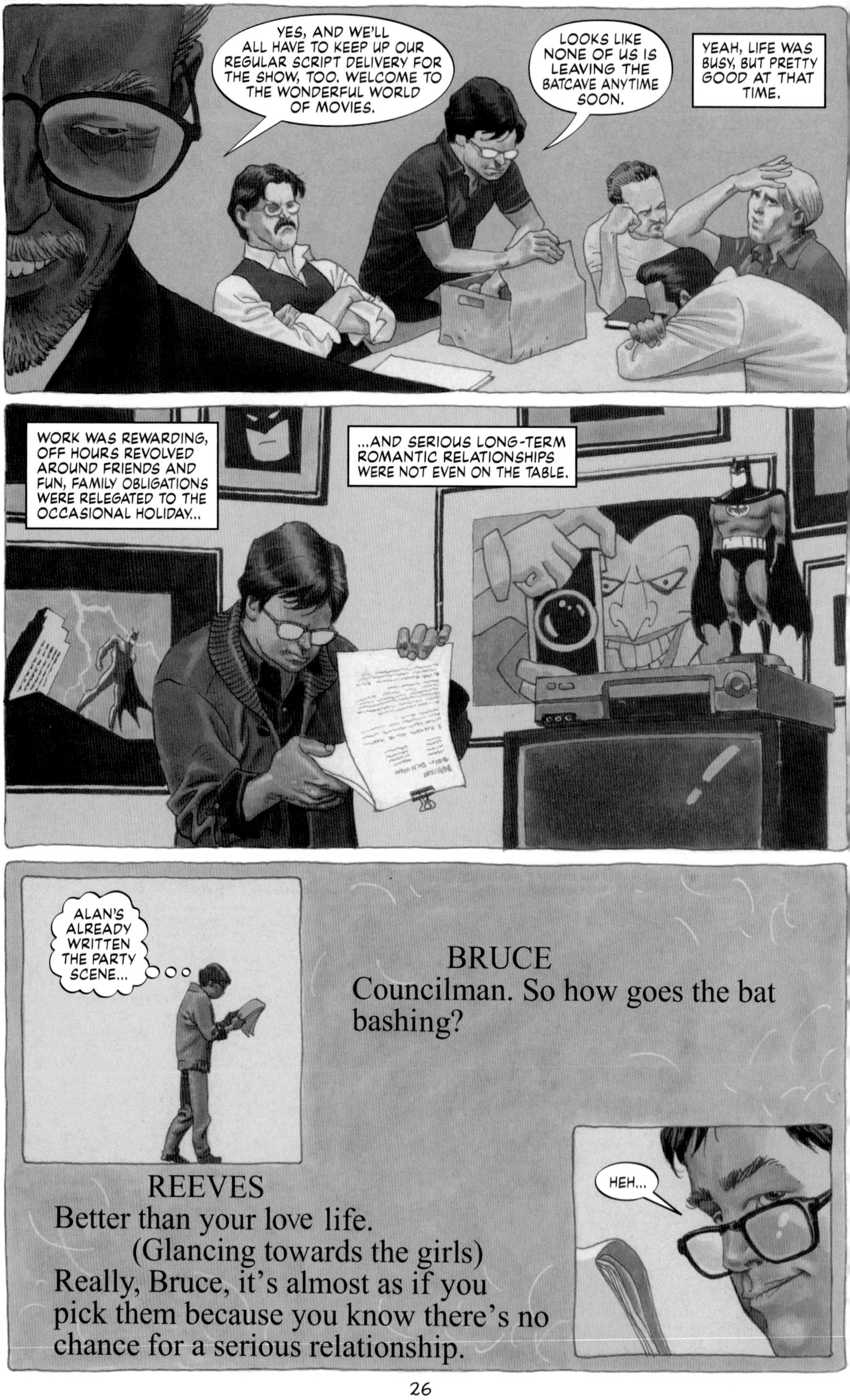
YES, AND WE'LL ALL HAVE TO KEEP UP OUR REGULAR SCRIPT DELIVERY FOR THE SHOW, TOO. WELCOME TO THE WONDERFUL WORLD OF MOVIES.
LOOKS LIKE NONE OF US IS LEAVING THE BATCAVE ANYTIME SOON.
YEAH, LIFE WAS BUSY, BUT PRETTY GOOD AT THAT TIME.
WORK WAS REWARDING, OFF HOURS REVOLVED AROUND FRIENDS AND FUN, FAMILY OBLIGATIONS WERE RELEGATED TO THE OCCASIONAL HOLIDAY...
...AND SERIOUS LONG-TERM ROMANTIC RELATIONSHIPS WERE NOT EVEN ON THE TABLE.
ALAN'S ALREADY WRITTEN THE PARTY SCENE...
BRUCE
Councilman. So how goes the bat bashing?
REEVES
Better than your love life.
(Glancing towards the girls)
Really, Bruce, it's almost as if you pick them because you know there's no chance for a serious relationship.
HEH...

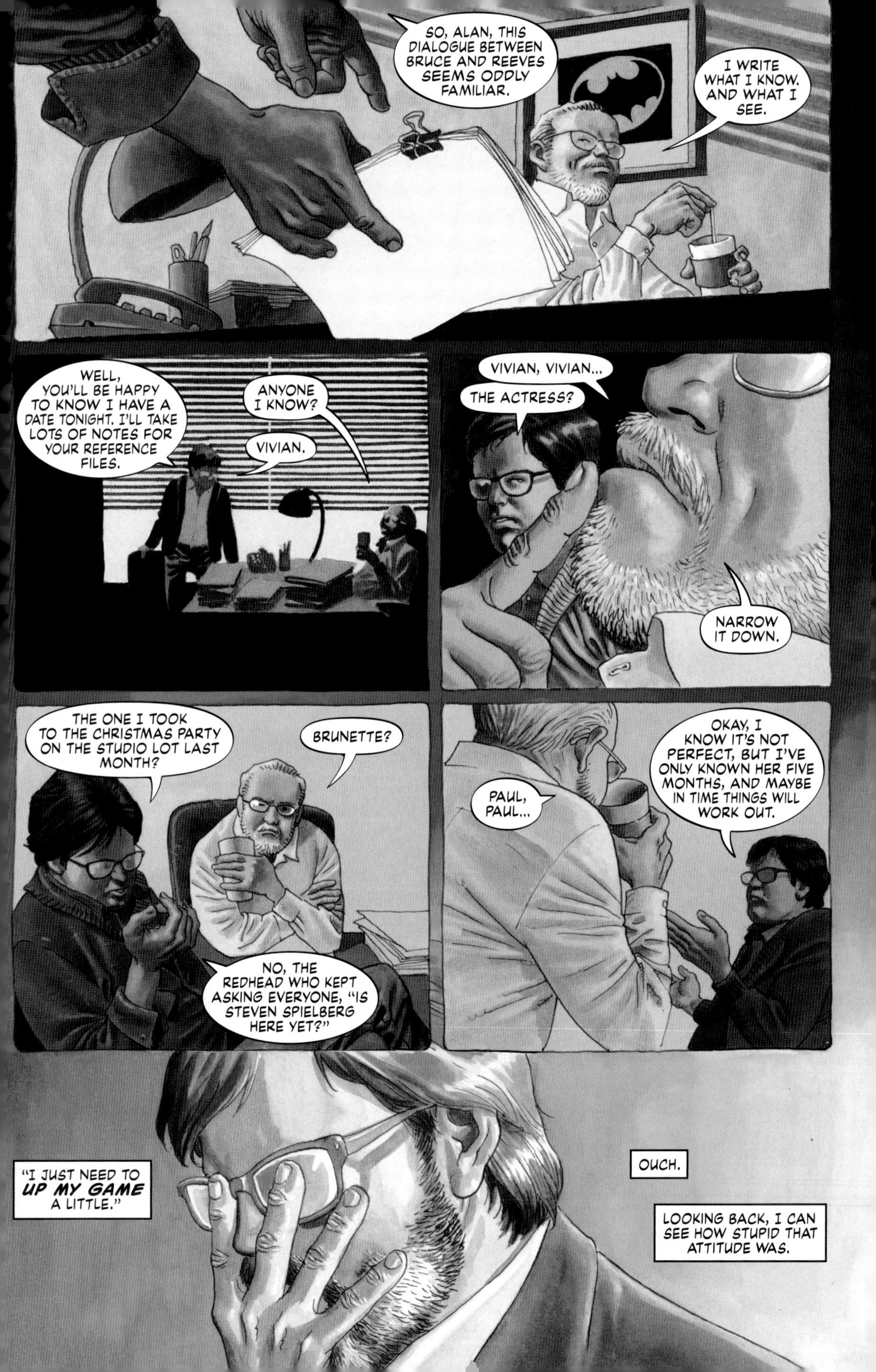

SO, ALAN, THIS DIALOGUE BETWEEN BRUCE AND REEVES SEEMS ODDLY FAMILIAR.
I WRITE WHAT I KNOW. AND WHAT I SEE.
WELL, YOU'LL BE HAPPY TO KNOW I HAVE A DATE TONIGHT. I'LL TAKE LOTS OF NOTES FOR YOUR REFERENCE FILES.
ANYONE I KNOW?
VIVIAN.
VIVIAN, VIVIAN...
THE ACTRESS?
NARROW IT DOWN.
THE ONE I TOOK TO THE CHRISTMAS PARTY ON THE STUDIO LOT LAST MONTH?
BRUNETTE?
NO, THE REDHEAD WHO KEPT ASKING EVERYONE, "IS STEVEN SPIELBERG HERE YET?"
PAUL, PAUL...
OKAY, I KNOW IT'S NOT PERFECT, BUT I'VE ONLY KNOWN HER FIVE MONTHS, AND MAYBE IN TIME THINGS WILL WORK OUT.
"I JUST NEED TO ***UP MY GAME*** A LITTLE."
OUCH.
LOOKING BACK, I CAN SEE HOW STUPID THAT ATTITUDE WAS.

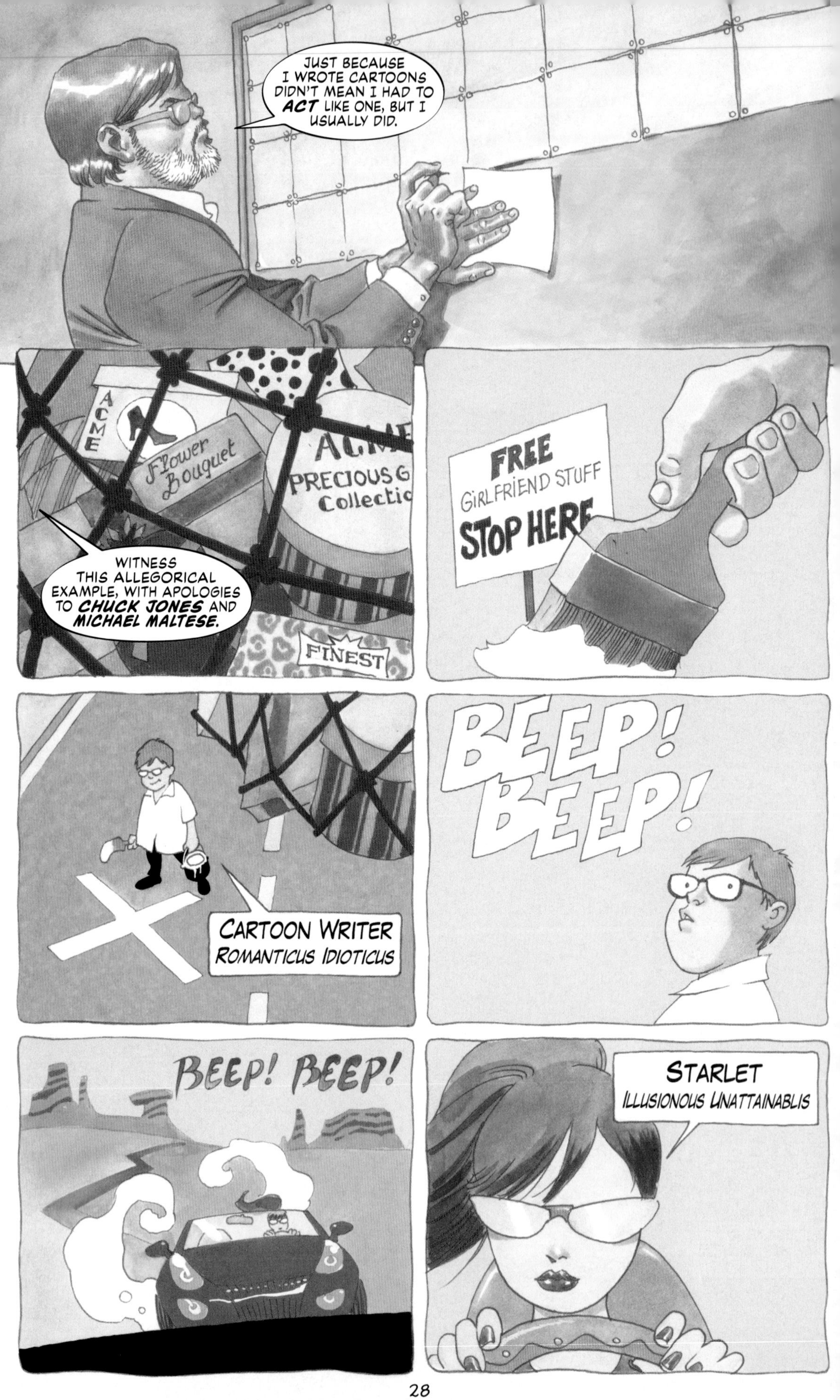
JUST BECAUSE I WROTE CARTOONS DIDN'T MEAN I HAD TO **ACT** LIKE ONE, BUT I USUALLY DID.
ACME
Flower Bouquet
ACME
PRECIOUS G
Collectic
FINEST
WITNESS THIS ALLEGORICAL EXAMPLE, WITH APOLOGIES TO **CHUCK JONES** AND **MICHAEL MALTESE.**
FREE
GIRLFRIEND STUFF
STOP HERE
CARTOON WRITER
ROMANTICUS IDIOTICUS
BEEP! BEEP!
BEEP! BEEP!
STARLET
ILLUSIONOUS UNATTAINABLIS

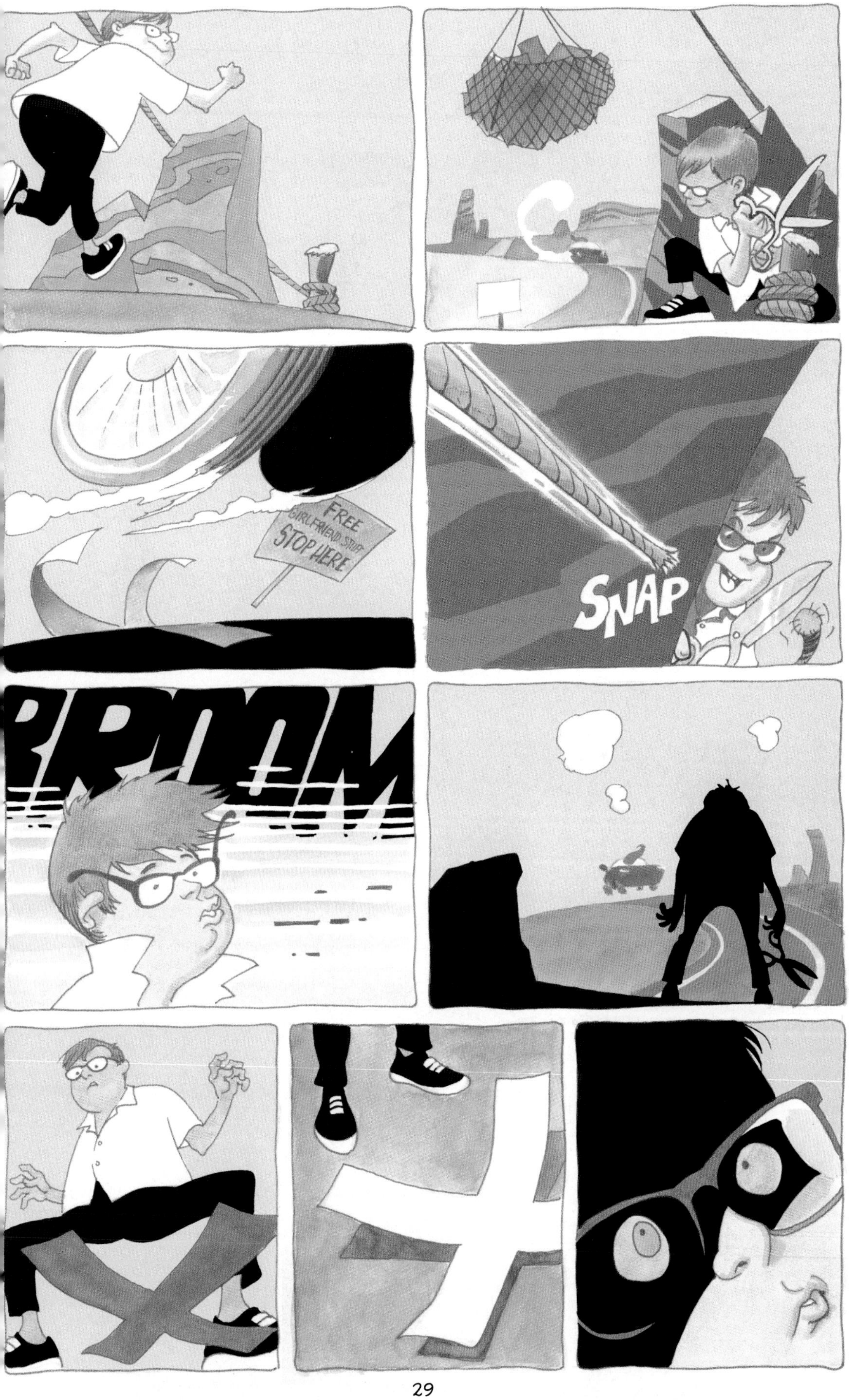
FREE
GIRLFRIEND STUFF
STOP HERE
SNAP
RROOM

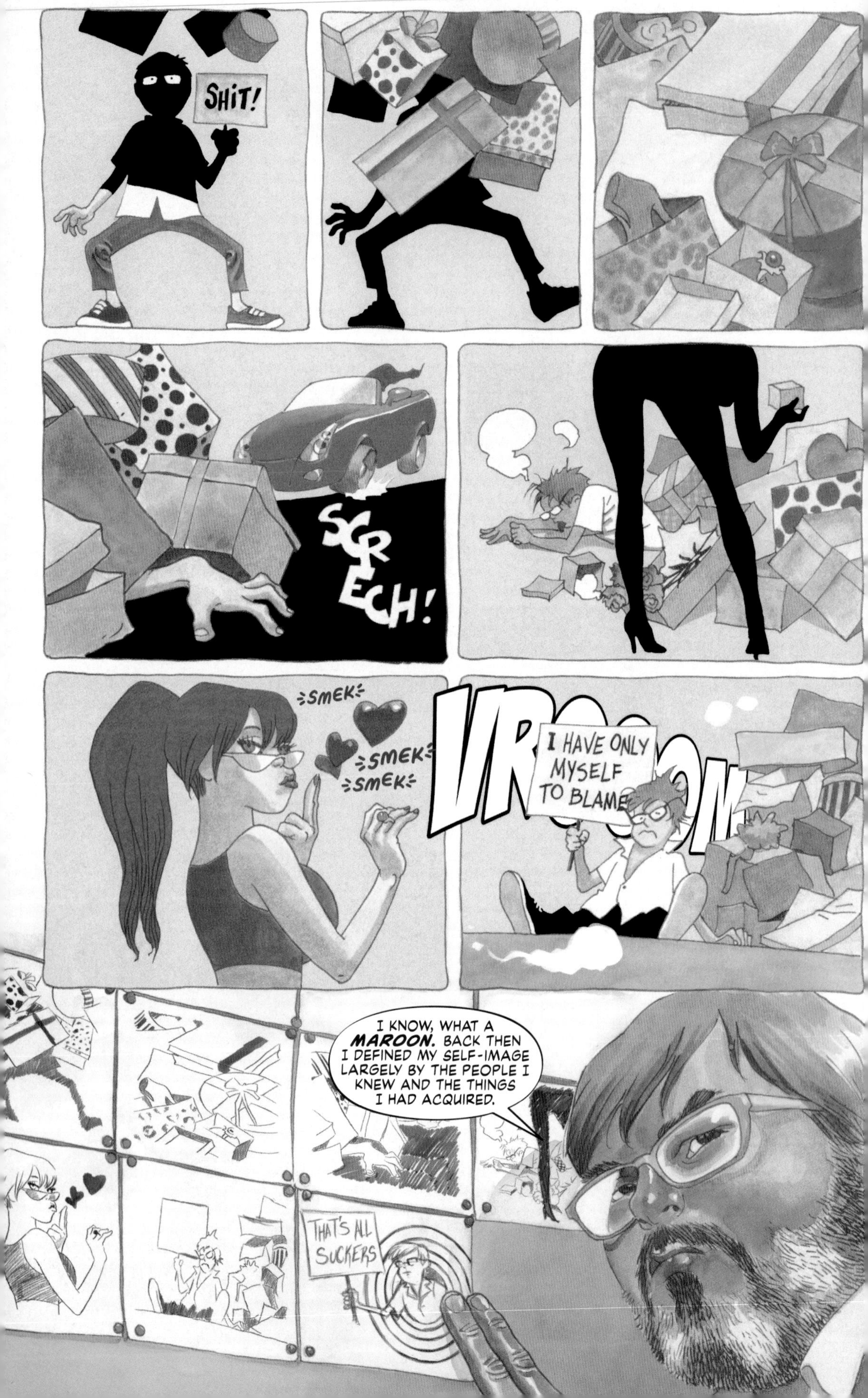
SHIT!
SCREECH!
SMEK
SMEK
SMEK
VROOOM
I HAVE ONLY MYSELF TO BLAME
I KNOW, WHAT A **MAROON.** BACK THEN I DEFINED MY SELF-IMAGE LARGELY BY THE PEOPLE I KNEW AND THE THINGS I HAD ACQUIRED.
THAT'S ALL SUCKERS

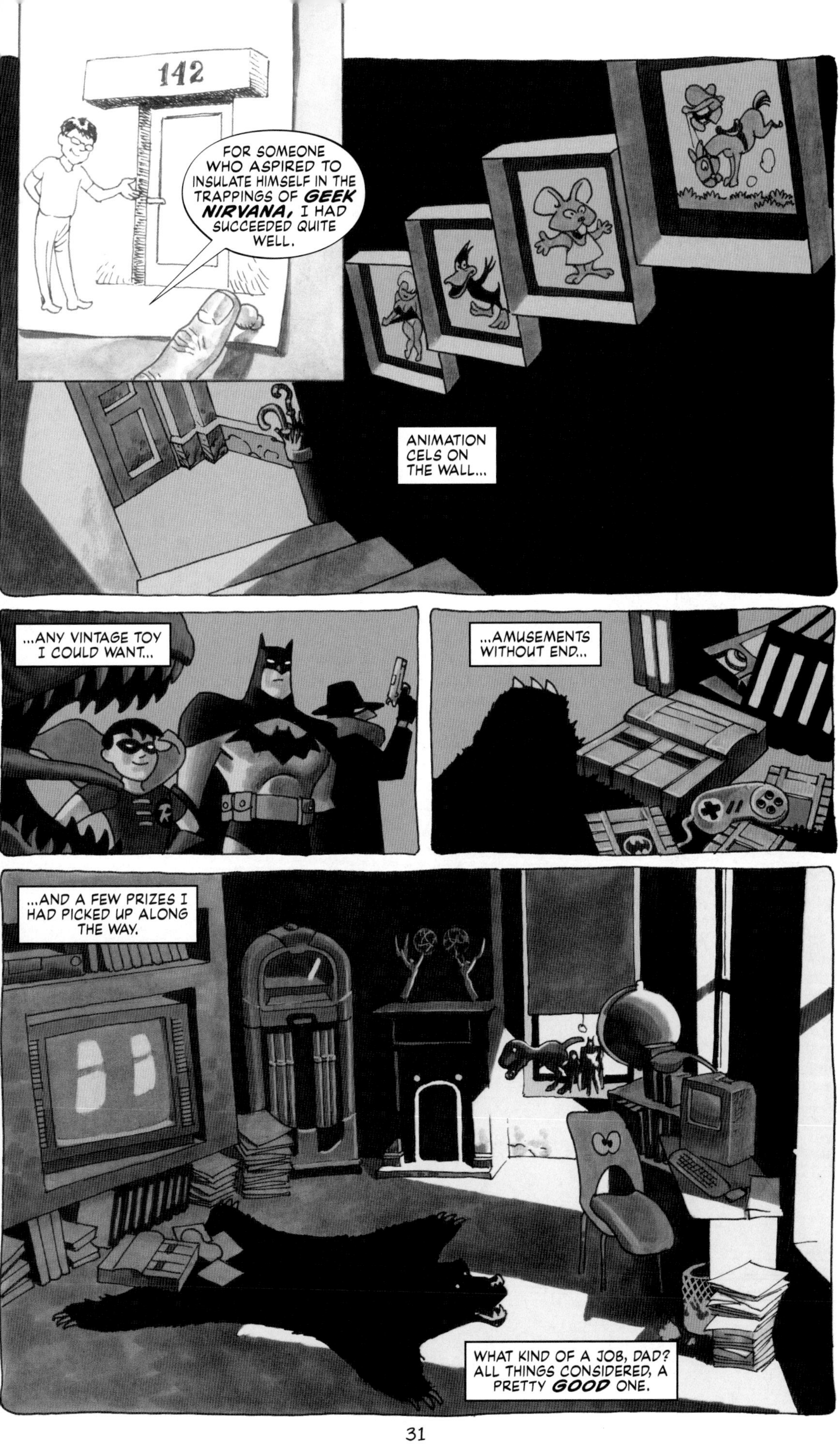
142
FOR SOMEONE WHO ASPIRED TO INSULATE HIMSELF IN THE TRAPPINGS OF GEEK NIRVANA, I HAD SUCCEEDED QUITE WELL.
ANIMATION CELS ON THE WALL...
...ANY VINTAGE TOY I COULD WANT...
...AMUSEMENTS WITHOUT END...
...AND A FEW PRIZES I HAD PICKED UP ALONG THE WAY.
WHAT KIND OF A JOB, DAD? ALL THINGS CONSIDERED, A PRETTY GOOD ONE.

NOW, DON'T THINK FOR A SECOND THAT I'M DUMPING ON MY FOLKS.

THEY MIGHT HAVE *GRUMBLED* TO SEE ME GOOFED ON CARTOONS EVERY SATURDAY A.M., BUT THEY NEVER *TOSSED OUT* MY COMICS, OR GAVE AWAY MY OLD TOYS, OR *BALKED* AT DRIVING ME INTO SAN FRANCISCO TO SEE THE LATEST DISNEY RELEASE.

AND MOST IMPORTANT, THEY ENCOURAGED ME TO KEEP DOING WHAT I *LOVED,* WHICH WAS DREAMING UP WEIRD STORIES.

MY ENTIRE FAMILY HAS BEEN NOTHING BUT SUPPORTIVE. MY SISTER, MY BROTHERS...

HEH. I REMEMBER WHEN I GOT MY FIRST WRITING JOB, RIGHT OUT OF COLLEGE, MY GRANDFATHER LOUIE...

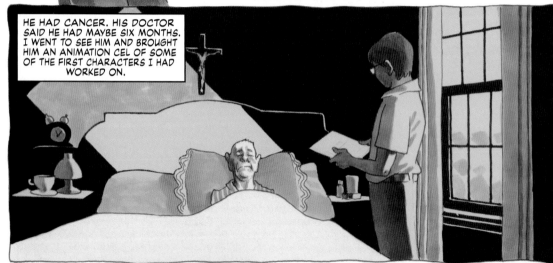

HE HAD CANCER. HIS DOCTOR SAID HE HAD MAYBE SIX MONTHS. I WENT TO SEE HIM AND BROUGHT HIM AN ANIMATION CEL OF SOME OF THE FIRST CHARACTERS I HAD WORKED ON.

TYPICAL SATURDAY MORNING STUFF, FUNNY ANIMALS, SOME OLD SUPER-HEROES...

CRAZY CRAP HE'D NEVER *HEARD* OF, BUT JUST SOMETHING TO SHOW THAT I WAS WORKING.

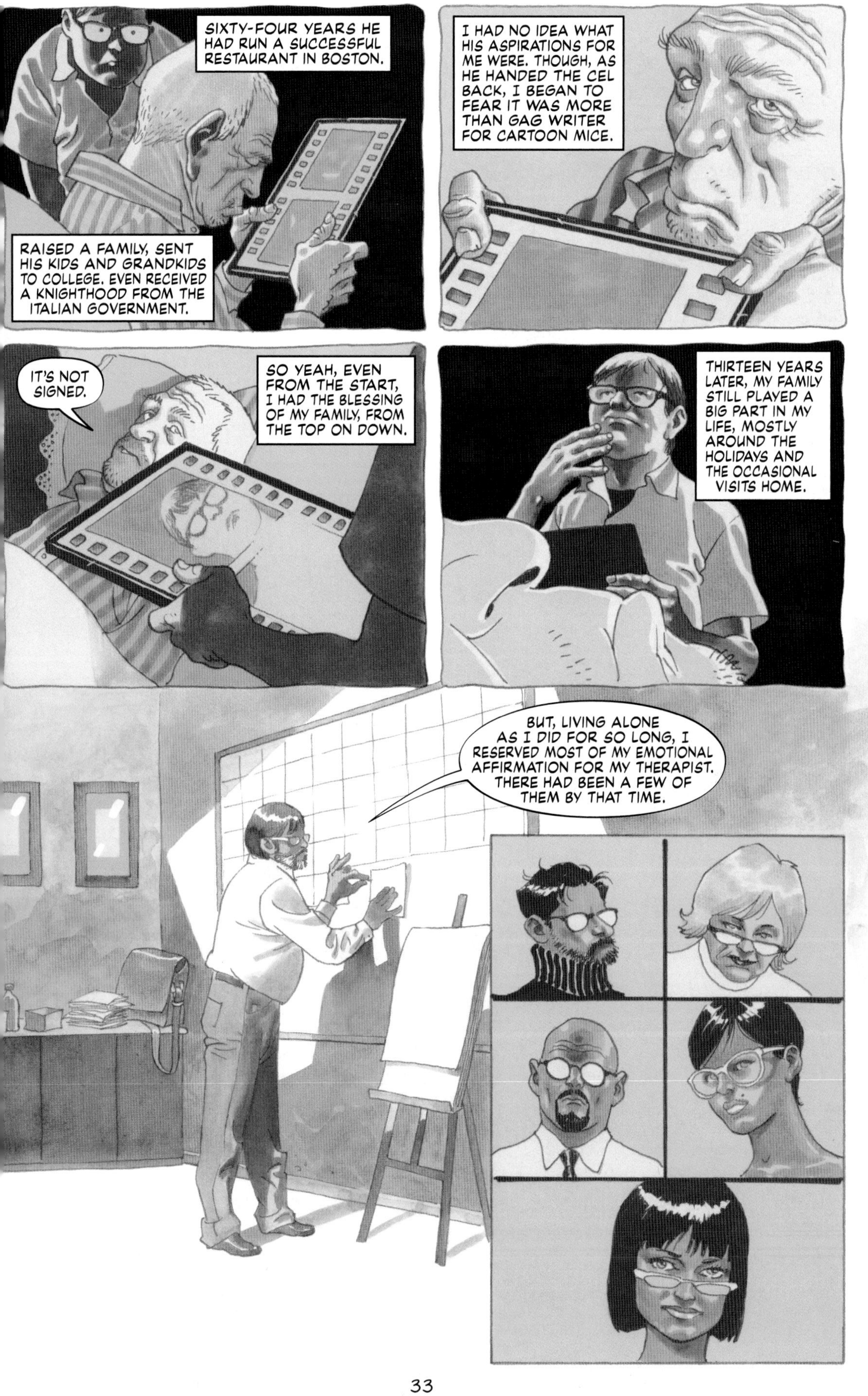

SIXTY-FOUR YEARS HE HAD RUN A SUCCESSFUL RESTAURANT IN BOSTON.
RAISED A FAMILY, SENT HIS KIDS AND GRANDKIDS TO COLLEGE. EVEN RECEIVED A KNIGHTHOOD FROM THE ITALIAN GOVERNMENT.
I HAD NO IDEA WHAT HIS ASPIRATIONS FOR ME WERE. THOUGH, AS HE HANDED THE CEL BACK, I BEGAN TO FEAR IT WAS MORE THAN GAG WRITER FOR CARTOON MICE.
IT'S NOT SIGNED.
SO YEAH, EVEN FROM THE START, I HAD THE BLESSING OF MY FAMILY, FROM THE TOP ON DOWN.
THIRTEEN YEARS LATER, MY FAMILY STILL PLAYED A BIG PART IN MY LIFE, MOSTLY AROUND THE HOLIDAYS AND THE OCCASIONAL VISITS HOME.
BUT, LIVING ALONE AS I DID FOR SO LONG, I RESERVED MOST OF MY EMOTIONAL AFFIRMATION FOR MY THERAPIST. THERE HAD BEEN A FEW OF THEM BY THAT TIME.

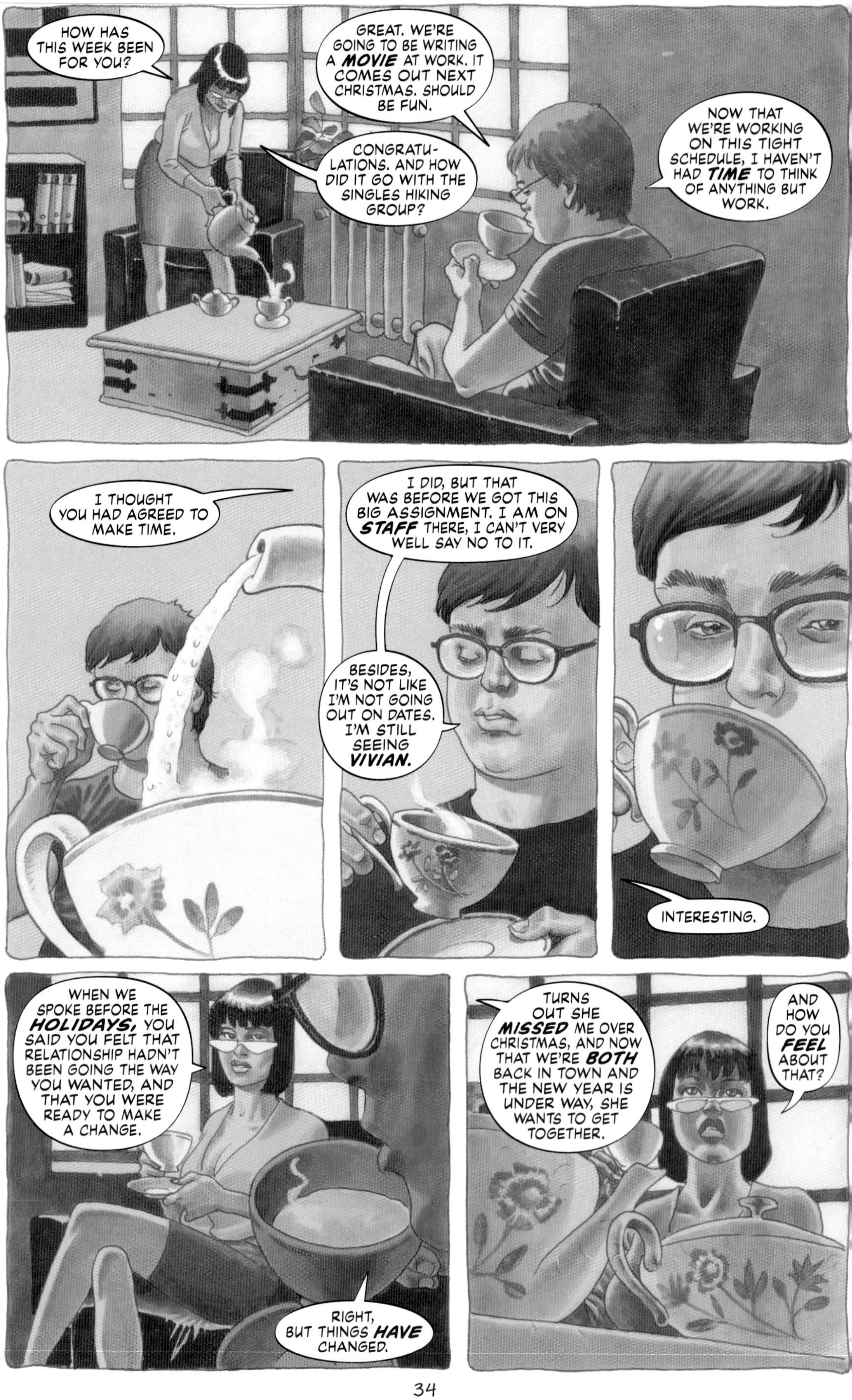

HOW HAS THIS WEEK BEEN FOR YOU?
GREAT. WE'RE GOING TO BE WRITING A **MOVIE** AT WORK. IT COMES OUT NEXT CHRISTMAS. SHOULD BE FUN.
CONGRATU-LATIONS. AND HOW DID IT GO WITH THE SINGLES HIKING GROUP?
NOW THAT WE'RE WORKING ON THIS TIGHT SCHEDULE, I HAVEN'T HAD **TIME** TO THINK OF ANYTHING BUT WORK.
I THOUGHT YOU HAD AGREED TO MAKE TIME.
I DID, BUT THAT WAS BEFORE WE GOT THIS BIG ASSIGNMENT. I AM ON **STAFF** THERE, I CAN'T VERY WELL SAY NO TO IT.
BESIDES, IT'S NOT LIKE I'M NOT GOING OUT ON DATES. I'M STILL SEEING **VIVIAN.**
INTERESTING.
WHEN WE SPOKE BEFORE THE **HOLIDAYS,** YOU SAID YOU FELT THAT RELATIONSHIP HADN'T BEEN GOING THE WAY YOU WANTED, AND THAT YOU WERE READY TO MAKE A CHANGE.
RIGHT, BUT THINGS **HAVE** CHANGED.
TURNS OUT SHE **MISSED** ME OVER CHRISTMAS, AND NOW THAT WE'RE **BOTH** BACK IN TOWN AND THE NEW YEAR IS UNDER WAY, SHE WANTS TO GET TOGETHER.
AND HOW DO YOU **FEEL** ABOUT THAT?

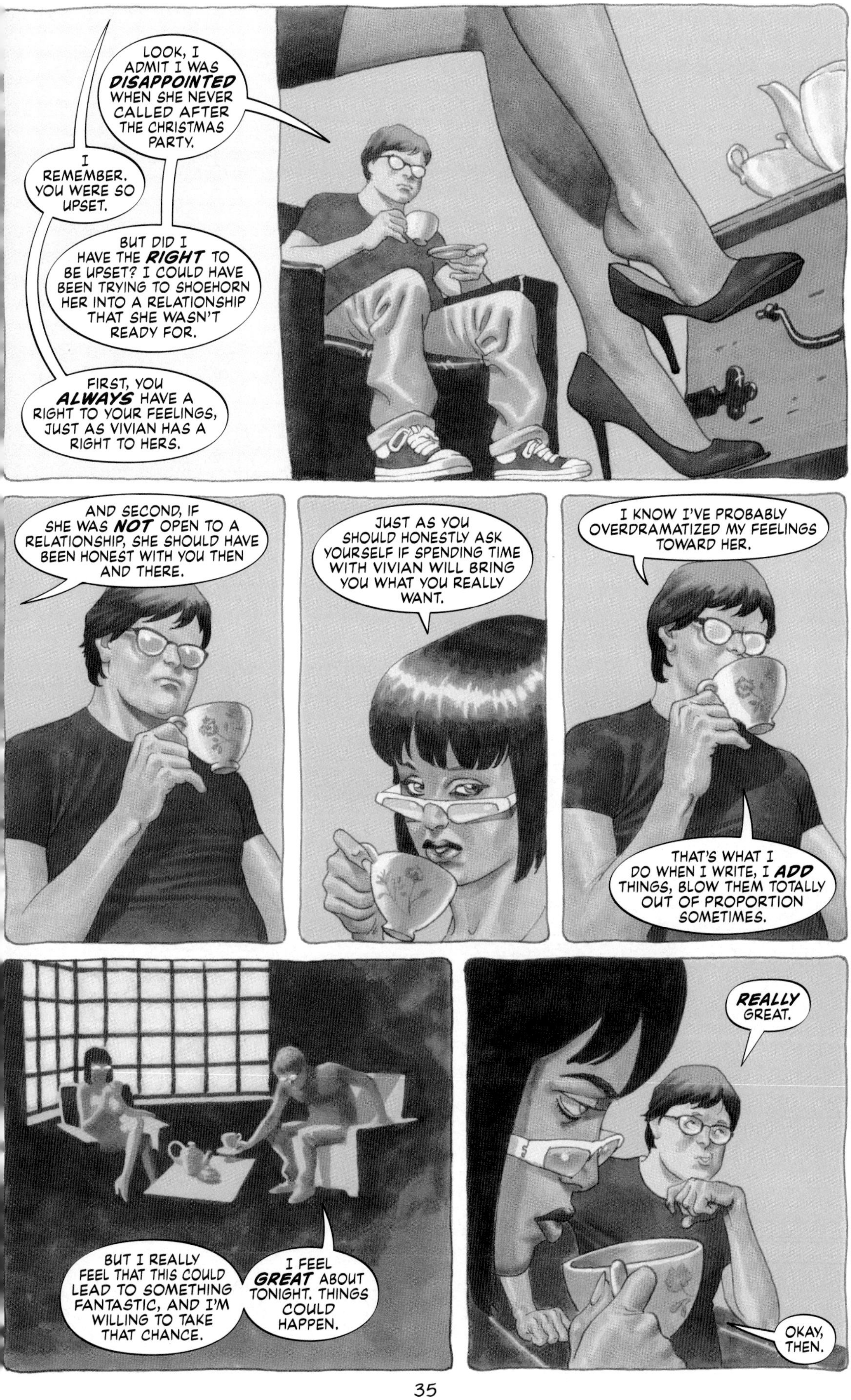
LOOK, I ADMIT I WAS DISAPPOINTED WHEN SHE NEVER CALLED AFTER THE CHRISTMAS PARTY.
I REMEMBER. YOU WERE SO UPSET.
BUT DID I HAVE THE RIGHT TO BE UPSET? I COULD HAVE BEEN TRYING TO SHOEHORN HER INTO A RELATIONSHIP THAT SHE WASN'T READY FOR.
FIRST, YOU ALWAYS HAVE A RIGHT TO YOUR FEELINGS, JUST AS VIVIAN HAS A RIGHT TO HERS.
AND SECOND, IF SHE WAS NOT OPEN TO A RELATIONSHIP, SHE SHOULD HAVE BEEN HONEST WITH YOU THEN AND THERE.
JUST AS YOU SHOULD HONESTLY ASK YOURSELF IF SPENDING TIME WITH VIVIAN WILL BRING YOU WHAT YOU REALLY WANT.
I KNOW I'VE PROBABLY OVERDRAMATIZED MY FEELINGS TOWARD HER.
THAT'S WHAT I DO WHEN I WRITE, I ADD THINGS, BLOW THEM TOTALLY OUT OF PROPORTION SOMETIMES.
BUT I REALLY FEEL THAT THIS COULD LEAD TO SOMETHING FANTASTIC, AND I'M WILLING TO TAKE THAT CHANCE.
I FEEL GREAT ABOUT TONIGHT. THINGS COULD HAPPEN.
REALLY GREAT.
OKAY, THEN.

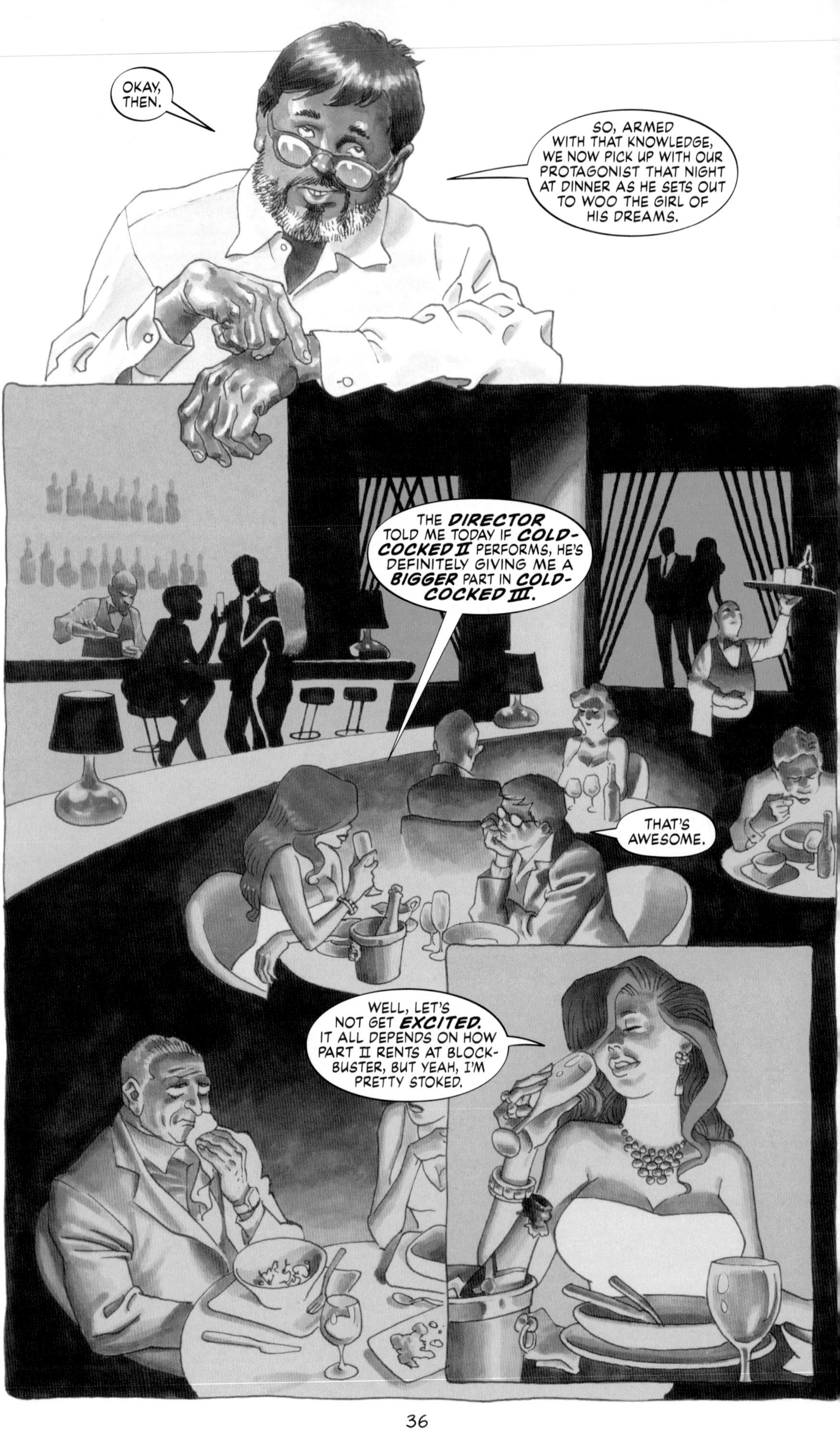

OKAY, THEN.
SO, ARMED WITH THAT KNOWLEDGE, WE NOW PICK UP WITH OUR PROTAGONIST THAT NIGHT AT DINNER AS HE SETS OUT TO WOO THE GIRL OF HIS DREAMS.
THE DIRECTOR TOLD ME TODAY IF COLD-COCKED II PERFORMS, HE'S DEFINITELY GIVING ME A BIGGER PART IN COLD-COCKED III.
THAT'S AWESOME.
WELL, LET'S NOT GET EXCITED. IT ALL DEPENDS ON HOW PART II RENTS AT BLOCK-BUSTER, BUT YEAH, I'M PRETTY STOKED.

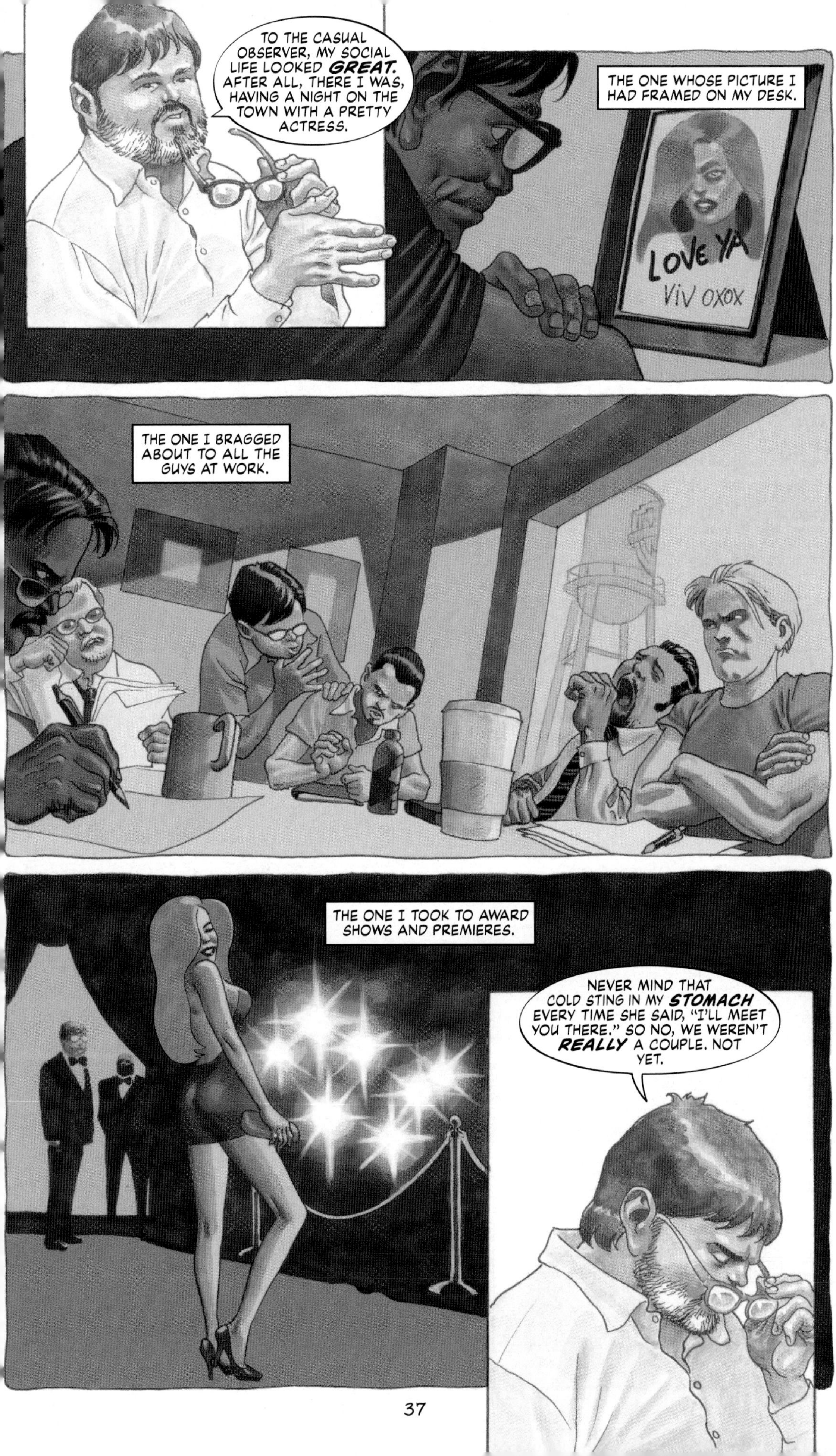
TO THE CASUAL OBSERVER, MY SOCIAL LIFE LOOKED GREAT. AFTER ALL, THERE I WAS, HAVING A NIGHT ON THE TOWN WITH A PRETTY ACTRESS.
THE ONE WHOSE PICTURE I HAD FRAMED ON MY DESK.
LOVE YA
VIV OXOX
THE ONE I BRAGGED ABOUT TO ALL THE GUYS AT WORK.
THE ONE I TOOK TO AWARD SHOWS AND PREMIERES.
NEVER MIND THAT COLD STING IN MY STOMACH EVERY TIME SHE SAID, "I'LL MEET YOU THERE." SO NO, WE WEREN'T REALLY A COUPLE. NOT YET.

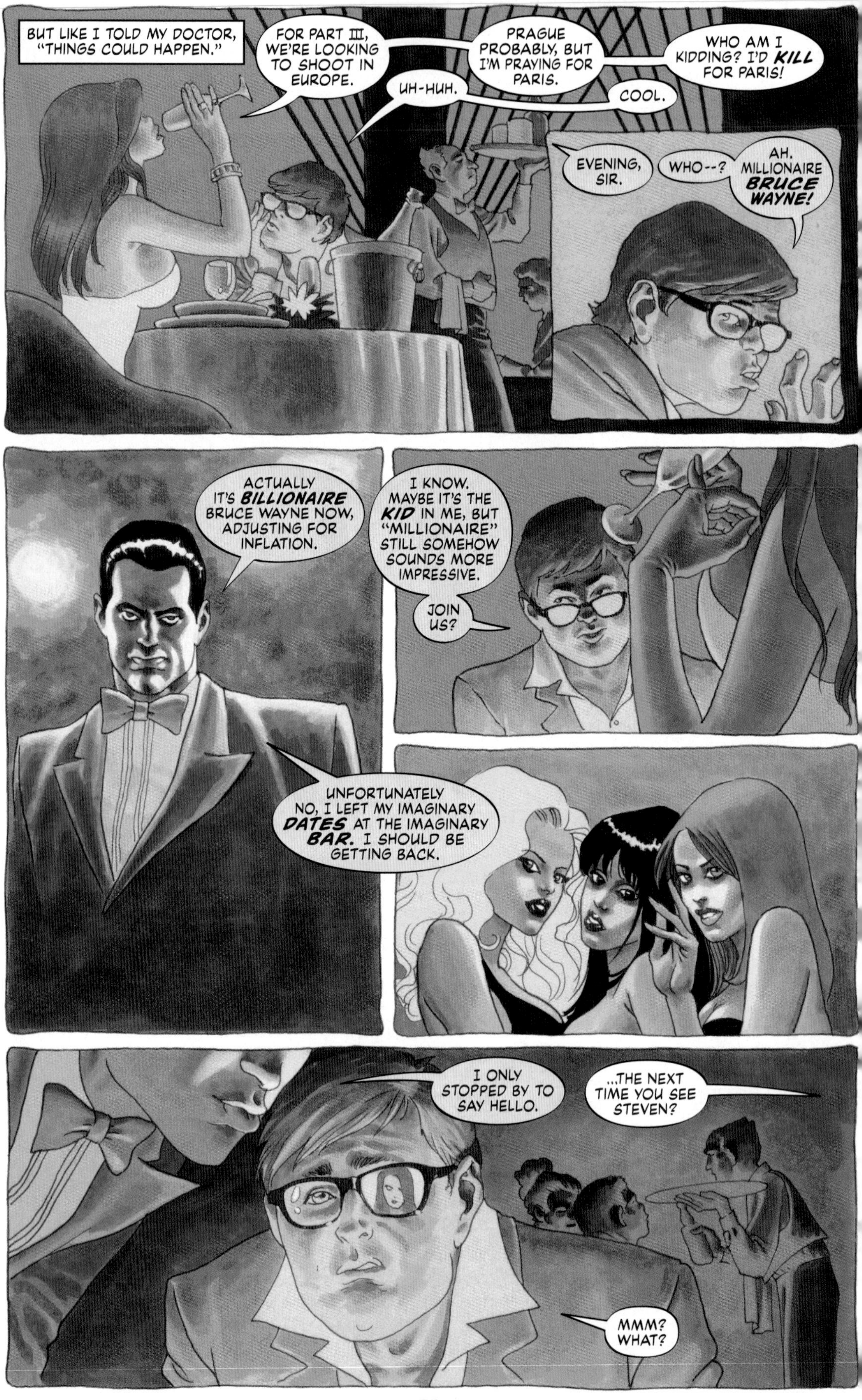
BUT LIKE I TOLD MY DOCTOR, "THINGS COULD HAPPEN."
FOR PART III, WE'RE LOOKING TO SHOOT IN EUROPE.
UH-HUH.
PRAGUE PROBABLY, BUT I'M PRAYING FOR PARIS.
COOL.
WHO AM I KIDDING? I'D KILL FOR PARIS!
EVENING, SIR.
WHO--?
AH. MILLIONAIRE BRUCE WAYNE!
ACTUALLY IT'S BILLIONAIRE BRUCE WAYNE NOW, ADJUSTING FOR INFLATION.
I KNOW. MAYBE IT'S THE KID IN ME, BUT "MILLIONAIRE" STILL SOMEHOW SOUNDS MORE IMPRESSIVE.
JOIN US?
UNFORTUNATELY NO, I LEFT MY IMAGINARY DATES AT THE IMAGINARY BAR. I SHOULD BE GETTING BACK.
I ONLY STOPPED BY TO SAY HELLO.
...THE NEXT TIME YOU SEE STEVEN?
MMM? WHAT?

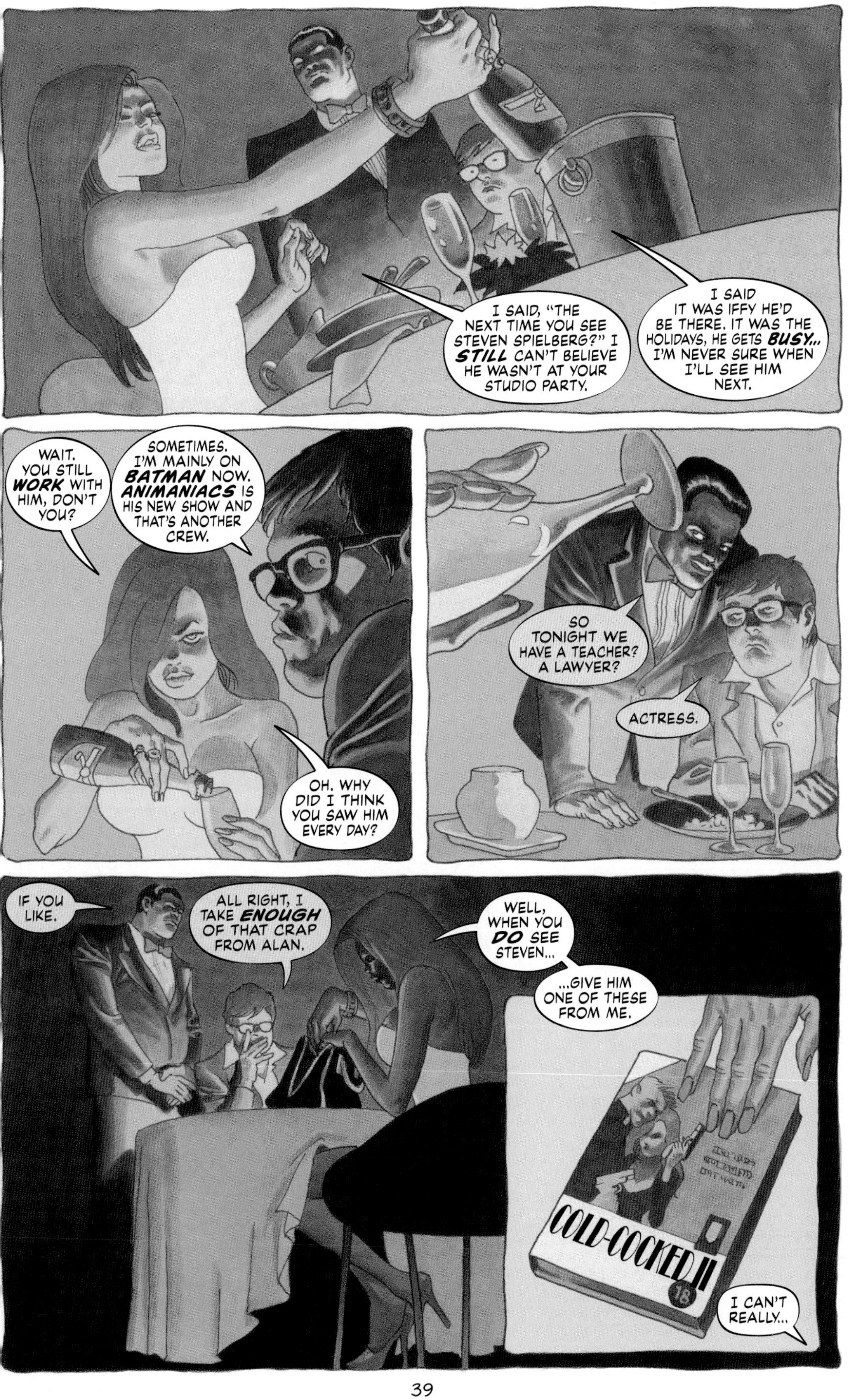
I SAID, "THE NEXT TIME YOU SEE STEVEN SPIELBERG?" I **STILL** CAN'T BELIEVE HE WASN'T AT YOUR STUDIO PARTY.
I SAID IT WAS IFFY HE'D BE THERE. IT WAS THE HOLIDAYS, HE GETS **BUSY...** I'M NEVER SURE WHEN I'LL SEE HIM NEXT.
WAIT. YOU STILL **WORK** WITH HIM, DON'T YOU?
SOMETIMES. I'M MAINLY ON **BATMAN** NOW. **ANIMANIACS** IS HIS NEW SHOW AND THAT'S ANOTHER CREW.
OH. WHY DID I THINK YOU SAW HIM EVERY DAY?
SO TONIGHT WE HAVE A TEACHER? A LAWYER?
ACTRESS.
IF YOU LIKE.
ALL RIGHT, I TAKE **ENOUGH** OF THAT CRAP FROM ALAN.
WELL, WHEN YOU **DO** SEE STEVEN...
...GIVE HIM ONE OF THESE FROM ME.
COLD-COCKED II
18
I CAN'T REALLY...

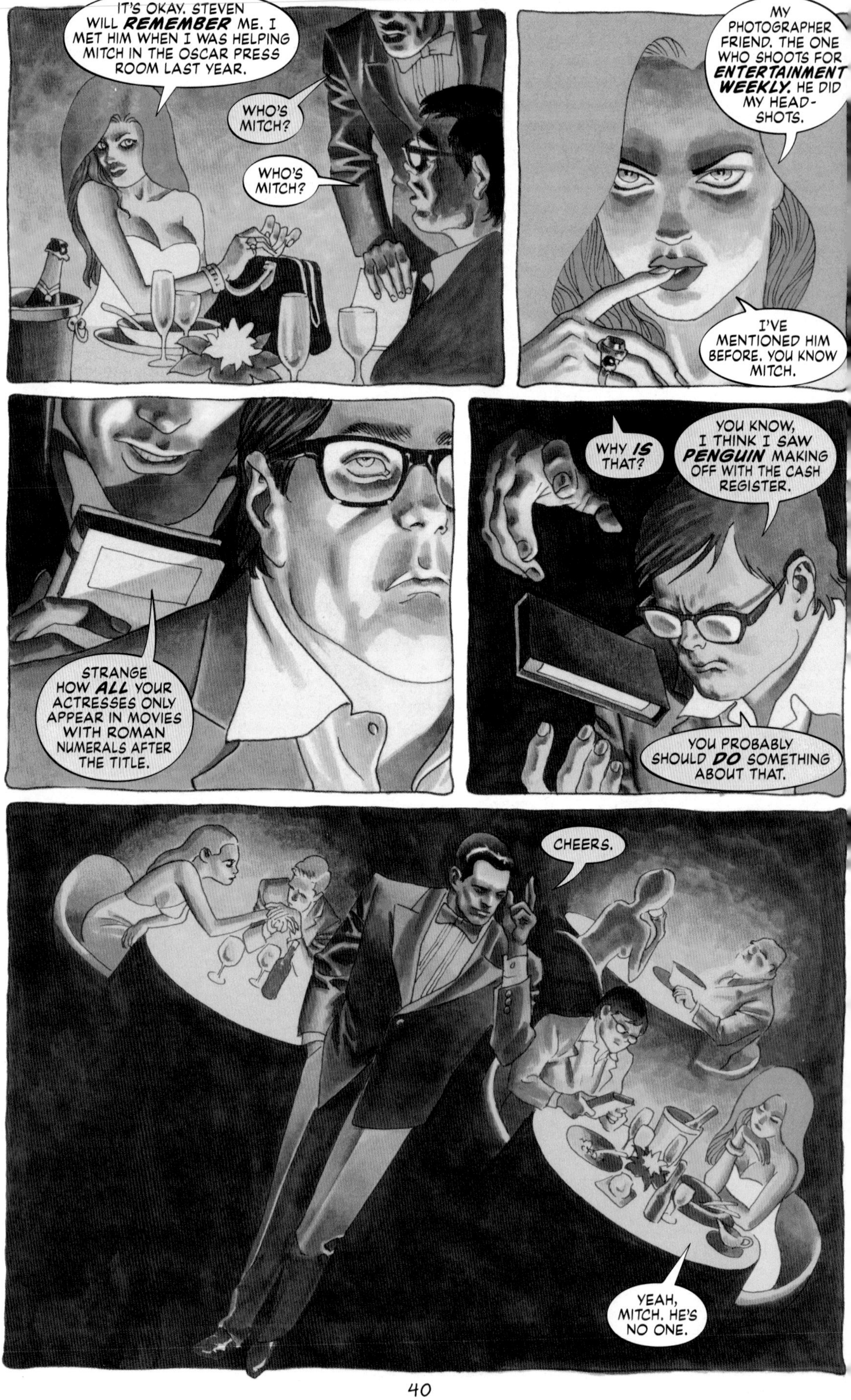
IT'S OKAY. STEVEN WILL **REMEMBER** ME. I MET HIM WHEN I WAS HELPING MITCH IN THE OSCAR PRESS ROOM LAST YEAR.
WHO'S MITCH?
WHO'S MITCH?
MY PHOTOGRAPHER FRIEND. THE ONE WHO SHOOTS FOR ***ENTERTAINMENT WEEKLY.*** HE DID MY HEAD-SHOTS.
I'VE MENTIONED HIM BEFORE. YOU KNOW MITCH.
STRANGE HOW **ALL** YOUR ACTRESSES ONLY APPEAR IN MOVIES WITH ROMAN NUMERALS AFTER THE TITLE.
WHY ***IS*** THAT?
YOU KNOW, I THINK I SAW ***PENGUIN*** MAKING OFF WITH THE CASH REGISTER.
YOU PROBABLY SHOULD ***DO*** SOMETHING ABOUT THAT.
CHEERS.
YEAH, MITCH. HE'S NO ONE.

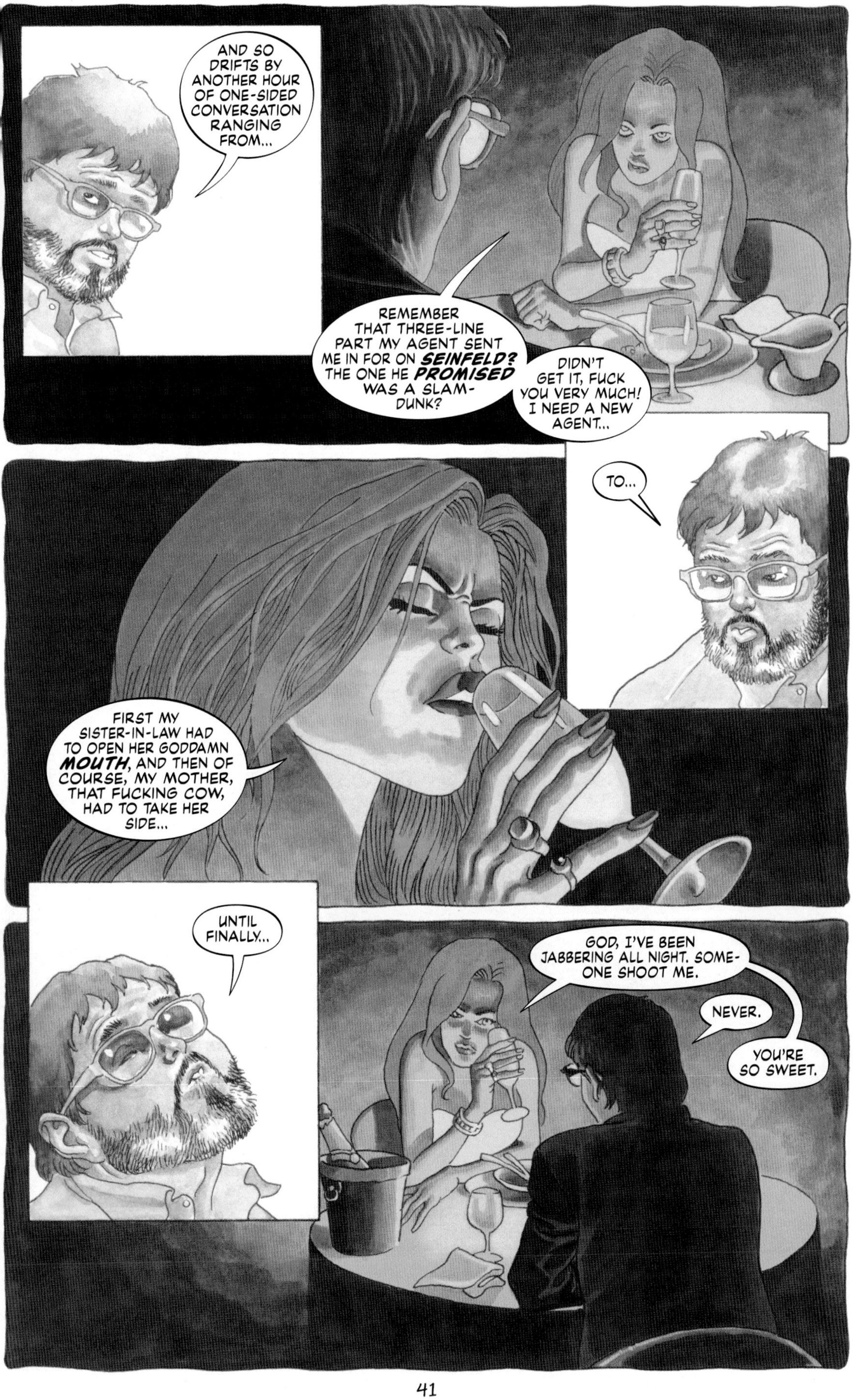
AND SO DRIFTS BY ANOTHER HOUR OF ONE-SIDED CONVERSATION RANGING FROM...
REMEMBER THAT THREE-LINE PART MY AGENT SENT ME IN FOR ON SEINFELD? THE ONE HE PROMISED WAS A SLAM-DUNK?
DIDN'T GET IT, FUCK YOU VERY MUCH! I NEED A NEW AGENT...
TO...
FIRST MY SISTER-IN-LAW HAD TO OPEN HER GODDAMN MOUTH, AND THEN OF COURSE, MY MOTHER, THAT FUCKING COW, HAD TO TAKE HER SIDE...
UNTIL FINALLY...
GOD, I'VE BEEN JABBERING ALL NIGHT. SOME-ONE SHOOT ME.
NEVER.
YOU'RE SO SWEET.

AND YOU. HOW ARE *YOU?* TELL ME EVERY-THING.

ARE YOU SEEING SOMEONE WONDERFUL? YOU CERTAINLY *DESERVE* SOMEONE WONDERFUL.

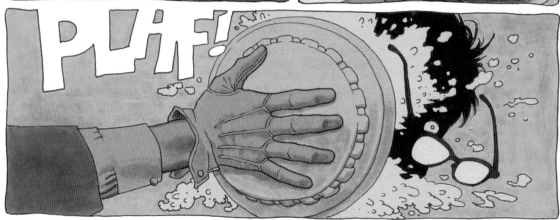
PLIF!

NOW *THAT* WAS WORTH SITTING THROUGH THE SISTER-IN-LAW STORY FOR!

OH, WANH-WANH-*WANH!* DON'T LOOK SO GLUM...

YOU'RE SO QUIET. THERE *IS* SOMEONE, AM I RIGHT?

YOU *KNEW* IT WAS COMING. WRAP IT UP, CHUMP.

WE'VE GOT *WORK* IN THE A.M., AND *GOD KNOWS* HOW LONG A DRIVE SHE'S GOT TO MITCH'S PLACE.

SO WHAT'S HER NAME?

WHAT'S SHE LIKE?

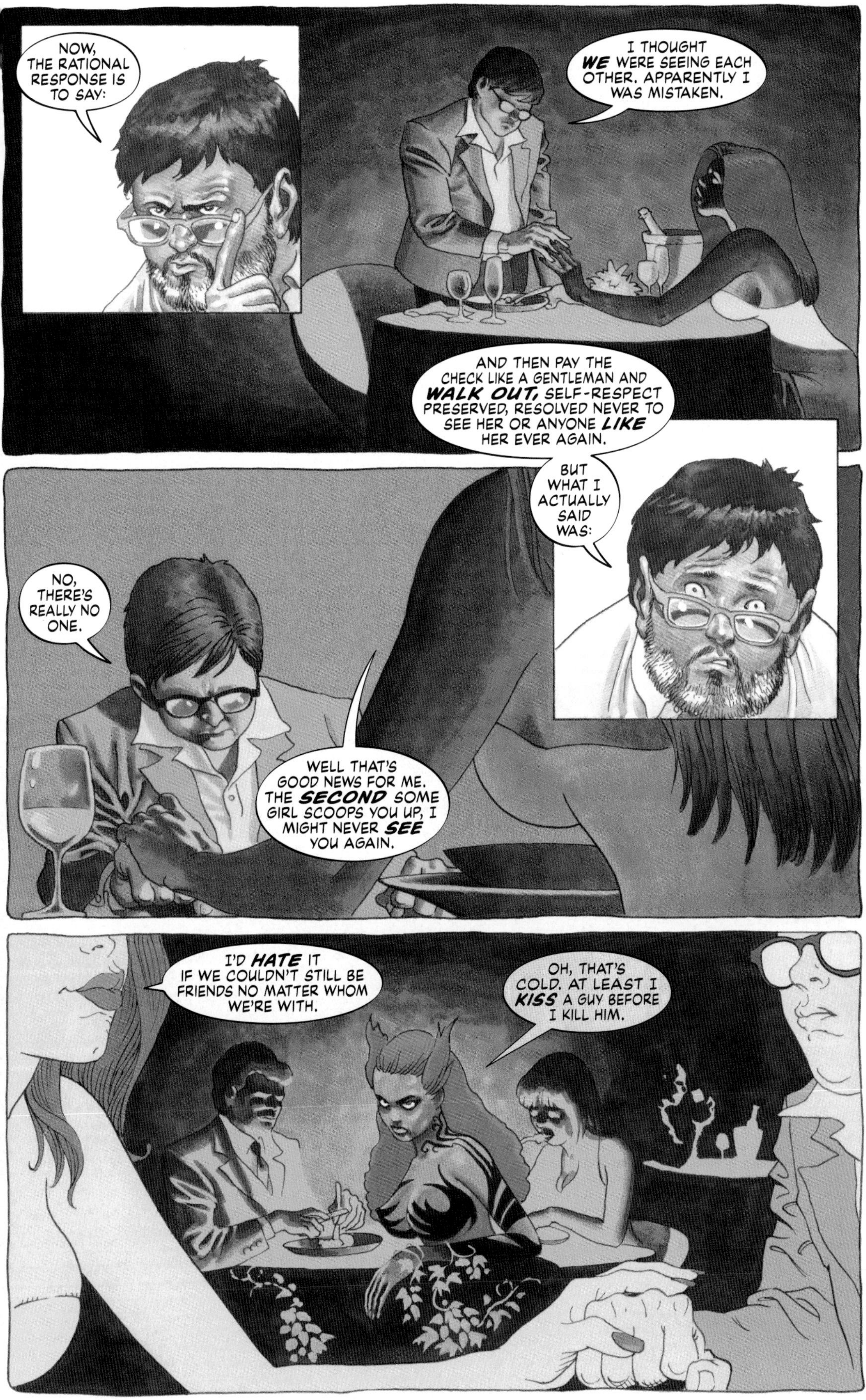

NOW, THE RATIONAL RESPONSE IS TO SAY:
I THOUGHT WE WERE SEEING EACH OTHER. APPARENTLY I WAS MISTAKEN.
AND THEN PAY THE CHECK LIKE A GENTLEMAN AND WALK OUT, SELF-RESPECT PRESERVED, RESOLVED NEVER TO SEE HER OR ANYONE LIKE HER EVER AGAIN.
BUT WHAT I ACTUALLY SAID WAS:
NO, THERE'S REALLY NO ONE.
WELL THAT'S GOOD NEWS FOR ME. THE SECOND SOME GIRL SCOOPS YOU UP, I MIGHT NEVER SEE YOU AGAIN.
I'D HATE IT IF WE COULDN'T STILL BE FRIENDS NO MATTER WHOM WE'RE WITH.
OH, THAT'S COLD. AT LEAST I KISS A GUY BEFORE I KILL HIM.

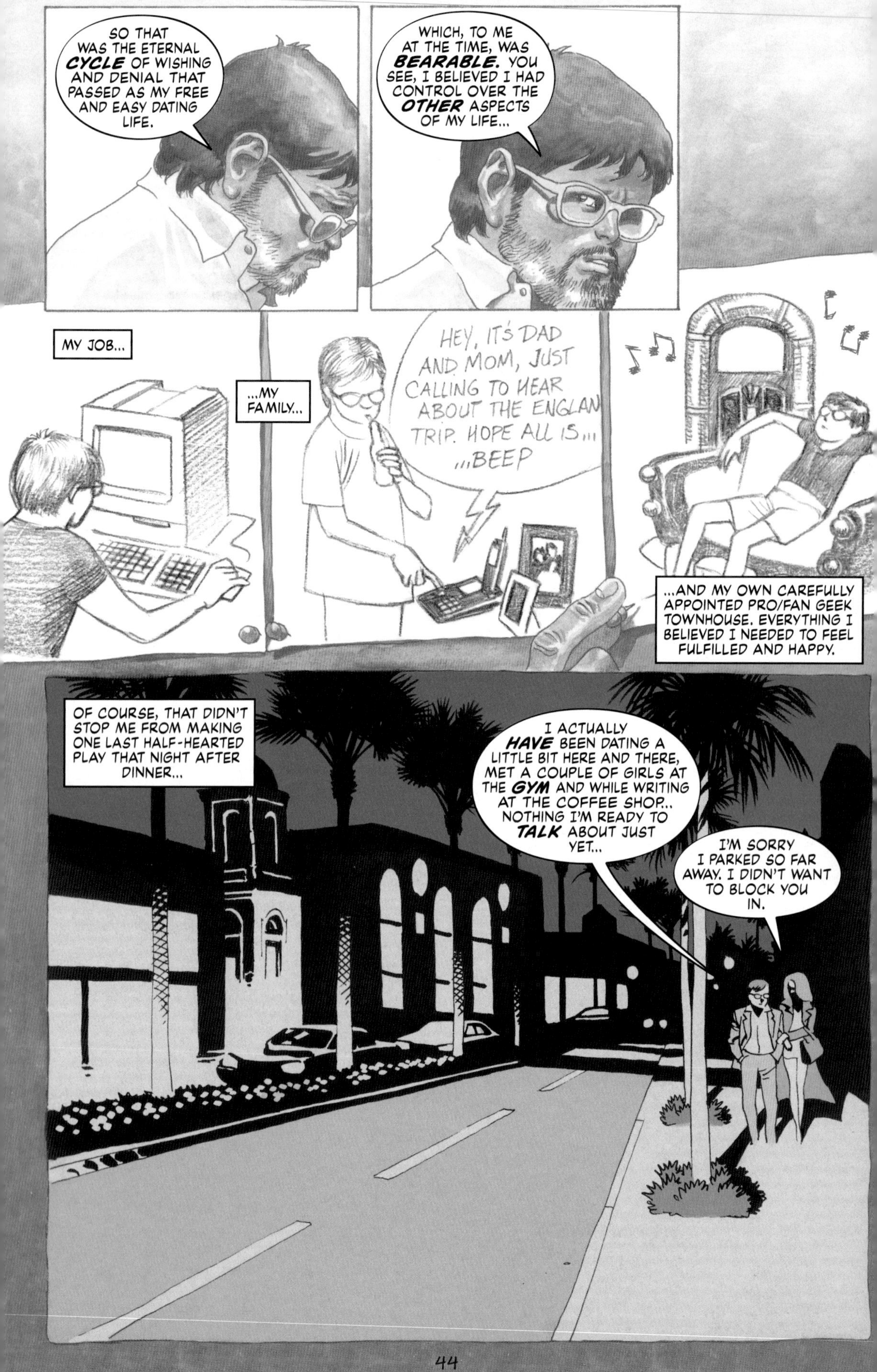
SO THAT WAS THE ETERNAL CYCLE OF WISHING AND DENIAL THAT PASSED AS MY FREE AND EASY DATING LIFE.
WHICH, TO ME AT THE TIME, WAS BEARABLE. YOU SEE, I BELIEVED I HAD CONTROL OVER THE OTHER ASPECTS OF MY LIFE...
MY JOB...
...MY FAMILY...
HEY, IT'S DAD AND MOM, JUST CALLING TO HEAR ABOUT THE ENGLAN TRIP. HOPE ALL IS... ...BEEP
...AND MY OWN CAREFULLY APPOINTED PRO/FAN GEEK TOWNHOUSE. EVERYTHING I BELIEVED I NEEDED TO FEEL FULFILLED AND HAPPY.
OF COURSE, THAT DIDN'T STOP ME FROM MAKING ONE LAST HALF-HEARTED PLAY THAT NIGHT AFTER DINNER...
I ACTUALLY HAVE BEEN DATING A LITTLE BIT HERE AND THERE, MET A COUPLE OF GIRLS AT THE GYM AND WHILE WRITING AT THE COFFEE SHOP.. NOTHING I'M READY TO TALK ABOUT JUST YET...
I'M SORRY I PARKED SO FAR AWAY. I DIDN'T WANT TO BLOCK YOU IN.

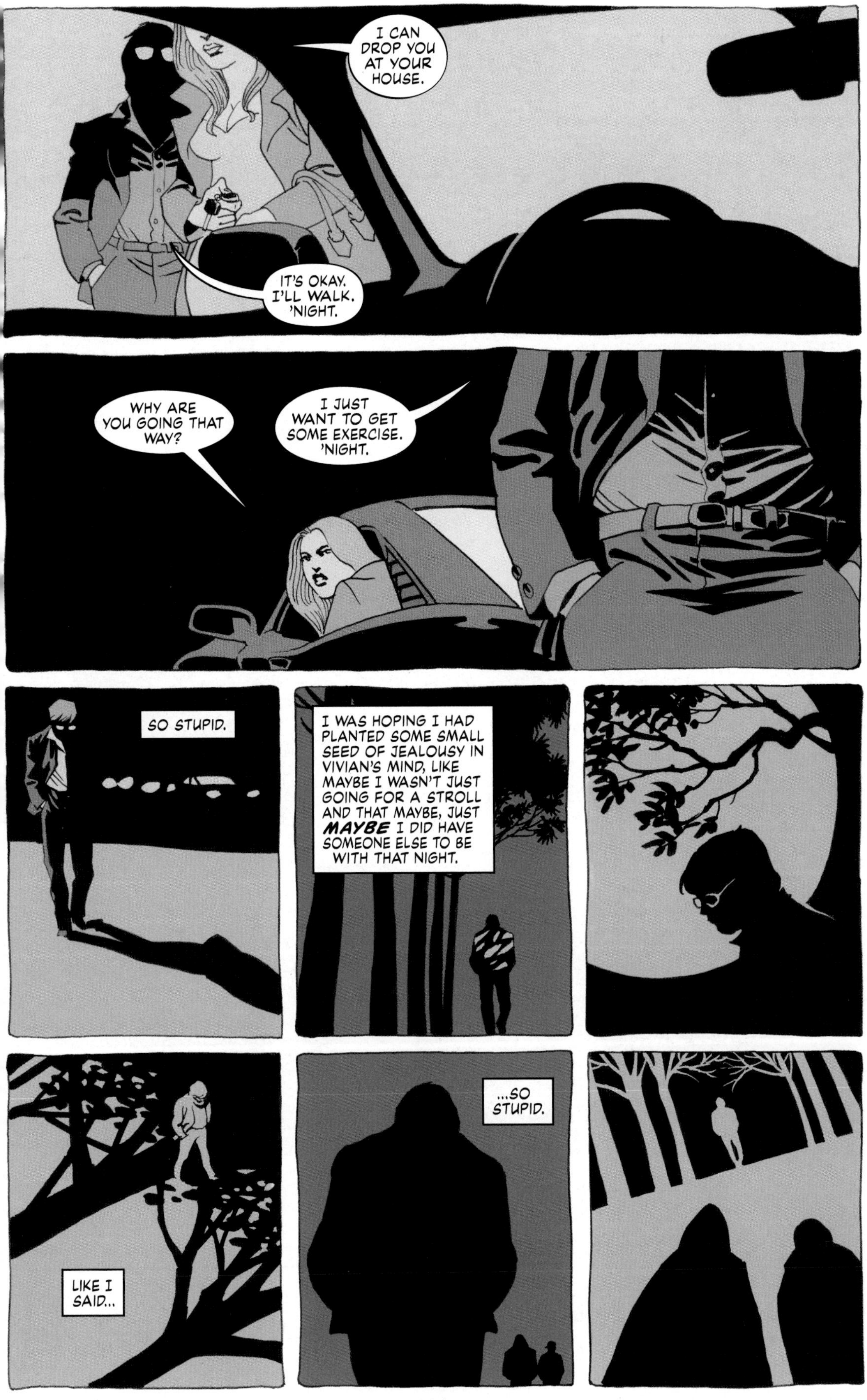
I CAN DROP YOU AT YOUR HOUSE.
IT'S OKAY. I'LL WALK. 'NIGHT.
WHY ARE YOU GOING THAT WAY?
I JUST WANT TO GET SOME EXERCISE. 'NIGHT.
SO STUPID.
I WAS HOPING I HAD PLANTED SOME SMALL SEED OF JEALOUSY IN VIVIAN'S MIND, LIKE MAYBE I WASN'T JUST GOING FOR A STROLL AND THAT MAYBE, JUST *MAYBE* I DID HAVE SOMEONE ELSE TO BE WITH THAT NIGHT.
LIKE I SAID...
...SO STUPID.

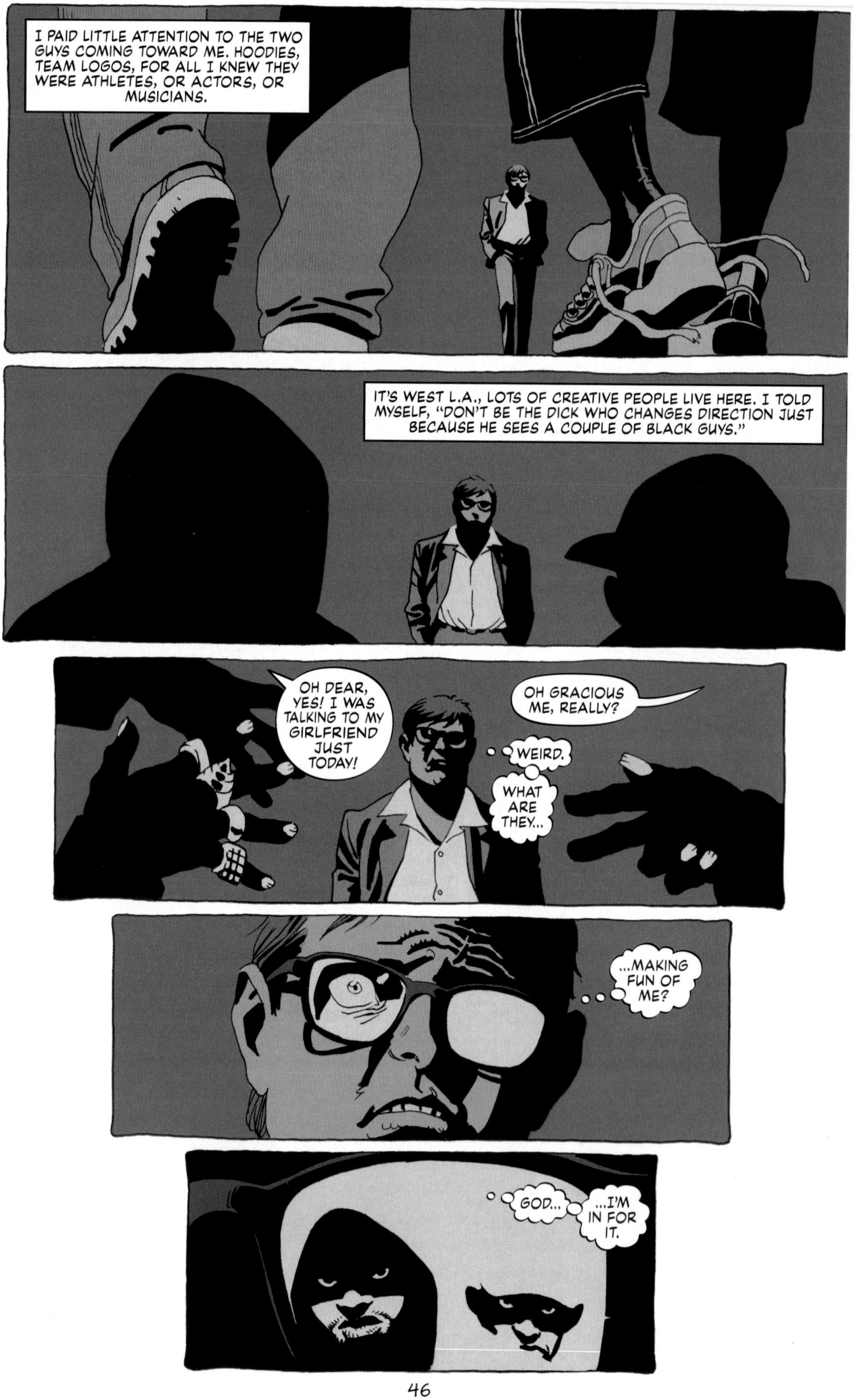
I PAID LITTLE ATTENTION TO THE TWO GUYS COMING TOWARD ME. HOODIES, TEAM LOGOS, FOR ALL I KNEW THEY WERE ATHLETES, OR ACTORS, OR MUSICIANS.
IT'S WEST L.A., LOTS OF CREATIVE PEOPLE LIVE HERE. I TOLD MYSELF, "DON'T BE THE DICK WHO CHANGES DIRECTION JUST BECAUSE HE SEES A COUPLE OF BLACK GUYS."
OH DEAR, YES! I WAS TALKING TO MY GIRLFRIEND JUST TODAY!
OH GRACIOUS ME, REALLY?
WEIRD.
WHAT ARE THEY...
...MAKING FUN OF ME?
GOD...
...I'M IN FOR IT.

MOTHER-FUCKING PIECE OF *SHIT!*

HOLD HIM!

FUCKING *BITCH!*

TAKE IT, YOU FUCKING *BITCH!*

KILL HIM!

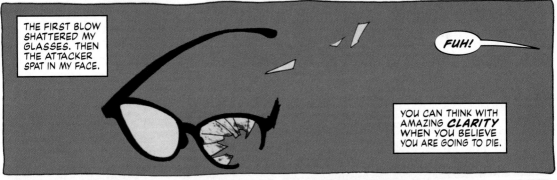

THE FIRST BLOW SHATTERED MY GLASSES. THEN THE ATTACKER SPAT IN MY FACE.

FUH!

YOU CAN THINK WITH AMAZING *CLARITY* WHEN YOU BELIEVE YOU ARE GOING TO DIE.

FOR ONE THING, I KNEW NO ONE WOULD HELP ME. IF ANYONE WAS GOING TO RUSH TO MY AID, THEY WOULD HAVE DONE SO ALREADY.

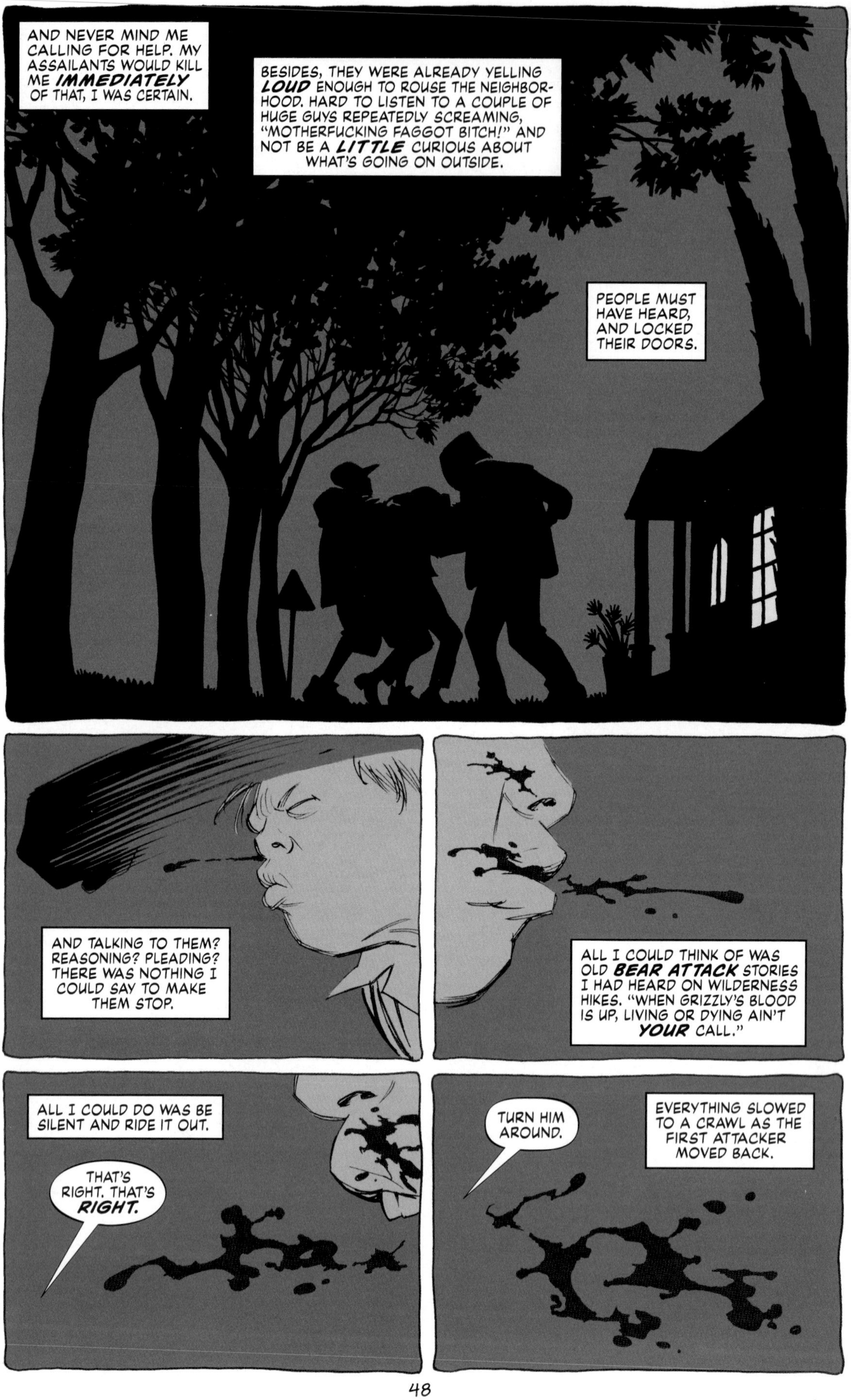

AND NEVER MIND ME CALLING FOR HELP. MY ASSAILANTS WOULD KILL ME *IMMEDIATELY* OF THAT, I WAS CERTAIN.
BESIDES, THEY WERE ALREADY YELLING *LOUD* ENOUGH TO ROUSE THE NEIGHBORHOOD. HARD TO LISTEN TO A COUPLE OF HUGE GUYS REPEATEDLY SCREAMING, "MOTHERFUCKING FAGGOT BITCH!" AND NOT BE A *LITTLE* CURIOUS ABOUT WHAT'S GOING ON OUTSIDE.
PEOPLE MUST HAVE HEARD, AND LOCKED THEIR DOORS.
AND TALKING TO THEM? REASONING? PLEADING? THERE WAS NOTHING I COULD SAY TO MAKE THEM STOP.
ALL I COULD THINK OF WAS OLD *BEAR ATTACK* STORIES I HAD HEARD ON WILDERNESS HIKES. "WHEN GRIZZLY'S BLOOD IS UP, LIVING OR DYING AIN'T *YOUR* CALL."
ALL I COULD DO WAS BE SILENT AND RIDE IT OUT.
THAT'S RIGHT. THAT'S *RIGHT.*
TURN HIM AROUND.
EVERYTHING SLOWED TO A CRAWL AS THE FIRST ATTACKER MOVED BACK.

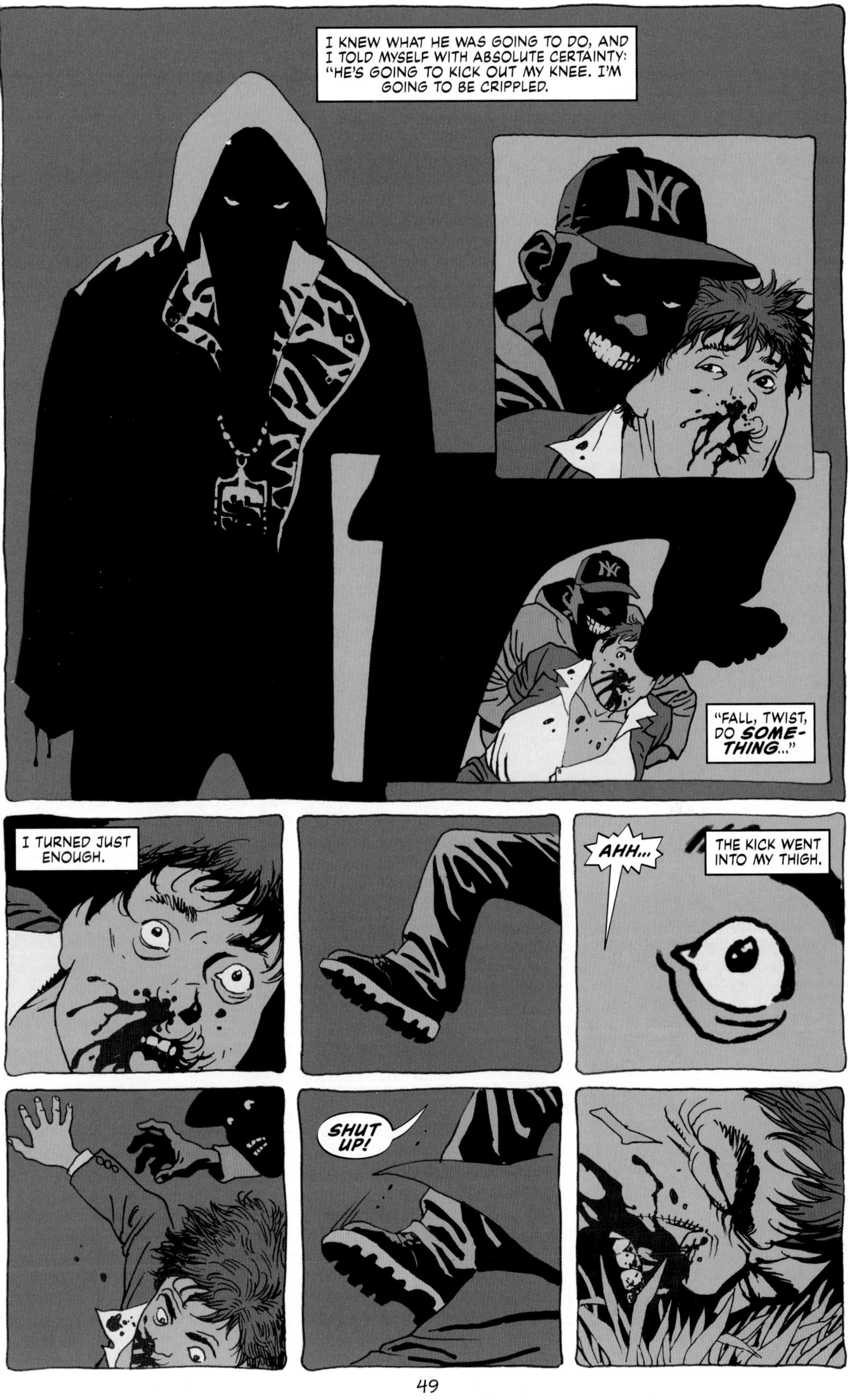
I KNEW WHAT HE WAS GOING TO DO, AND I TOLD MYSELF WITH ABSOLUTE CERTAINTY: "HE'S GOING TO KICK OUT MY KNEE. I'M GOING TO BE CRIPPLED.
"FALL, TWIST, DO **SOME-THING**..."
I TURNED JUST ENOUGH.
AHH...
THE KICK WENT INTO MY THIGH.
SHUT UP!

BITCH...

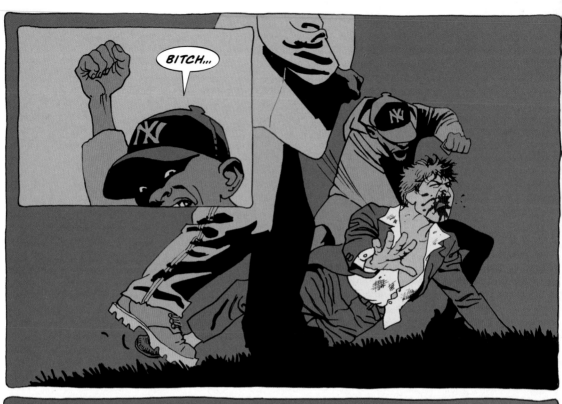

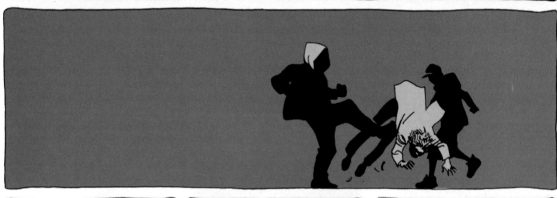

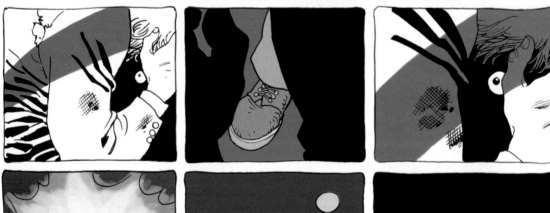

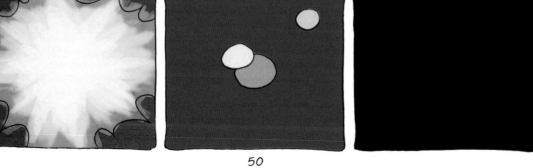

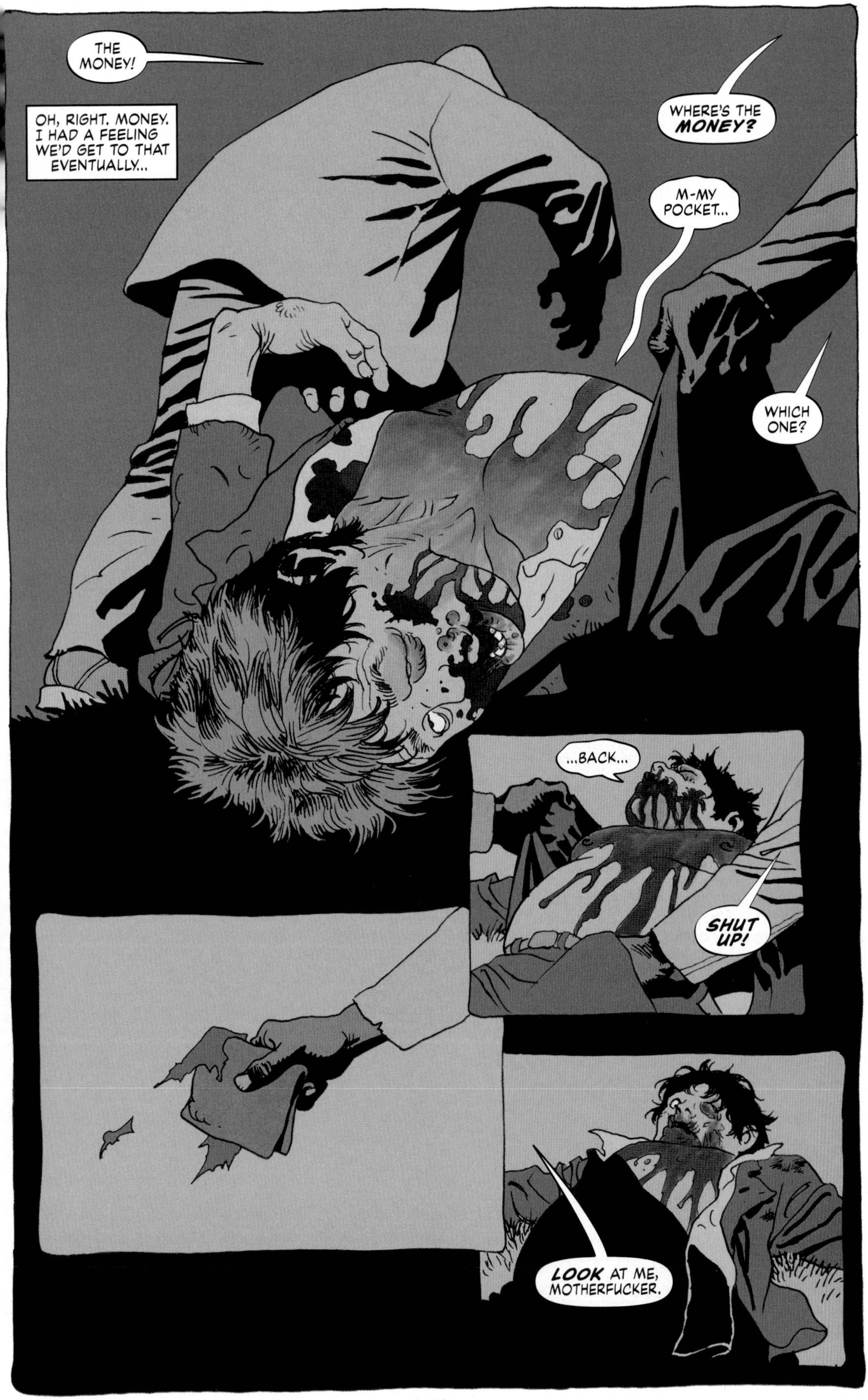
THE MONEY!
OH, RIGHT. MONEY. I HAD A FEELING WE'D GET TO THAT EVENTUALLY...
WHERE'S THE **MONEY?**
M-MY POCKET...
WHICH ONE?
...BACK...
SHUT UP!
LOOK AT ME, MOTHERFUCKER.

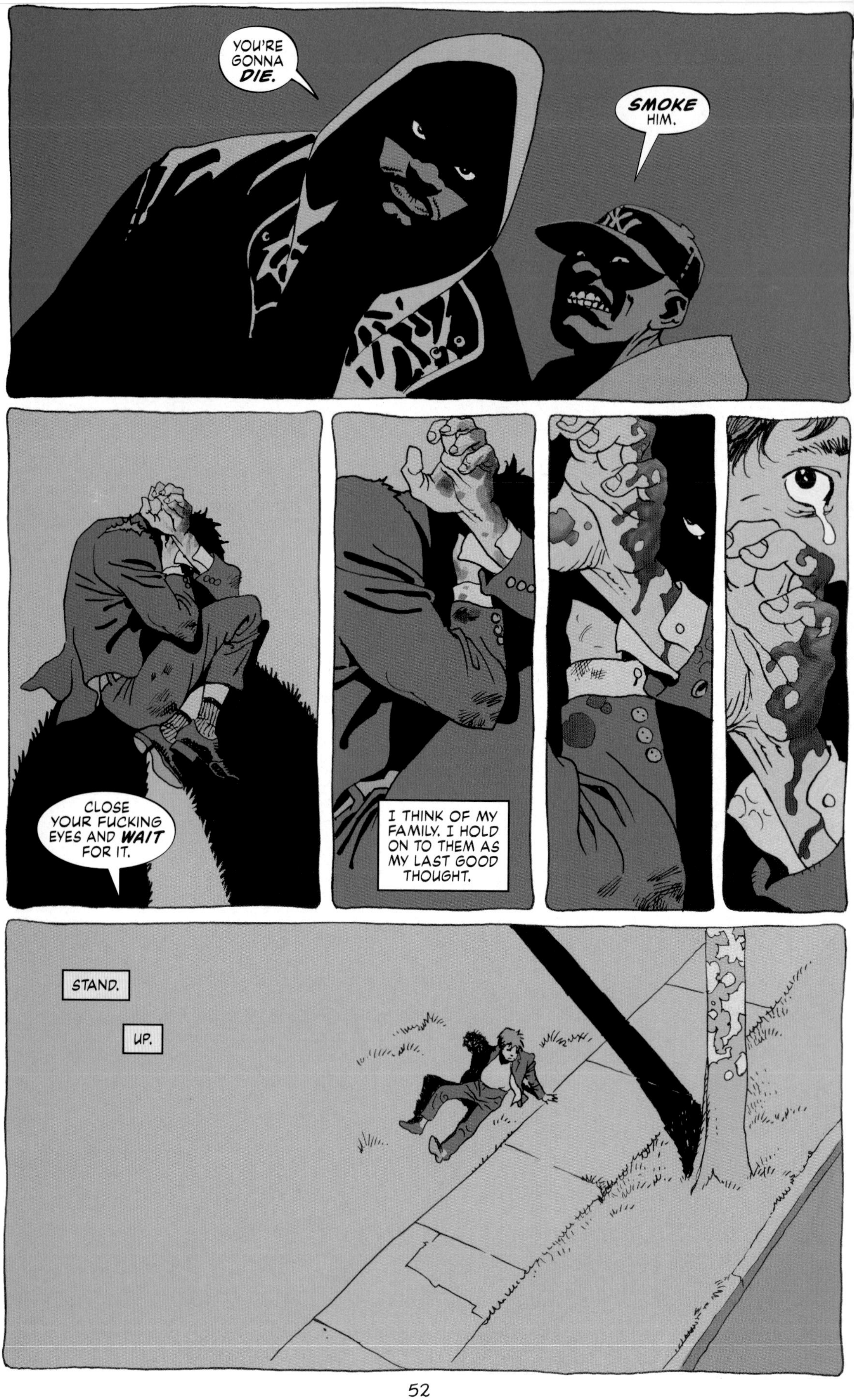

YOU'RE GONNA DIE.
SMOKE HIM.
CLOSE YOUR FUCKING EYES AND WAIT FOR IT.
I THINK OF MY FAMILY. I HOLD ON TO THEM AS MY LAST GOOD THOUGHT.
STAND.
UP.

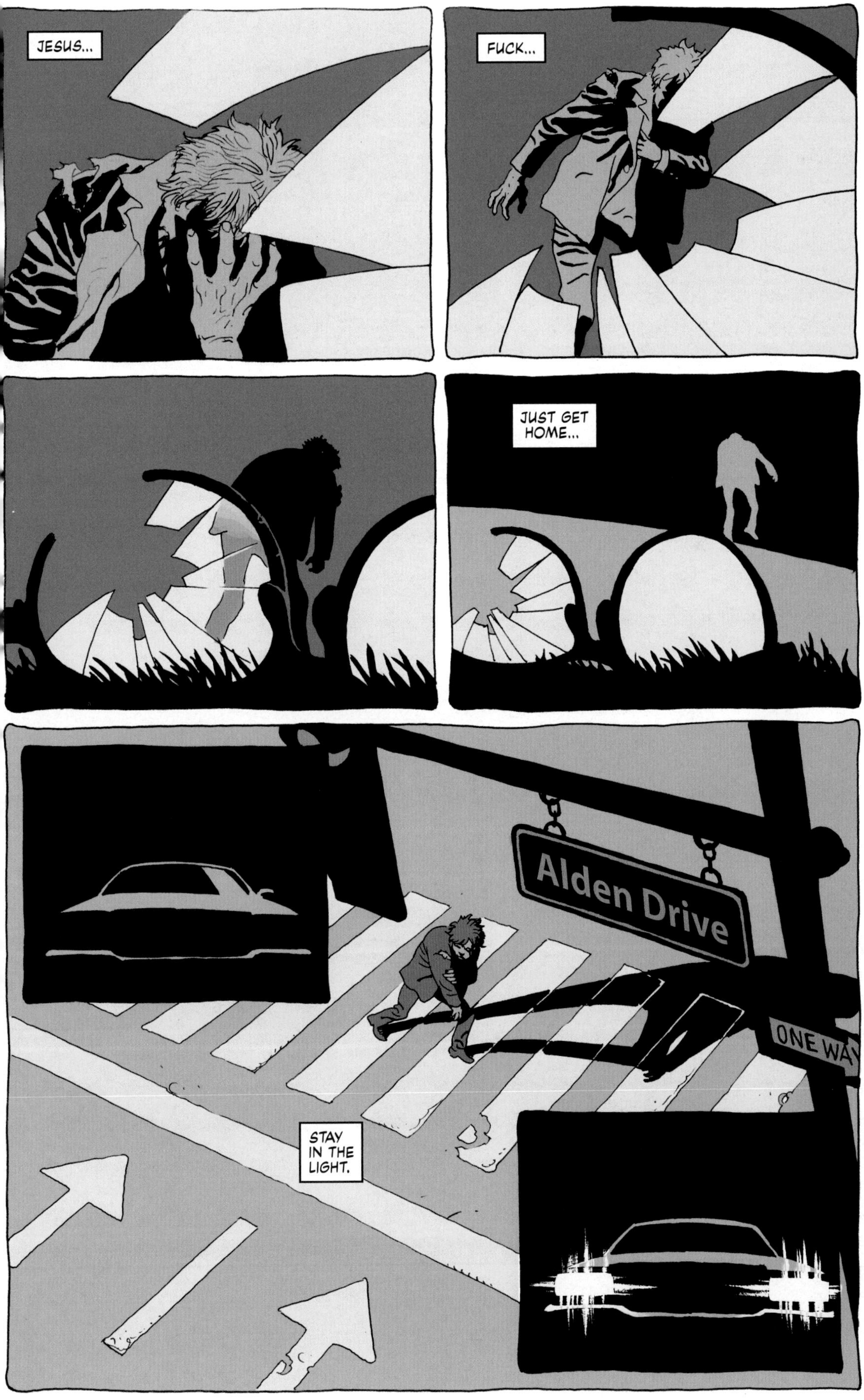
JESUS...
FUCK...
JUST GET HOME...
Alden Drive
ONE WAY
STAY IN THE LIGHT.

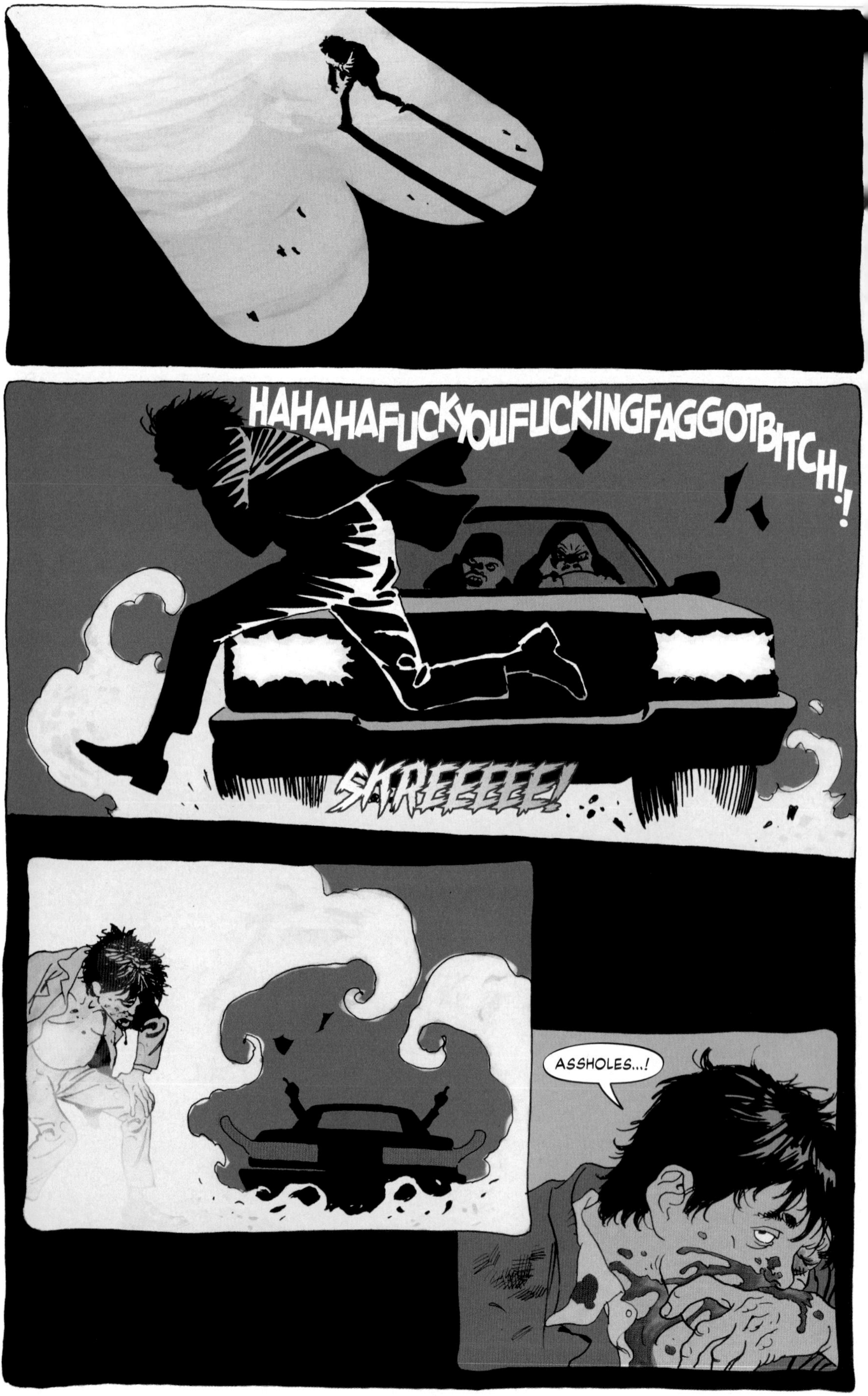
HAHAHAFUCKYOUFUCKINGFAGGOTBITCH!!
SKREEEEEE!
ASSHOLES...!

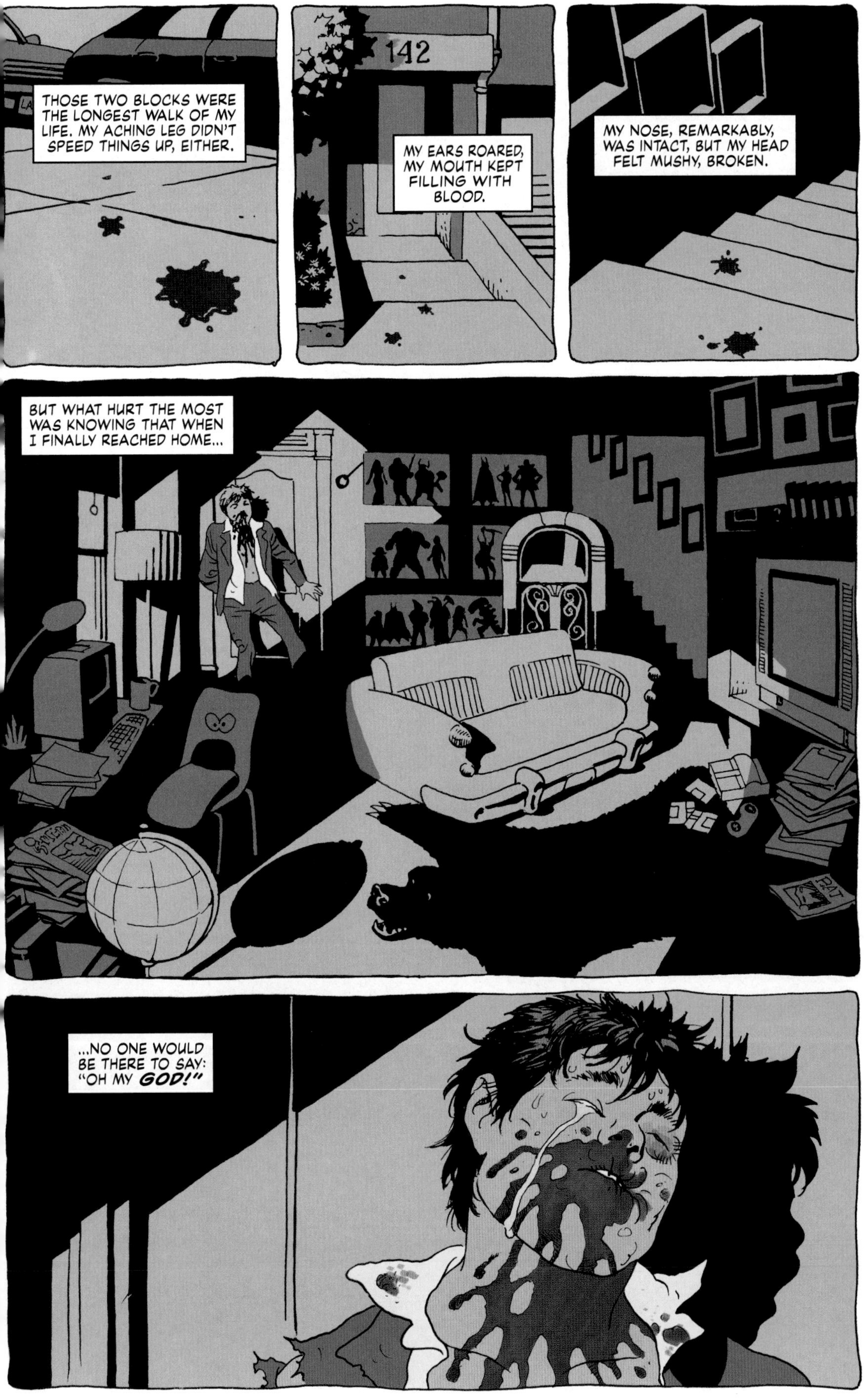
THOSE TWO BLOCKS WERE THE LONGEST WALK OF MY LIFE. MY ACHING LEG DIDN'T SPEED THINGS UP, EITHER.
142
MY EARS ROARED, MY MOUTH KEPT FILLING WITH BLOOD.
MY NOSE, REMARKABLY, WAS INTACT, BUT MY HEAD FELT MUSHY, BROKEN.
BUT WHAT HURT THE MOST WAS KNOWING THAT WHEN I FINALLY REACHED HOME...
...NO ONE WOULD BE THERE TO SAY: "OH MY *GOD!*"

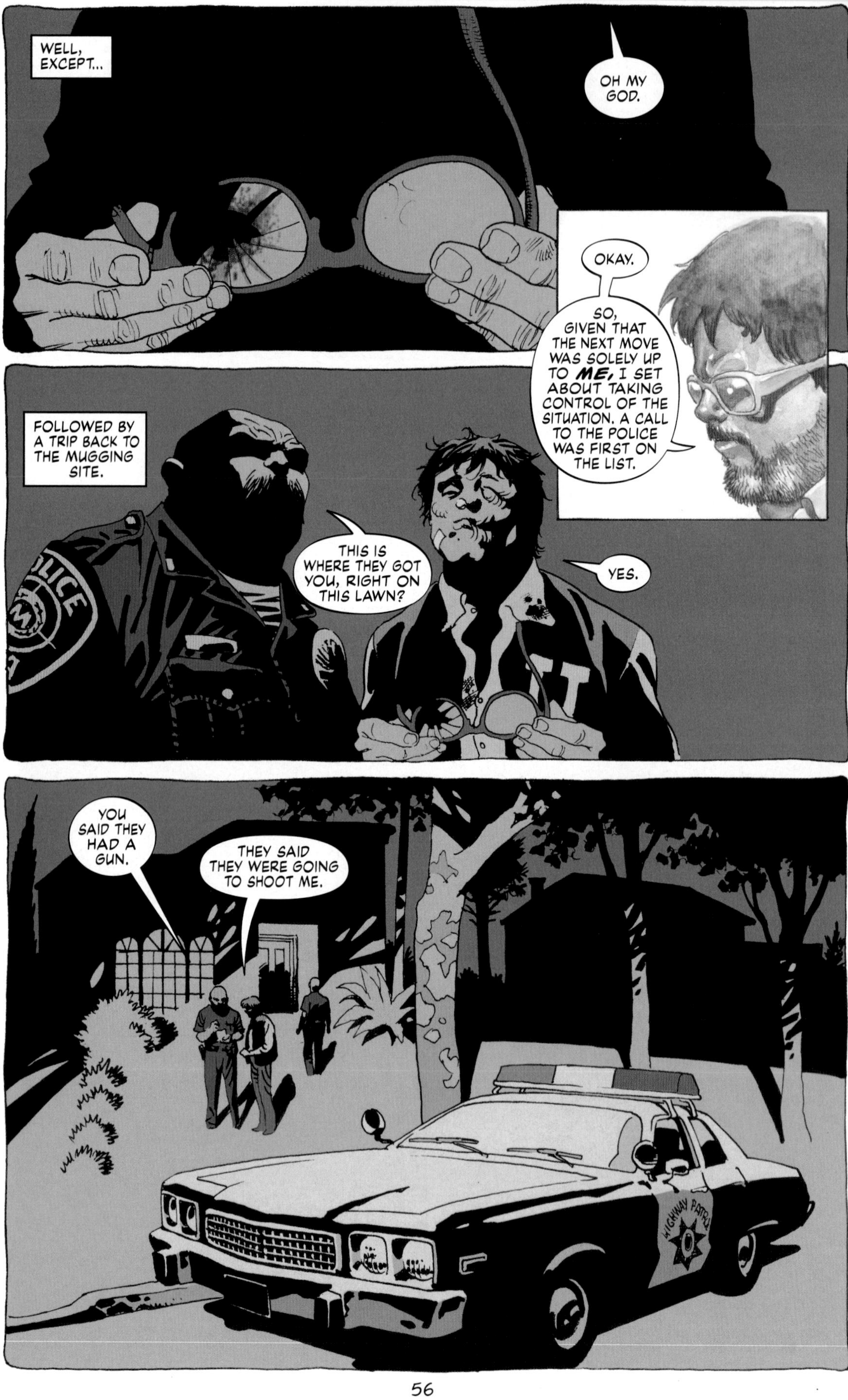
WELL, EXCEPT...
OH MY GOD.
OKAY.
SO, GIVEN THAT THE NEXT MOVE WAS SOLELY UP TO ME, I SET ABOUT TAKING CONTROL OF THE SITUATION. A CALL TO THE POLICE WAS FIRST ON THE LIST.
FOLLOWED BY A TRIP BACK TO THE MUGGING SITE.
POLICE
THIS IS WHERE THEY GOT YOU, RIGHT ON THIS LAWN?
YES.
YOU SAID THEY HAD A GUN.
THEY SAID THEY WERE GOING TO SHOOT ME.
HIGHWAY PATROL

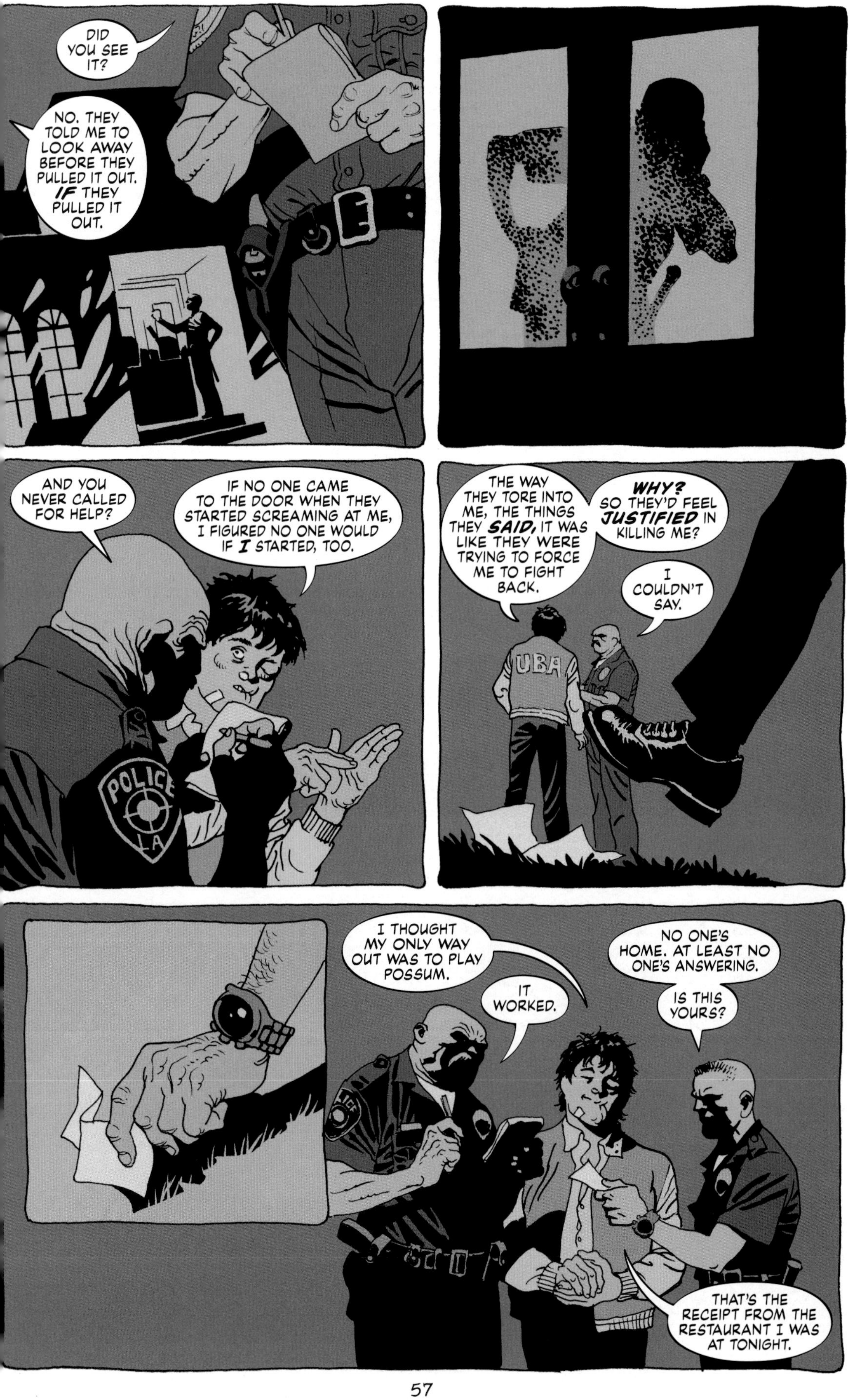

DID YOU SEE IT?
NO. THEY TOLD ME TO LOOK AWAY BEFORE THEY PULLED IT OUT. IF THEY PULLED IT OUT.
AND YOU NEVER CALLED FOR HELP?
IF NO ONE CAME TO THE DOOR WHEN THEY STARTED SCREAMING AT ME, I FIGURED NO ONE WOULD IF I STARTED, TOO.
POLICE
LA
THE WAY THEY TORE INTO ME, THE THINGS THEY SAID, IT WAS LIKE THEY WERE TRYING TO FORCE ME TO FIGHT BACK.
WHY? SO THEY'D FEEL JUSTIFIED IN KILLING ME?
I COULDN'T SAY.
UBA
I THOUGHT MY ONLY WAY OUT WAS TO PLAY POSSUM.
IT WORKED.
NO ONE'S HOME. AT LEAST NO ONE'S ANSWERING.
IS THIS YOURS?
THAT'S THE RECEIPT FROM THE RESTAURANT I WAS AT TONIGHT.

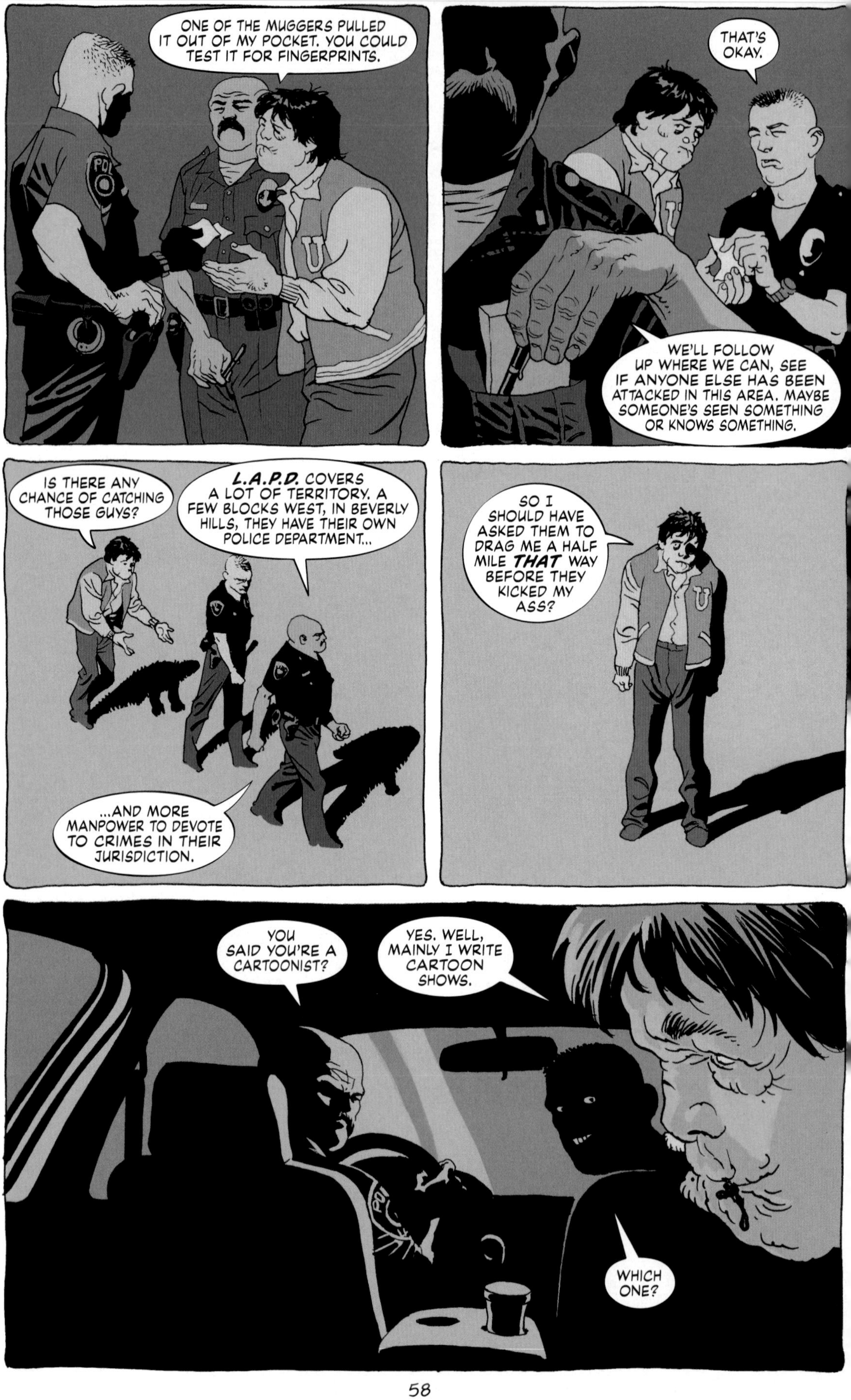
ONE OF THE MUGGERS PULLED IT OUT OF MY POCKET. YOU COULD TEST IT FOR FINGERPRINTS.
THAT'S OKAY.
WE'LL FOLLOW UP WHERE WE CAN, SEE IF ANYONE ELSE HAS BEEN ATTACKED IN THIS AREA. MAYBE SOMEONE'S SEEN SOMETHING OR KNOWS SOMETHING.
IS THERE ANY CHANCE OF CATCHING THOSE GUYS?
L.A.P.D. COVERS A LOT OF TERRITORY. A FEW BLOCKS WEST, IN BEVERLY HILLS, THEY HAVE THEIR OWN POLICE DEPARTMENT...
...AND MORE MANPOWER TO DEVOTE TO CRIMES IN THEIR JURISDICTION.
SO I SHOULD HAVE ASKED THEM TO DRAG ME A HALF MILE THAT WAY BEFORE THEY KICKED MY ASS?
YOU SAID YOU'RE A CARTOONIST?
YES. WELL, MAINLY I WRITE CARTOON SHOWS.
WHICH ONE?

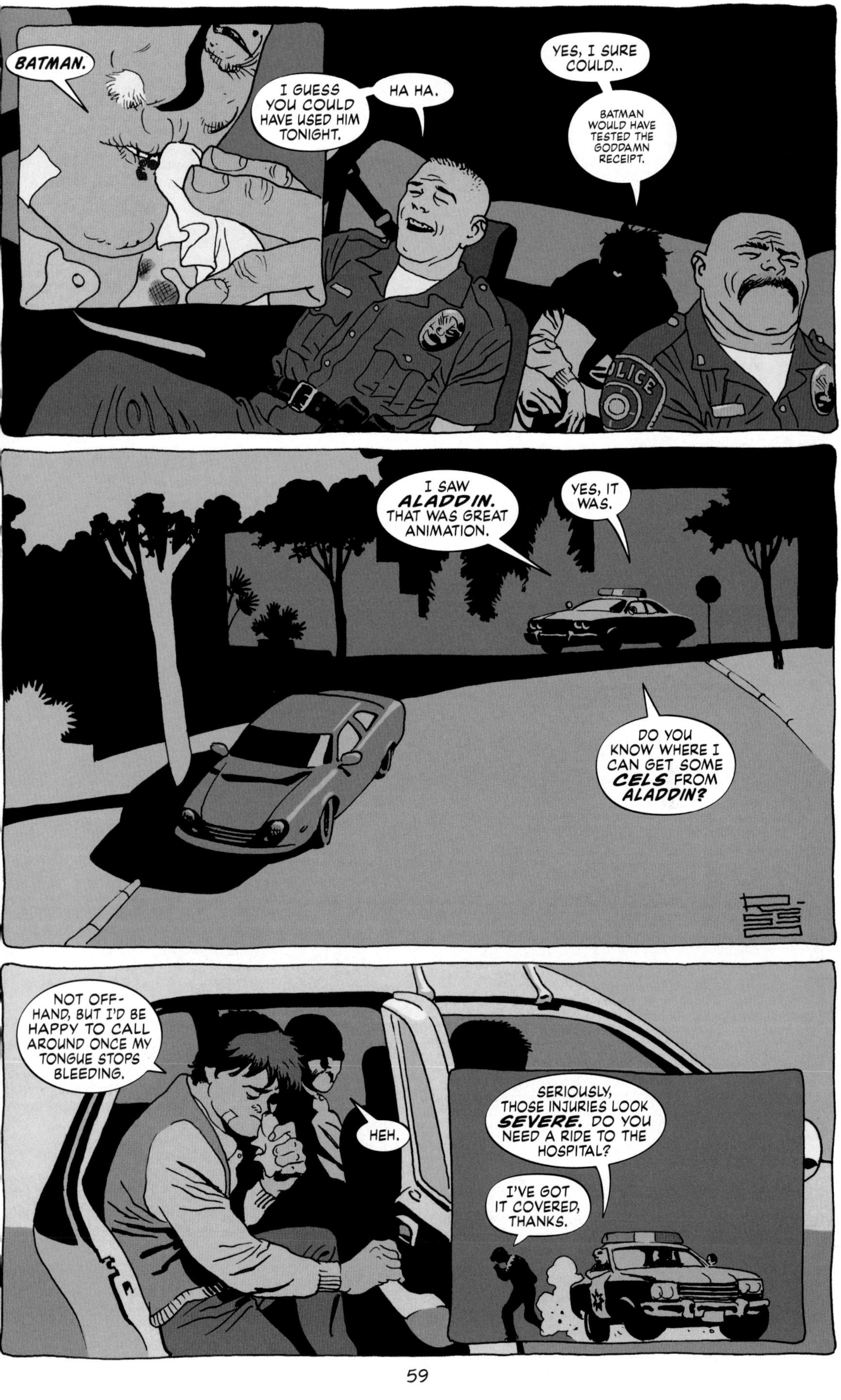
BATMAN.
I GUESS YOU COULD HAVE USED HIM TONIGHT.
HA HA.
YES, I SURE COULD...
BATMAN WOULD HAVE TESTED THE GODDAMN RECEIPT.
I SAW ALADDIN. THAT WAS GREAT ANIMATION.
YES, IT WAS.
DO YOU KNOW WHERE I CAN GET SOME CELS FROM ALADDIN?
NOT OFF-HAND, BUT I'D BE HAPPY TO CALL AROUND ONCE MY TONGUE STOPS BLEEDING.
HEH.
SERIOUSLY, THOSE INJURIES LOOK SEVERE. DO YOU NEED A RIDE TO THE HOSPITAL?
I'VE GOT IT COVERED, THANKS.

SO AFTER I WALKED YOU TO YOUR CAR, THESE TWO GUYS JUMPED ME.

"JUMPED"? YOU MEAN ATTACKED?

I MEAN THEY MASSACRED ME.

THAT'S SO AWFUL! THERE WAS THIS ONE TIME I WAS WALKING HOME FROM AN AUDITION AND THERE WERE THESE *GUYS* OUTSIDE A PARKING LOT IN HOLLY-WOOD...

...AND THEY STARTED FOLLOWING ME, WHISTLING AND MAKING CRUDE JOKES. THEY NEVER TOUCHED ME, THANK GOD...

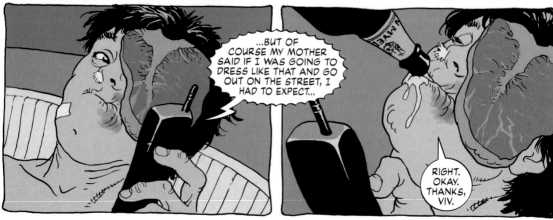

...BUT OF COURSE MY MOTHER SAID IF I WAS GOING TO DRESS LIKE THAT AND GO OUT ON THE STREET, I HAD TO EXPECT...

RIGHT. OKAY. THANKS, VIV.

60

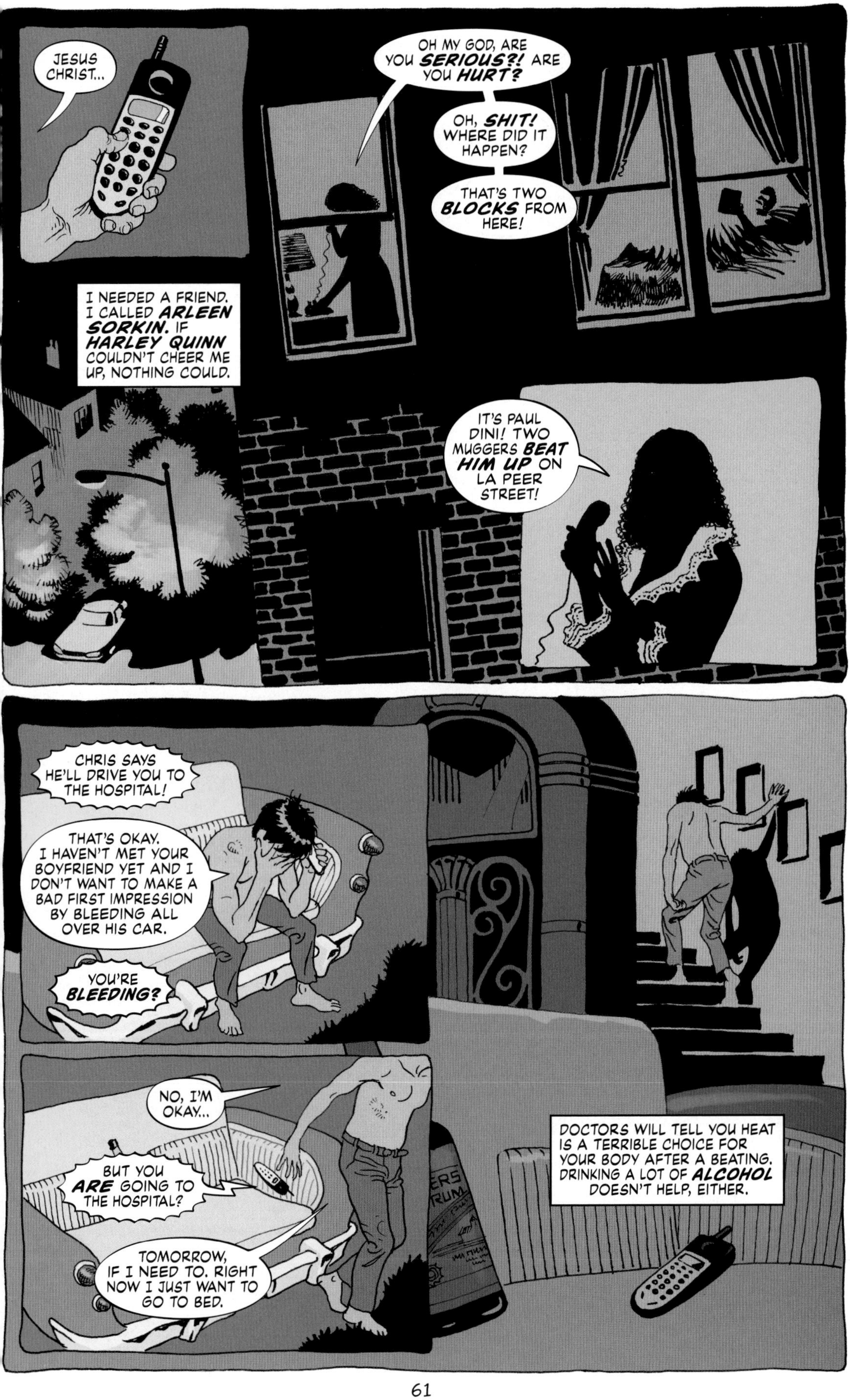
JESUS CHRIST...
OH MY GOD, ARE YOU SERIOUS?! ARE YOU HURT?
OH, SHIT! WHERE DID IT HAPPEN?
THAT'S TWO BLOCKS FROM HERE!
I NEEDED A FRIEND. I CALLED ARLEEN SORKIN. IF HARLEY QUINN COULDN'T CHEER ME UP, NOTHING COULD.
IT'S PAUL DINI! TWO MUGGERS BEAT HIM UP ON LA PEER STREET!
CHRIS SAYS HE'LL DRIVE YOU TO THE HOSPITAL!
THAT'S OKAY. I HAVEN'T MET YOUR BOYFRIEND YET AND I DON'T WANT TO MAKE A BAD FIRST IMPRESSION BY BLEEDING ALL OVER HIS CAR.
YOU'RE BLEEDING?
NO, I'M OKAY...
BUT YOU ARE GOING TO THE HOSPITAL?
TOMORROW, IF I NEED TO. RIGHT NOW I JUST WANT TO GO TO BED.
DOCTORS WILL TELL YOU HEAT IS A TERRIBLE CHOICE FOR YOUR BODY AFTER A BEATING. DRINKING A LOT OF ALCOHOL DOESN'T HELP, EITHER.

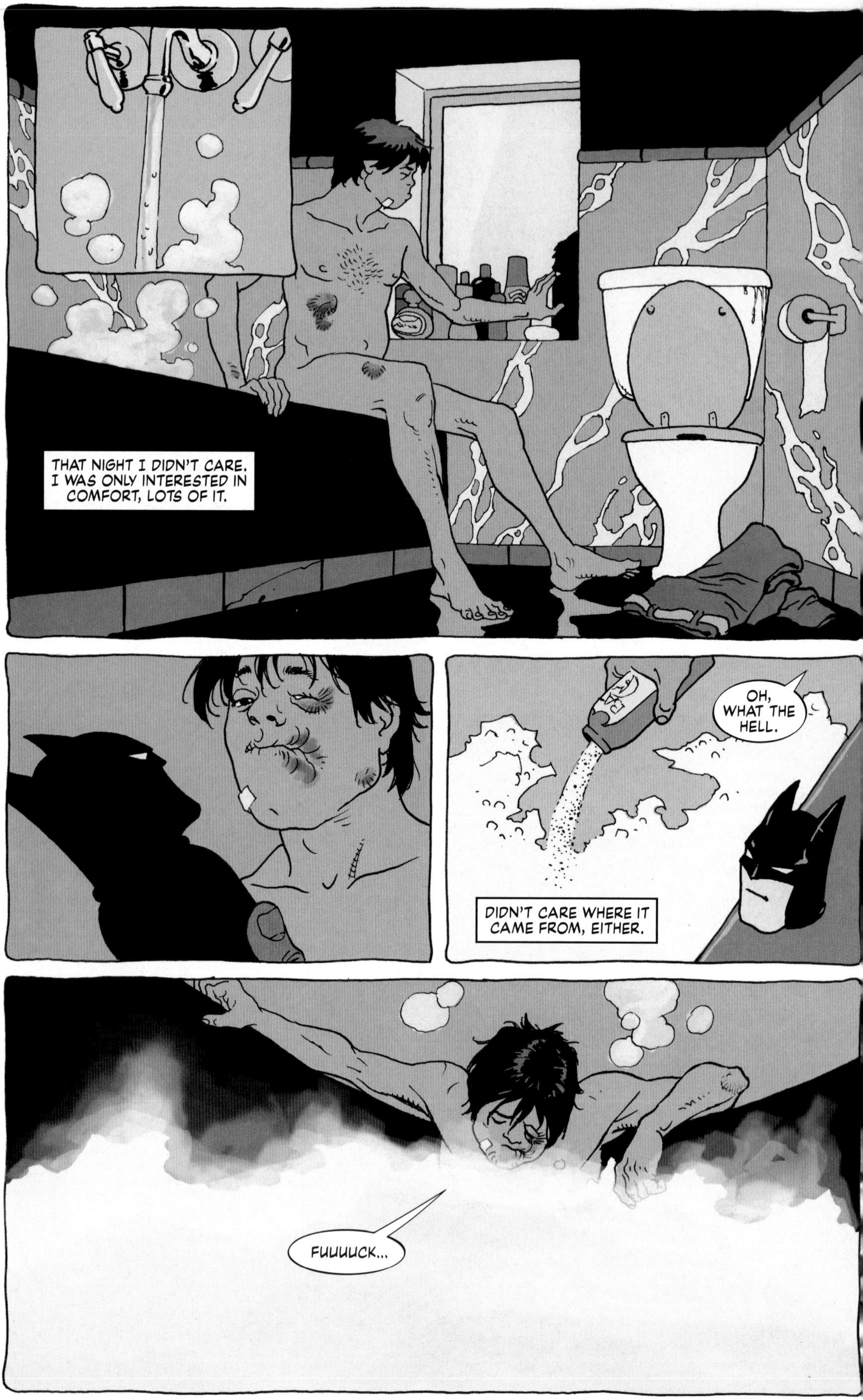
THAT NIGHT I DIDN'T CARE. I WAS ONLY INTERESTED IN COMFORT, LOTS OF IT.
OH, WHAT THE HELL.
DIDN'T CARE WHERE IT CAME FROM, EITHER.
FUUUUCK...

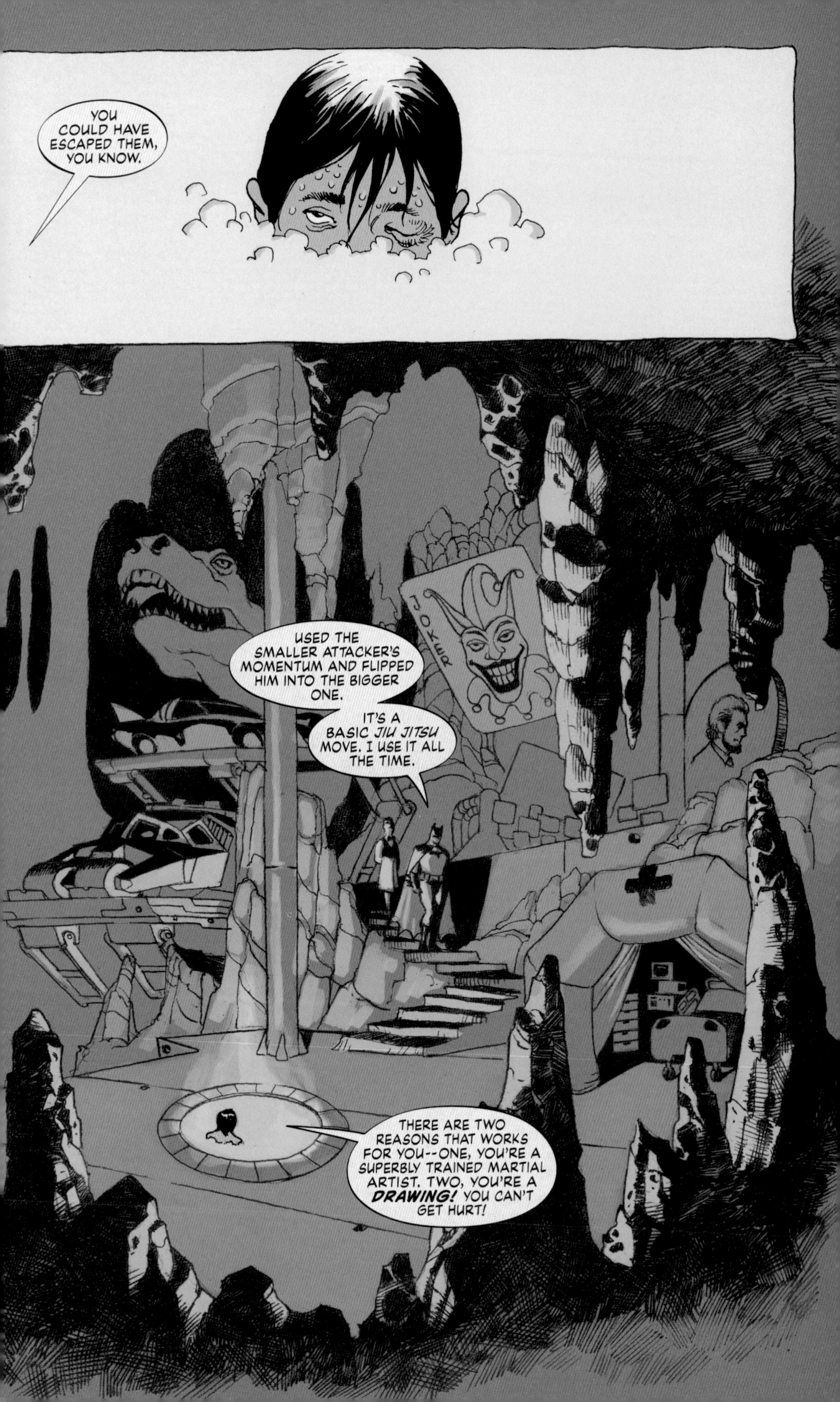
YOU COULD HAVE ESCAPED THEM, YOU KNOW.
JOKER
USED THE SMALLER ATTACKER'S MOMENTUM AND FLIPPED HIM INTO THE BIGGER ONE.
IT'S A BASIC JIU JITSU MOVE. I USE IT ALL THE TIME.
THERE ARE TWO REASONS THAT WORKS FOR YOU--ONE, YOU'RE A SUPERBLY TRAINED MARTIAL ARTIST. TWO, YOU'RE A DRAWING! YOU CAN'T GET HURT!

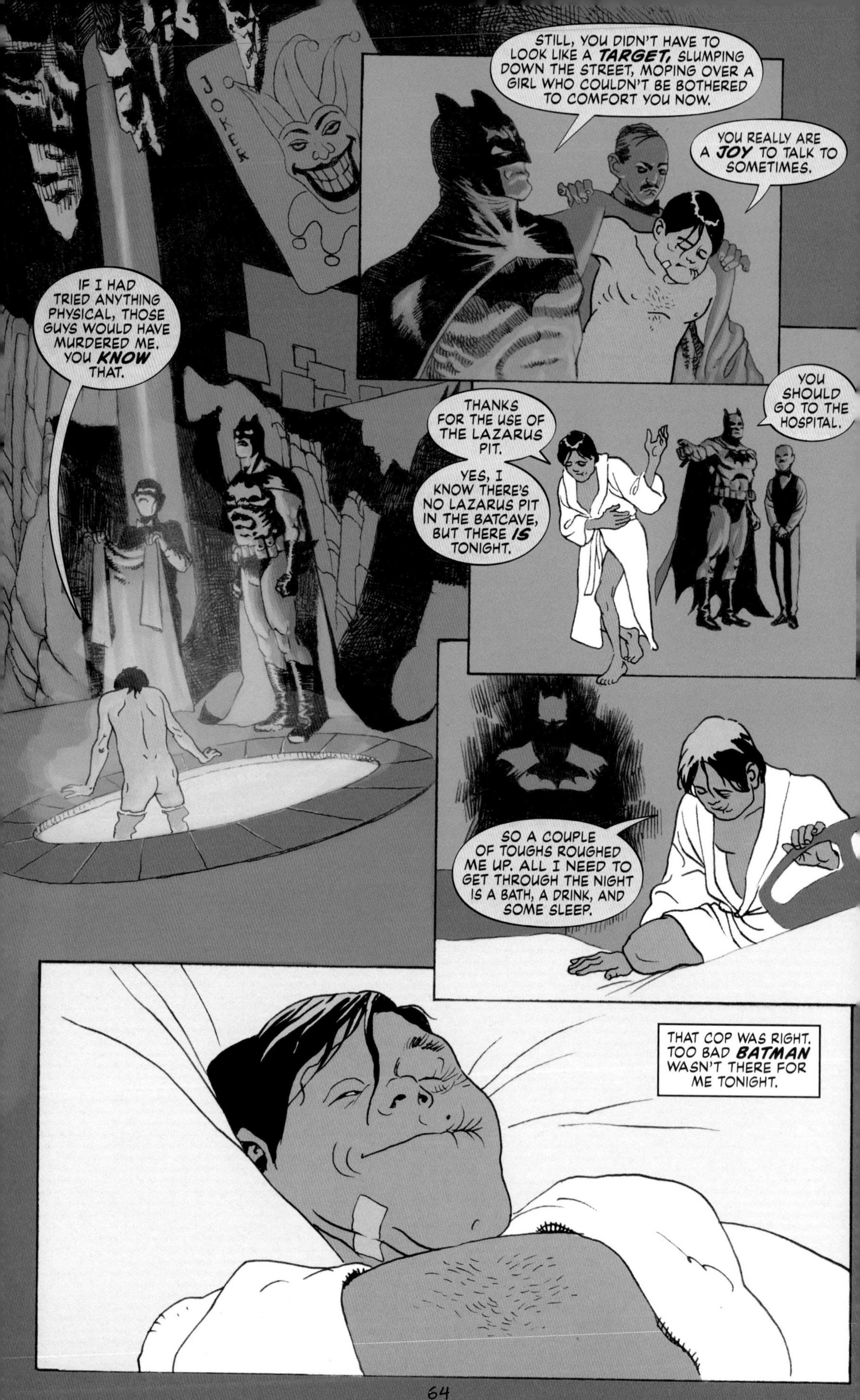
STILL, YOU DIDN'T HAVE TO LOOK LIKE A TARGET, SLUMPING DOWN THE STREET, MOPING OVER A GIRL WHO COULDN'T BE BOTHERED TO COMFORT YOU NOW.
YOU REALLY ARE A JOY TO TALK TO SOMETIMES.
JOKER
IF I HAD TRIED ANYTHING PHYSICAL, THOSE GUYS WOULD HAVE MURDERED ME. YOU KNOW THAT.
THANKS FOR THE USE OF THE LAZARUS PIT.
YES, I KNOW THERE'S NO LAZARUS PIT IN THE BATCAVE, BUT THERE IS TONIGHT.
YOU SHOULD GO TO THE HOSPITAL.
SO A COUPLE OF TOUGHS ROUGHED ME UP. ALL I NEED TO GET THROUGH THE NIGHT IS A BATH, A DRINK, AND SOME SLEEP.
THAT COP WAS RIGHT. TOO BAD BATMAN WASN'T THERE FOR ME TONIGHT.

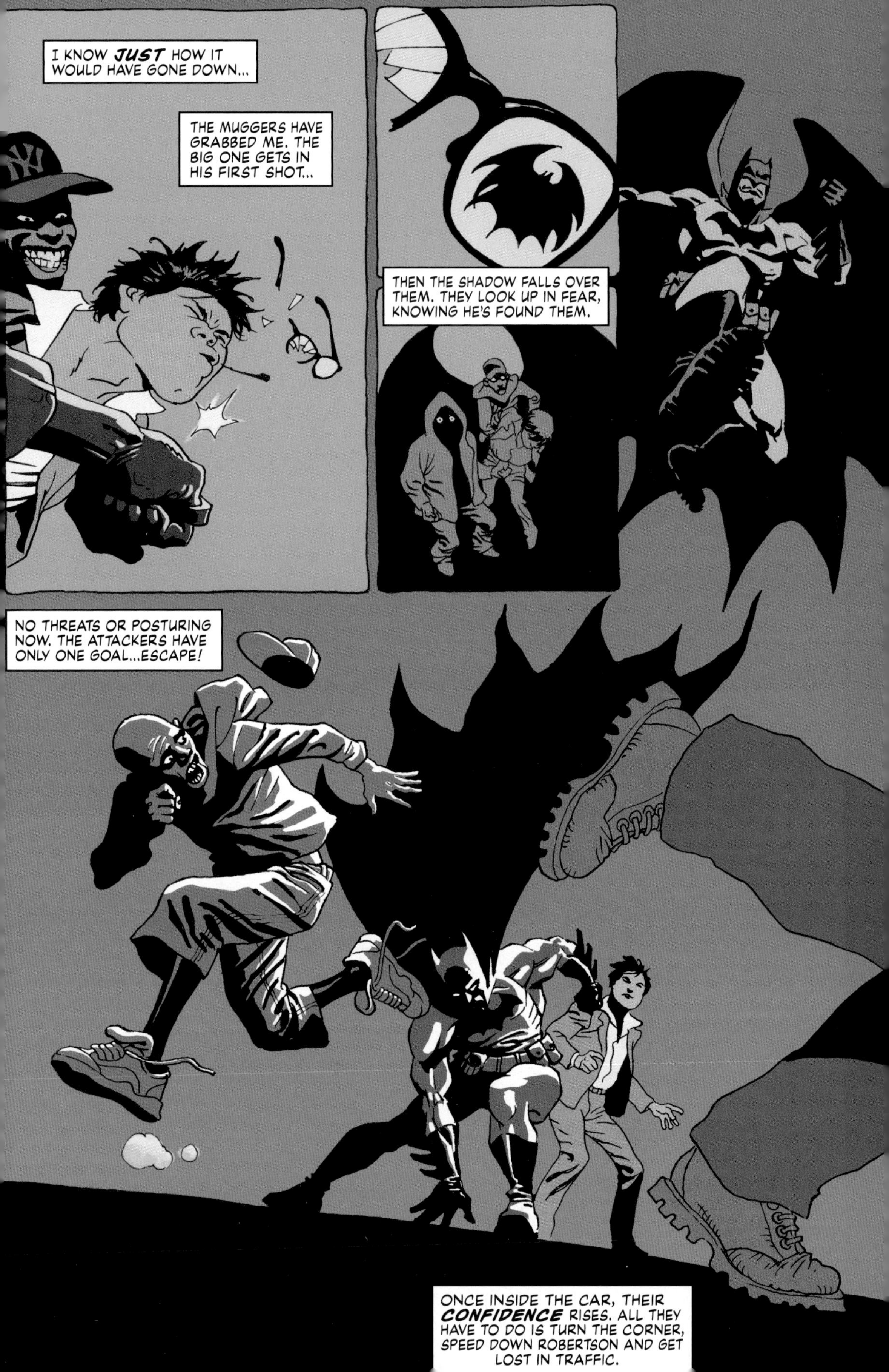
I KNOW JUST HOW IT WOULD HAVE GONE DOWN...
THE MUGGERS HAVE GRABBED ME. THE BIG ONE GETS IN HIS FIRST SHOT...
THEN THE SHADOW FALLS OVER THEM. THEY LOOK UP IN FEAR, KNOWING HE'S FOUND THEM.
NO THREATS OR POSTURING NOW. THE ATTACKERS HAVE ONLY ONE GOAL...ESCAPE!
ONCE INSIDE THE CAR, THEIR CONFIDENCE RISES. ALL THEY HAVE TO DO IS TURN THE CORNER, SPEED DOWN ROBERTSON AND GET LOST IN TRAFFIC.

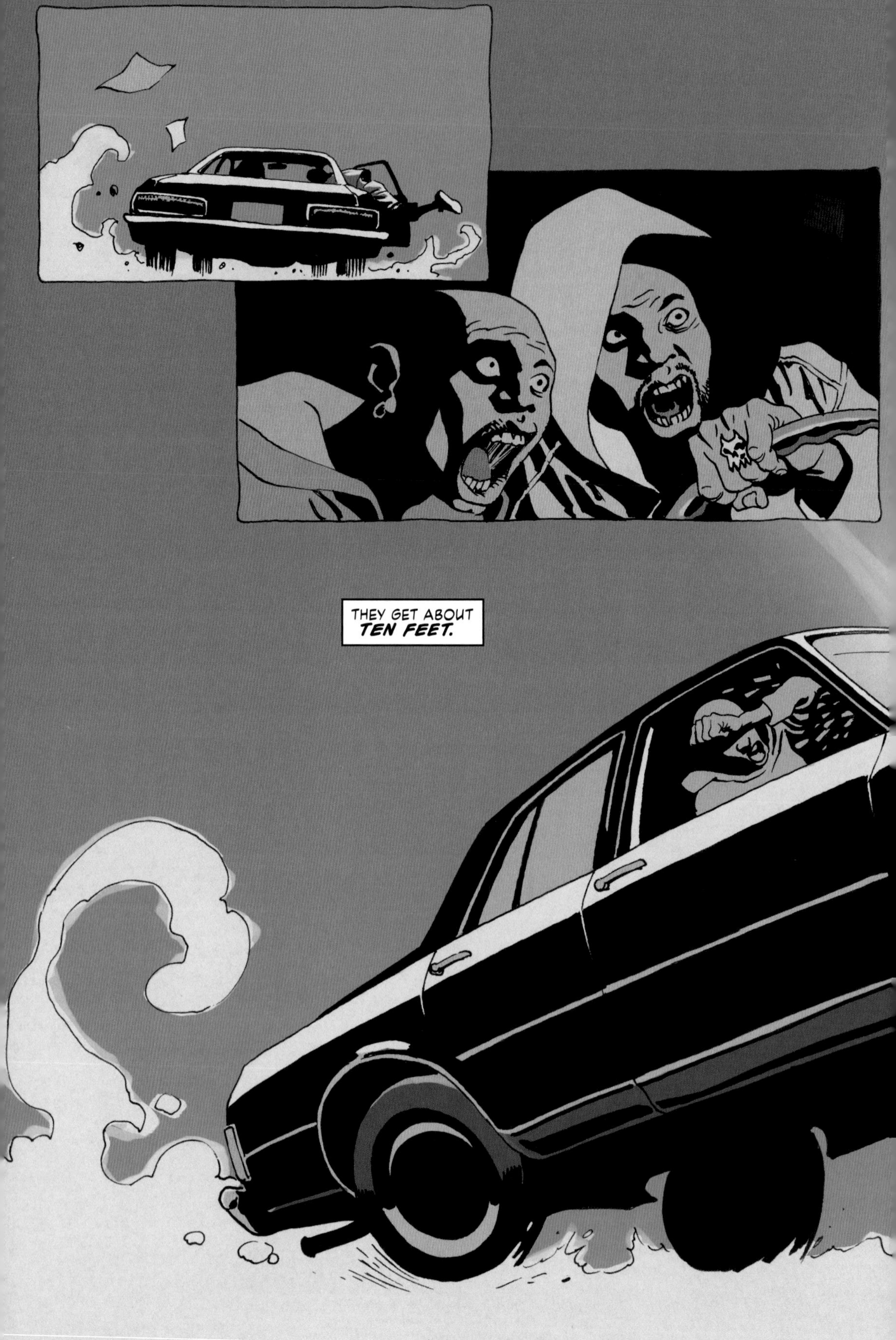
THEY GET ABOUT
TEN FEET.

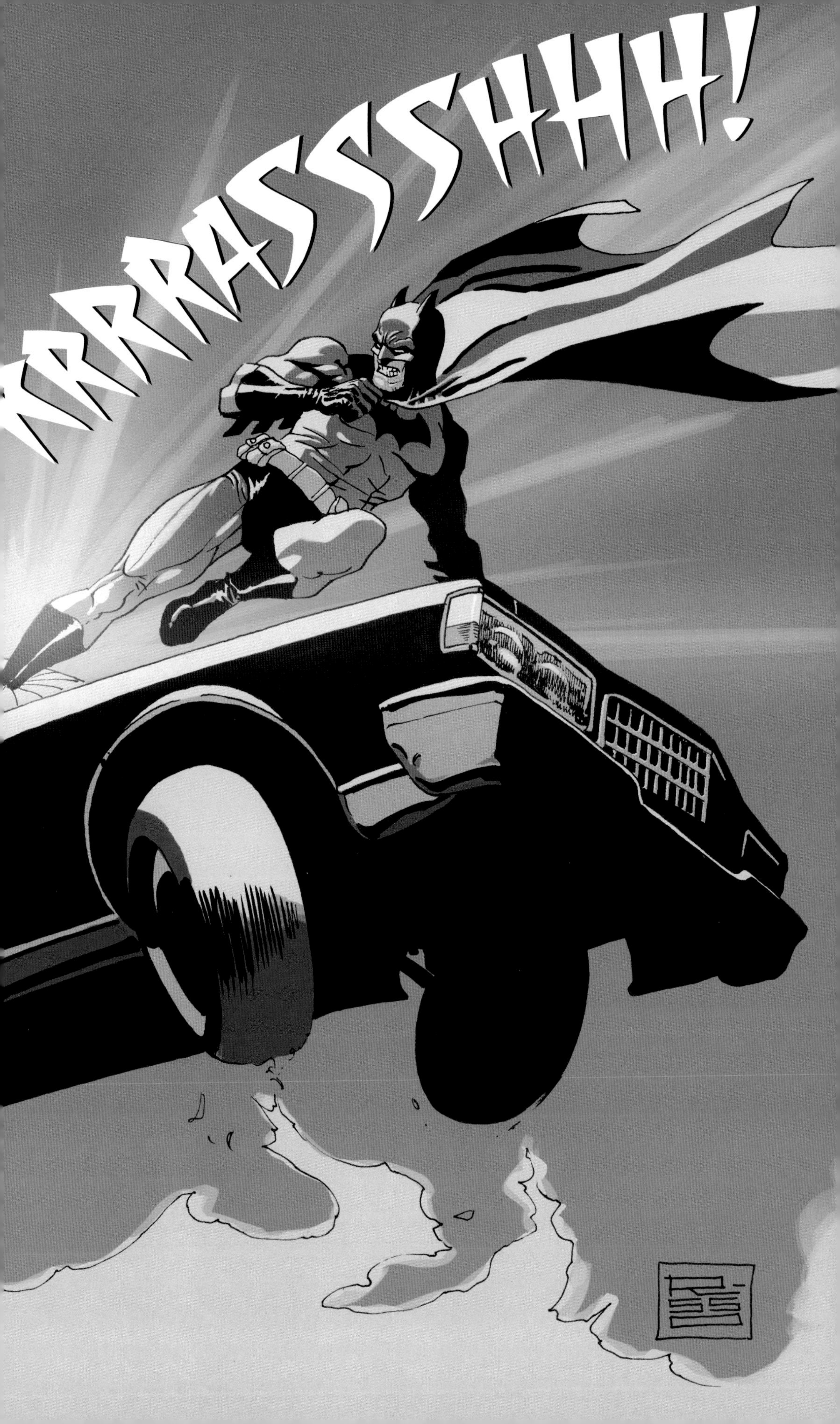
KRRRASSSHHH!

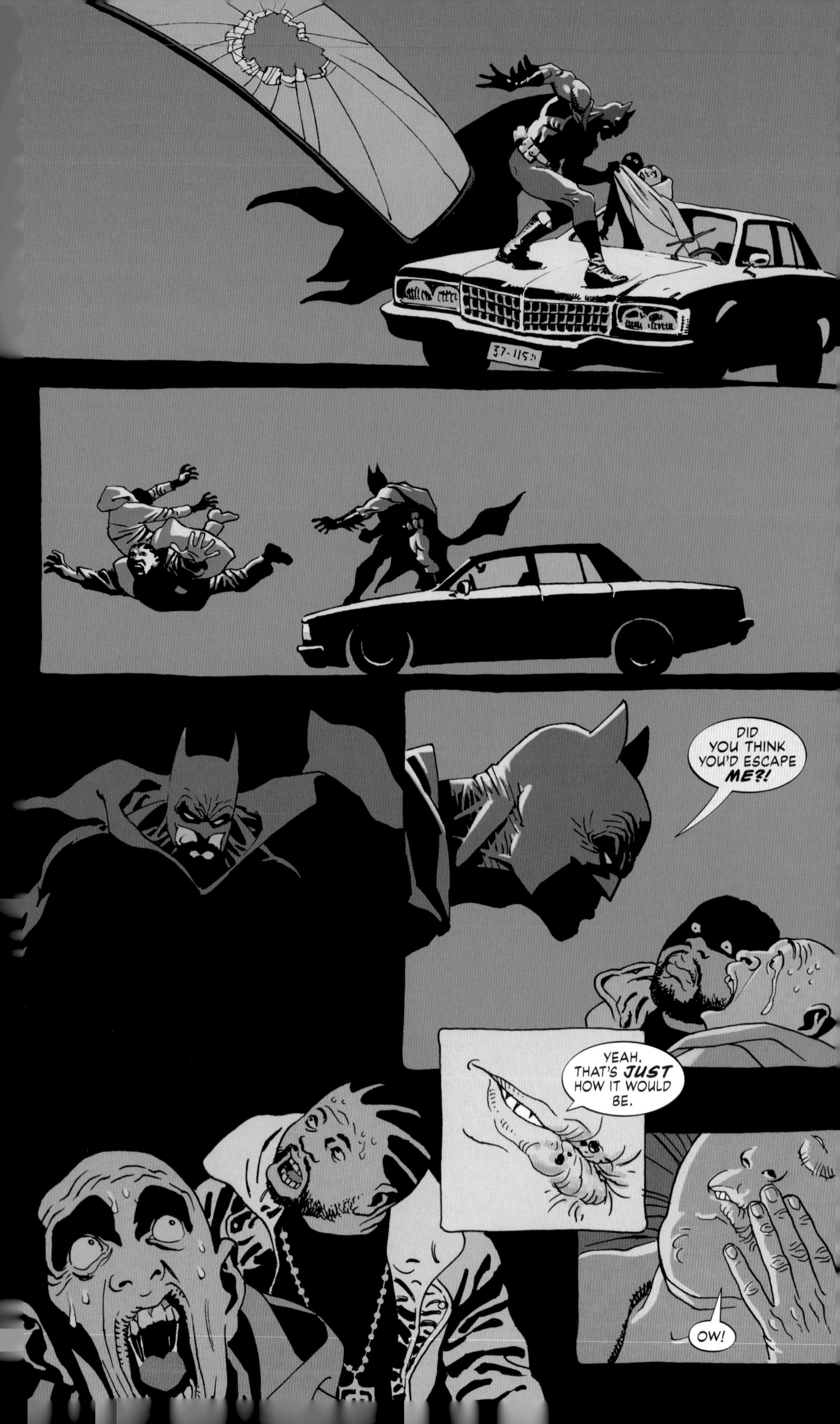
DID YOU THINK YOU'D ESCAPE *ME?!*
YEAH. THAT'S *JUST* HOW IT WOULD BE.
OW!

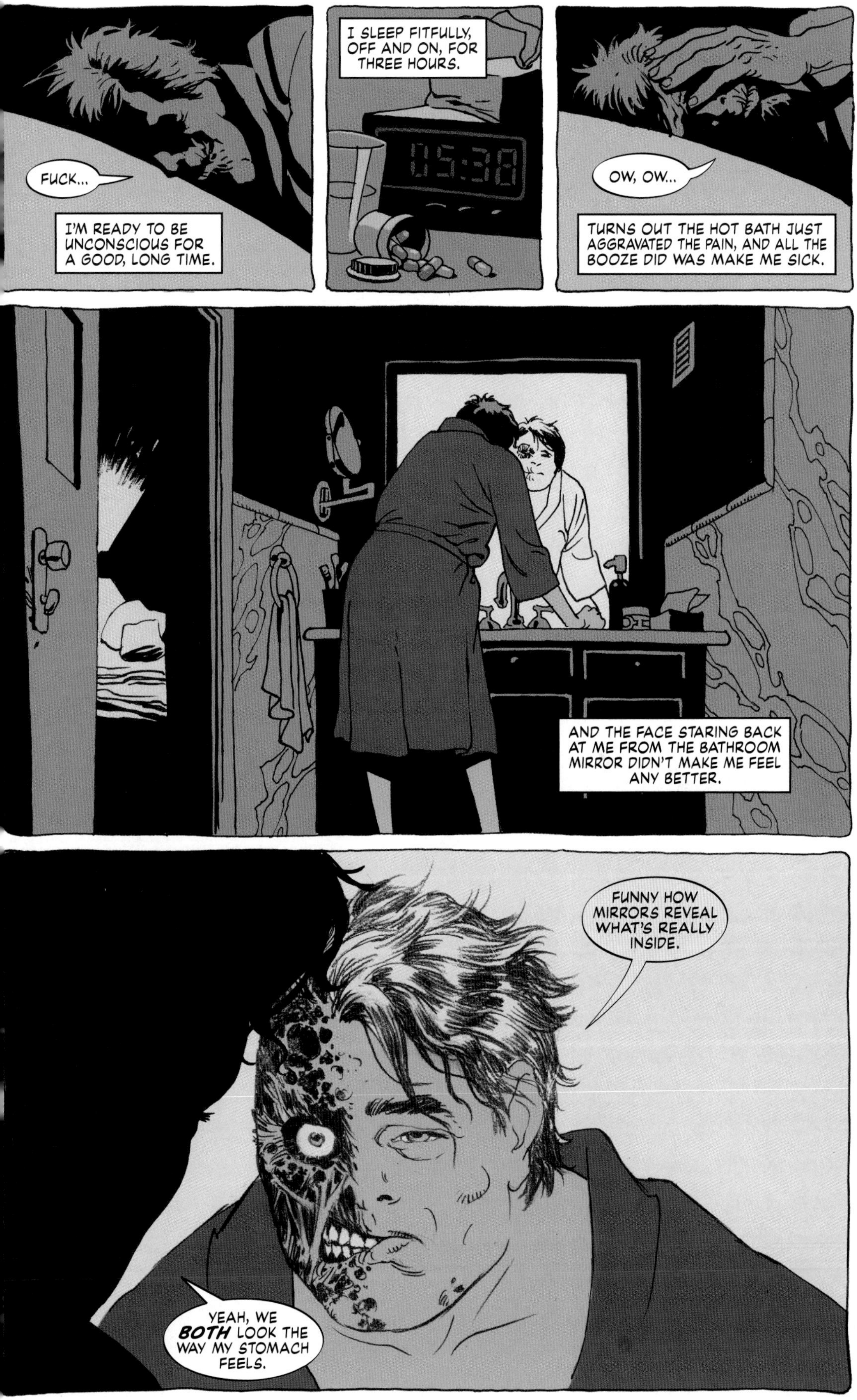
FUCK...
I'M READY TO BE UNCONSCIOUS FOR A GOOD, LONG TIME.
I SLEEP FITFULLY, OFF AND ON, FOR THREE HOURS.
05:38
OW, OW...
TURNS OUT THE HOT BATH JUST AGGRAVATED THE PAIN, AND ALL THE BOOZE DID WAS MAKE ME SICK.
AND THE FACE STARING BACK AT ME FROM THE BATHROOM MIRROR DIDN'T MAKE ME FEEL ANY BETTER.
FUNNY HOW MIRRORS REVEAL WHAT'S REALLY INSIDE.
YEAH, WE **BOTH** LOOK THE WAY MY STOMACH FEELS.

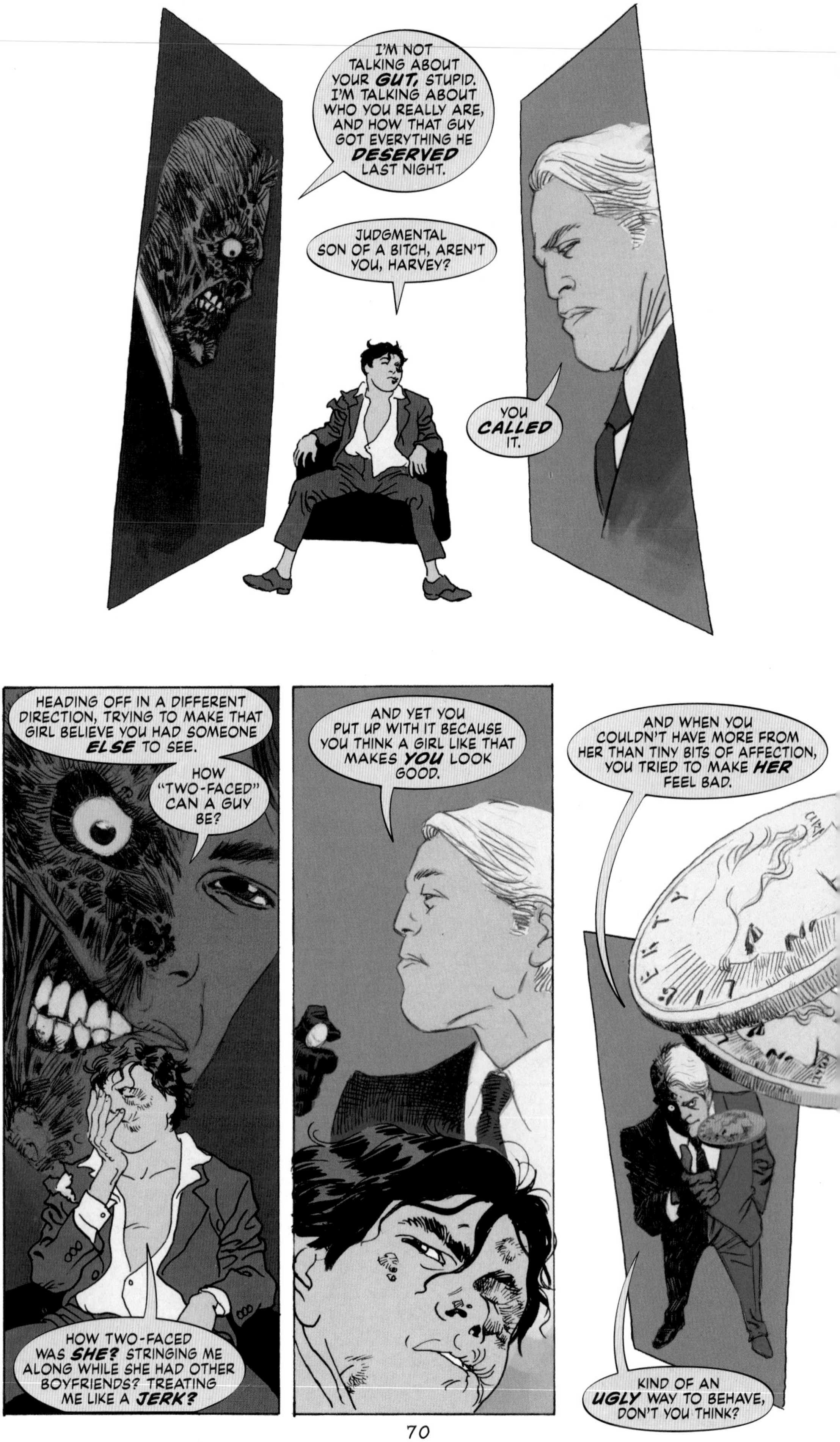
I'M NOT TALKING ABOUT YOUR GUT, STUPID. I'M TALKING ABOUT WHO YOU REALLY ARE, AND HOW THAT GUY GOT EVERYTHING HE DESERVED LAST NIGHT.
JUDGMENTAL SON OF A BITCH, AREN'T YOU, HARVEY?
YOU CALLED IT.
HEADING OFF IN A DIFFERENT DIRECTION, TRYING TO MAKE THAT GIRL BELIEVE YOU HAD SOMEONE ELSE TO SEE.
HOW "TWO-FACED" CAN A GUY BE?
HOW TWO-FACED WAS SHE? STRINGING ME ALONG WHILE SHE HAD OTHER BOYFRIENDS? TREATING ME LIKE A JERK?
AND YET YOU PUT UP WITH IT BECAUSE YOU THINK A GIRL LIKE THAT MAKES YOU LOOK GOOD.
AND WHEN YOU COULDN'T HAVE MORE FROM HER THAN TINY BITS OF AFFECTION, YOU TRIED TO MAKE HER FEEL BAD.
KIND OF AN UGLY WAY TO BEHAVE, DON'T YOU THINK?

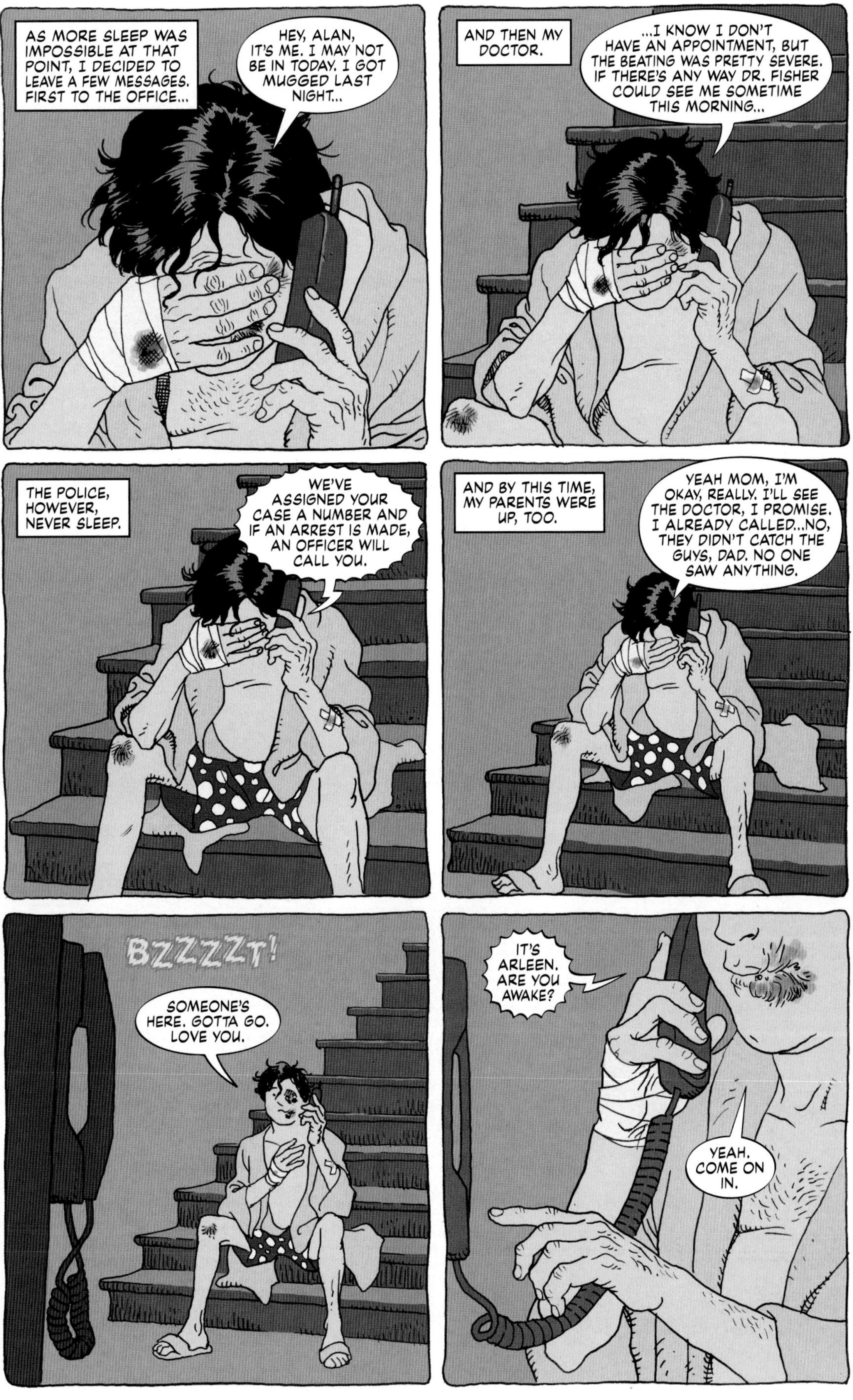
AS MORE SLEEP WAS IMPOSSIBLE AT THAT POINT, I DECIDED TO LEAVE A FEW MESSAGES. FIRST TO THE OFFICE...
HEY, ALAN, IT'S ME. I MAY NOT BE IN TODAY. I GOT MUGGED LAST NIGHT...
AND THEN MY DOCTOR.
...I KNOW I DON'T HAVE AN APPOINTMENT, BUT THE BEATING WAS PRETTY SEVERE. IF THERE'S ANY WAY DR. FISHER COULD SEE ME SOMETIME THIS MORNING...
THE POLICE, HOWEVER, NEVER SLEEP.
WE'VE ASSIGNED YOUR CASE A NUMBER AND IF AN ARREST IS MADE, AN OFFICER WILL CALL YOU.
AND BY THIS TIME, MY PARENTS WERE UP, TOO.
YEAH MOM, I'M OKAY, REALLY. I'LL SEE THE DOCTOR, I PROMISE. I ALREADY CALLED...NO, THEY DIDN'T CATCH THE GUYS, DAD. NO ONE SAW ANYTHING.
BZZZZT!
SOMEONE'S HERE. GOTTA GO. LOVE YOU.
IT'S ARLEEN. ARE YOU AWAKE?
YEAH. COME ON IN.

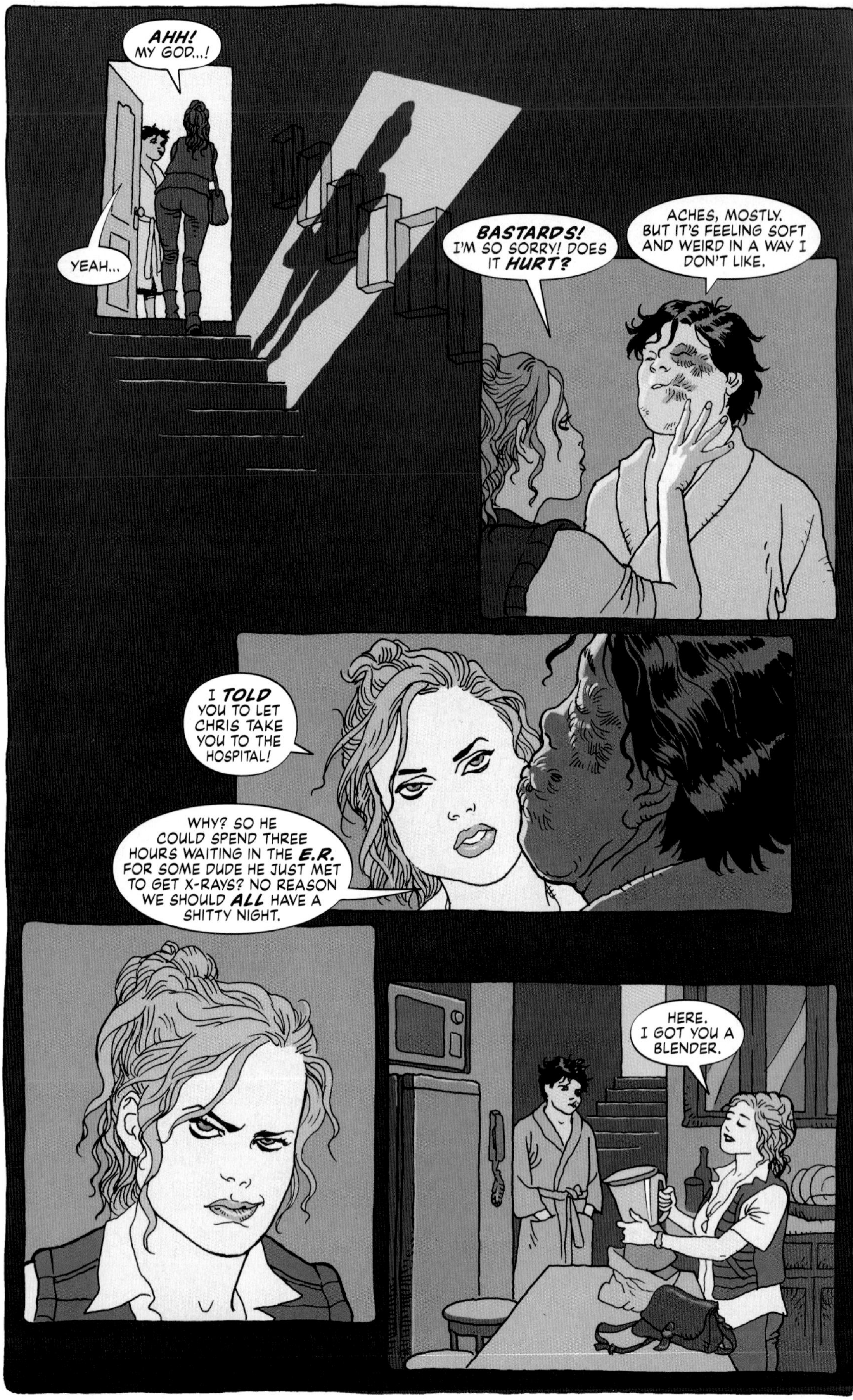
AHH! MY GOD...!
YEAH...
BASTARDS! I'M SO SORRY! DOES IT HURT?
ACHES, MOSTLY. BUT IT'S FEELING SOFT AND WEIRD IN A WAY I DON'T LIKE.
I TOLD YOU TO LET CHRIS TAKE YOU TO THE HOSPITAL!
WHY? SO HE COULD SPEND THREE HOURS WAITING IN THE E.R. FOR SOME DUDE HE JUST MET TO GET X-RAYS? NO REASON WE SHOULD ALL HAVE A SHITTY NIGHT.
HERE. I GOT YOU A BLENDER.

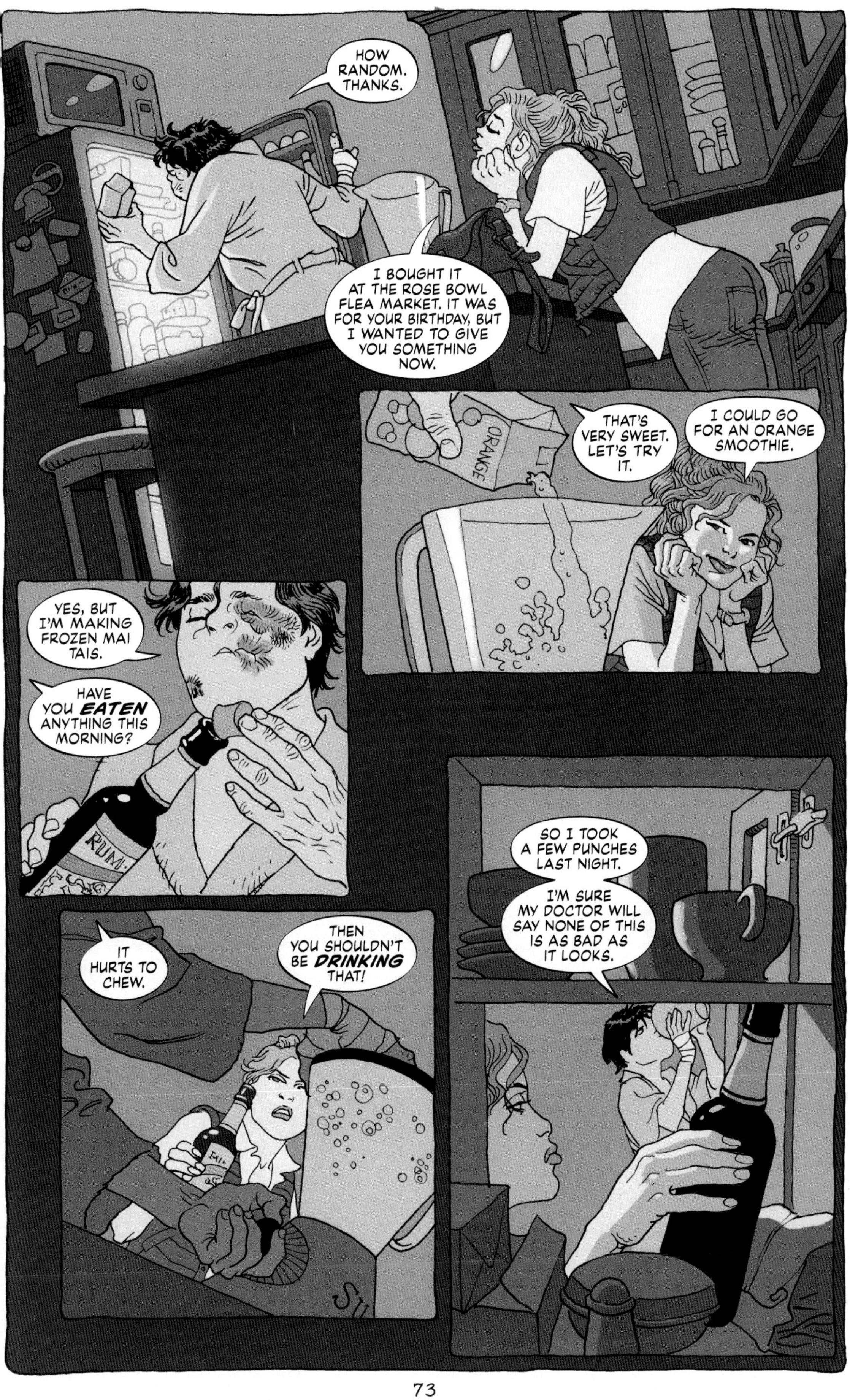
HOW RANDOM. THANKS.
I BOUGHT IT AT THE ROSE BOWL FLEA MARKET. IT WAS FOR YOUR BIRTHDAY, BUT I WANTED TO GIVE YOU SOMETHING NOW.
ORANGE
THAT'S VERY SWEET. LET'S TRY IT.
I COULD GO FOR AN ORANGE SMOOTHIE.
YES, BUT I'M MAKING FROZEN MAI TAIS.
HAVE YOU EATEN ANYTHING THIS MORNING?
RUM
IT HURTS TO CHEW.
THEN YOU SHOULDN'T BE DRINKING THAT!
SO I TOOK A FEW PUNCHES LAST NIGHT.
I'M SURE MY DOCTOR WILL SAY NONE OF THIS IS AS BAD AS IT LOOKS.

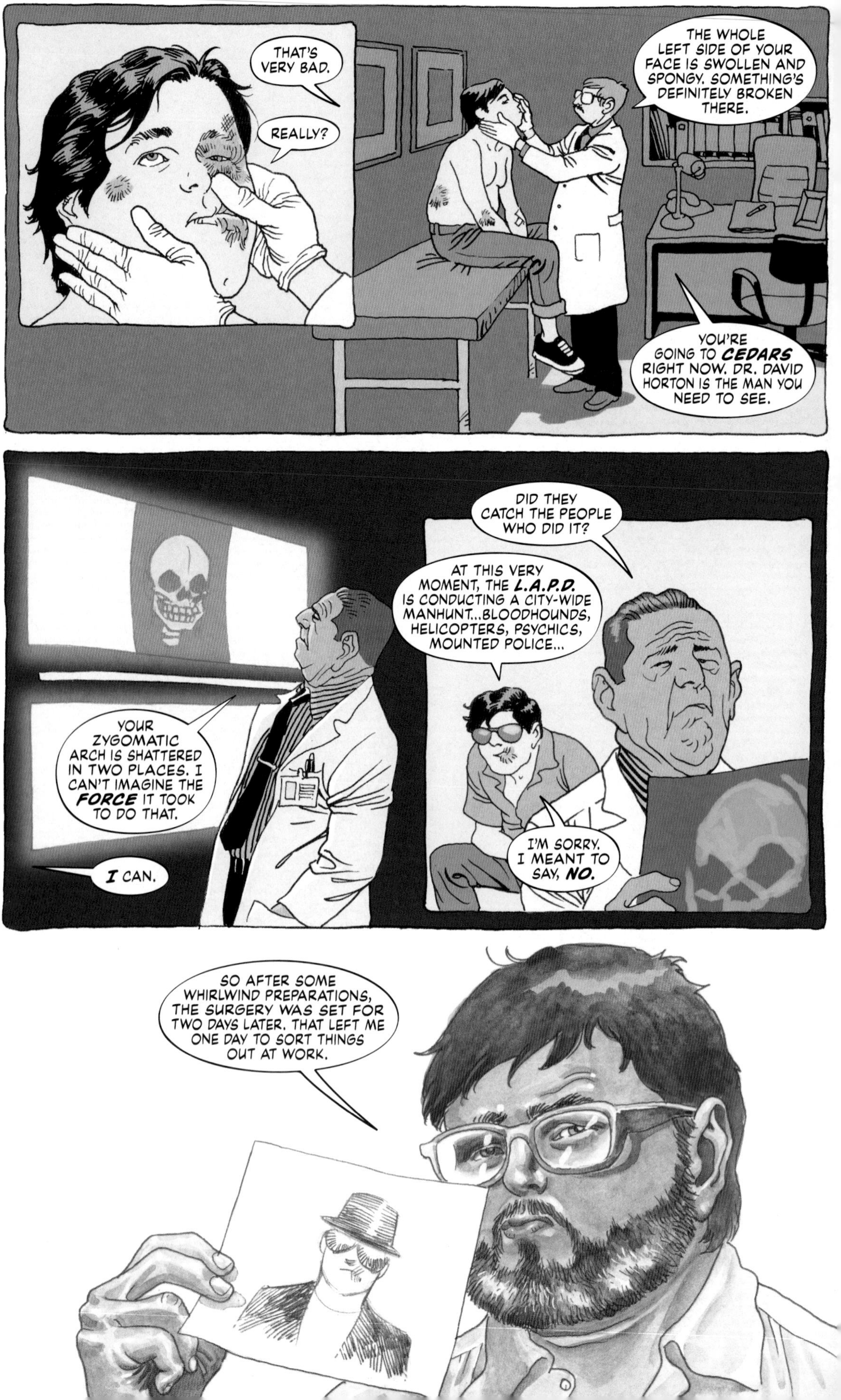

THAT'S VERY BAD.
REALLY?
THE WHOLE LEFT SIDE OF YOUR FACE IS SWOLLEN AND SPONGY. SOMETHING'S DEFINITELY BROKEN THERE.
YOU'RE GOING TO **CEDARS** RIGHT NOW. DR. DAVID HORTON IS THE MAN YOU NEED TO SEE.
YOUR ZYGOMATIC ARCH IS SHATTERED IN TWO PLACES. I CAN'T IMAGINE THE **FORCE** IT TOOK TO DO THAT.
I CAN.
DID THEY CATCH THE PEOPLE WHO DID IT?
AT THIS VERY MOMENT, THE ***L.A.P.D.*** IS CONDUCTING A CITY-WIDE MANHUNT...BLOODHOUNDS, HELICOPTERS, PSYCHICS, MOUNTED POLICE...
I'M SORRY. I MEANT TO SAY, ***NO.***
SO AFTER SOME WHIRLWIND PREPARATIONS, THE SURGERY WAS SET FOR TWO DAYS LATER. THAT LEFT ME ONE DAY TO SORT THINGS OUT AT WORK.

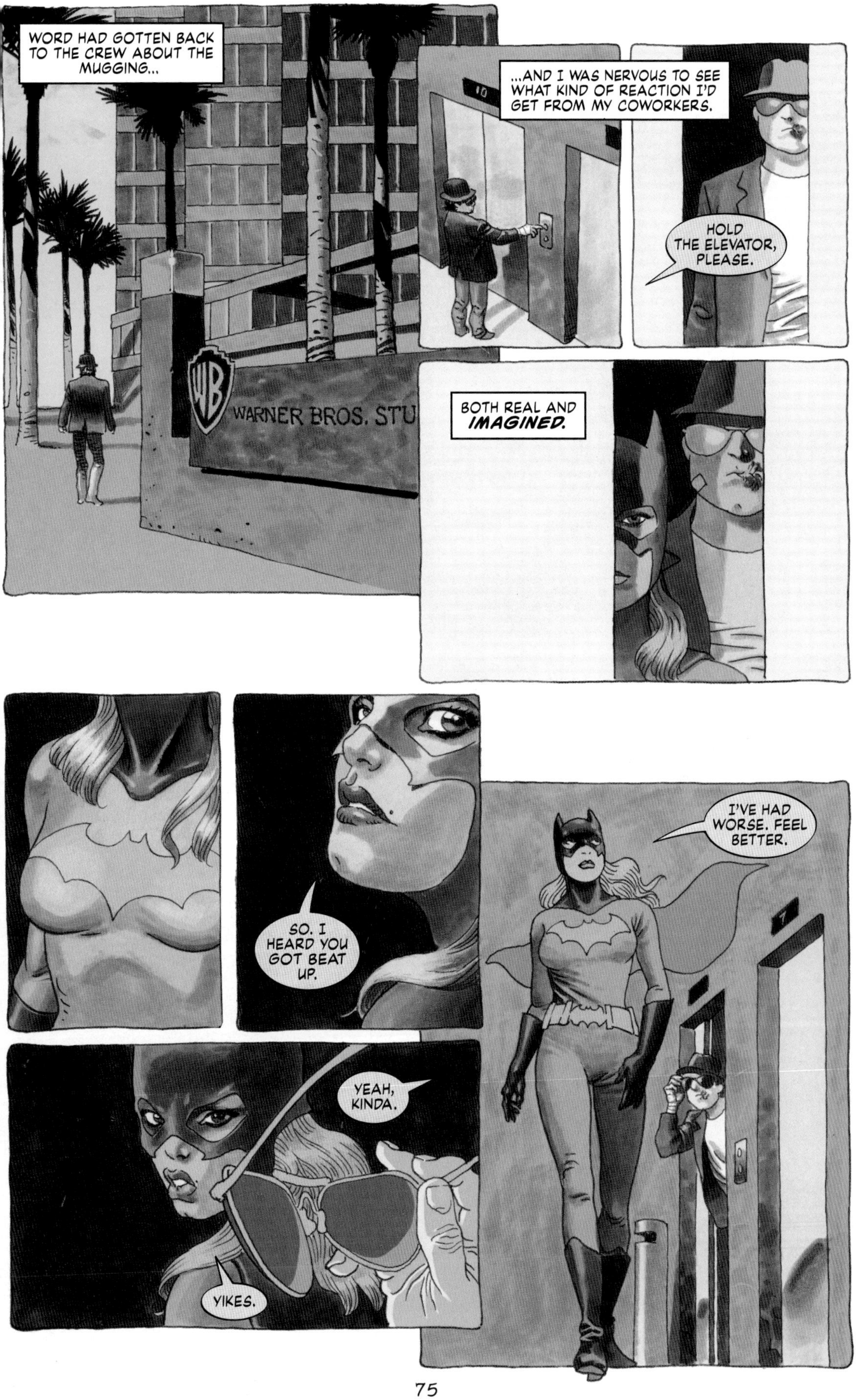
WORD HAD GOTTEN BACK TO THE CREW ABOUT THE MUGGING...
WARNER BROS. STU
...AND I WAS NERVOUS TO SEE WHAT KIND OF REACTION I'D GET FROM MY COWORKERS.
HOLD THE ELEVATOR, PLEASE.
BOTH REAL AND *IMAGINED.*
SO. I HEARD YOU GOT BEAT UP.
YEAH, KINDA.
YIKES.
I'VE HAD WORSE. FEEL BETTER.

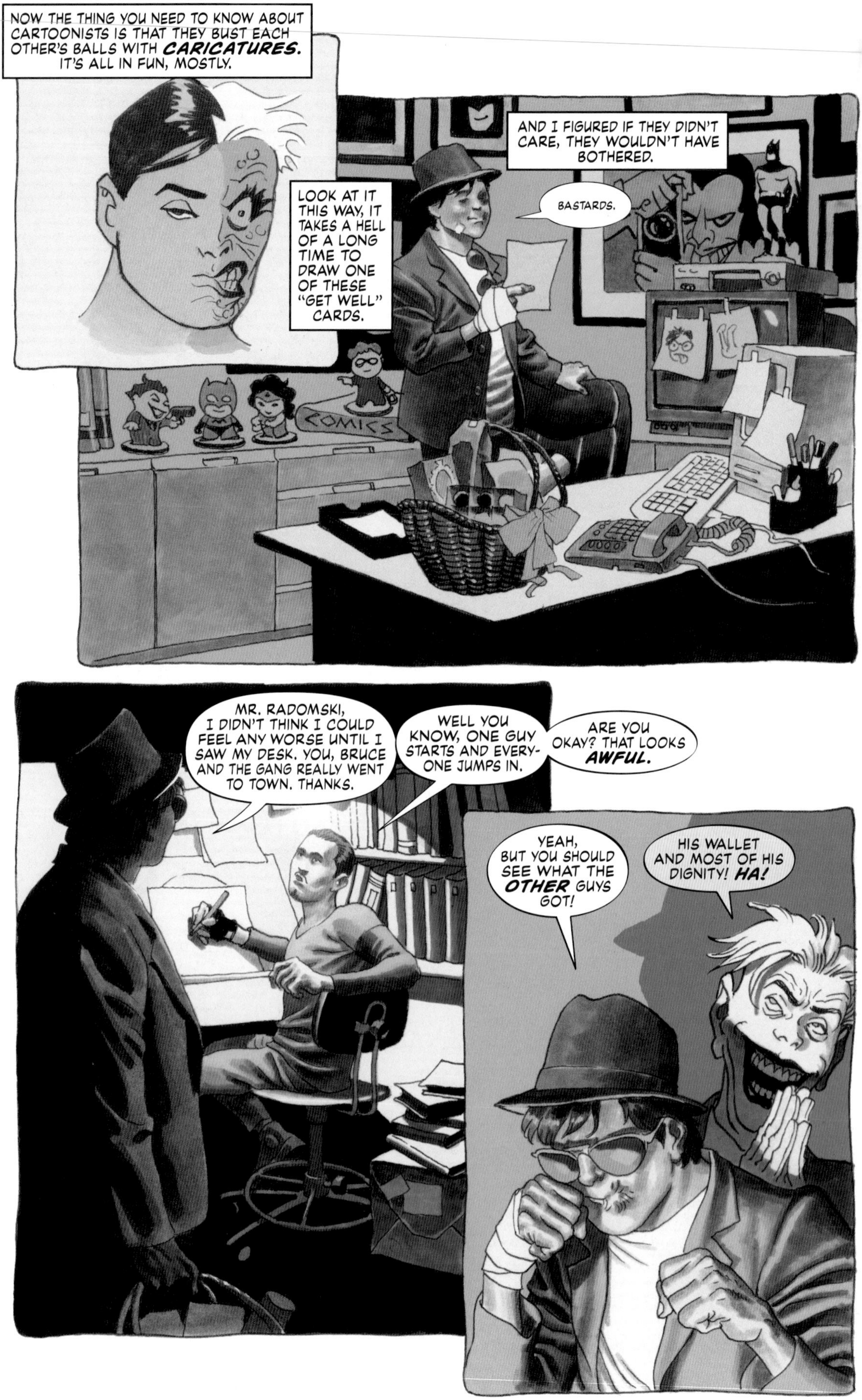
NOW THE THING YOU NEED TO KNOW ABOUT CARTOONISTS IS THAT THEY BUST EACH OTHER'S BALLS WITH CARICATURES. IT'S ALL IN FUN, MOSTLY.
LOOK AT IT THIS WAY, IT TAKES A HELL OF A LONG TIME TO DRAW ONE OF THESE "GET WELL" CARDS.
AND I FIGURED IF THEY DIDN'T CARE, THEY WOULDN'T HAVE BOTHERED.
BASTARDS.
COMICS
MR. RADOMSKI, I DIDN'T THINK I COULD FEEL ANY WORSE UNTIL I SAW MY DESK. YOU, BRUCE AND THE GANG REALLY WENT TO TOWN. THANKS.
WELL YOU KNOW, ONE GUY STARTS AND EVERY-ONE JUMPS IN.
ARE YOU OKAY? THAT LOOKS AWFUL.
YEAH, BUT YOU SHOULD SEE WHAT THE OTHER GUYS GOT!
HIS WALLET AND MOST OF HIS DIGNITY! HA!

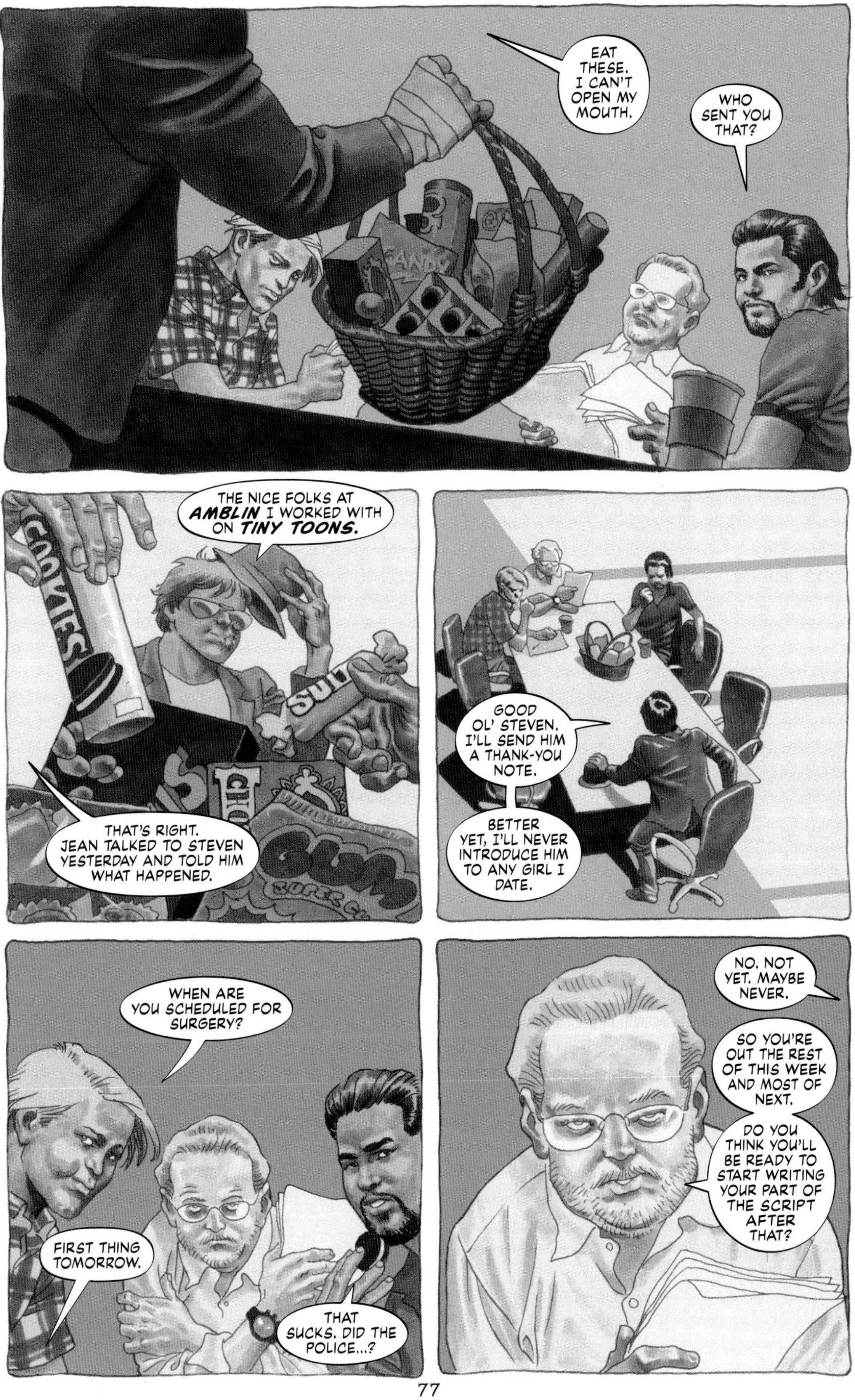

EAT THESE. I CAN'T OPEN MY MOUTH.
WHO SENT YOU THAT?
THE NICE FOLKS AT **AMBLIN** I WORKED WITH ON ***TINY TOONS.***
THAT'S RIGHT. JEAN TALKED TO STEVEN YESTERDAY AND TOLD HIM WHAT HAPPENED.
GOOD OL' STEVEN. I'LL SEND HIM A THANK-YOU NOTE.
BETTER YET, I'LL NEVER INTRODUCE HIM TO ANY GIRL I DATE.
WHEN ARE YOU SCHEDULED FOR SURGERY?
FIRST THING TOMORROW.
THAT SUCKS. DID THE POLICE...?
NO. NOT YET. MAYBE NEVER.
SO YOU'RE OUT THE REST OF THIS WEEK AND MOST OF NEXT.
DO YOU THINK YOU'LL BE READY TO START WRITING YOUR PART OF THE SCRIPT AFTER THAT?

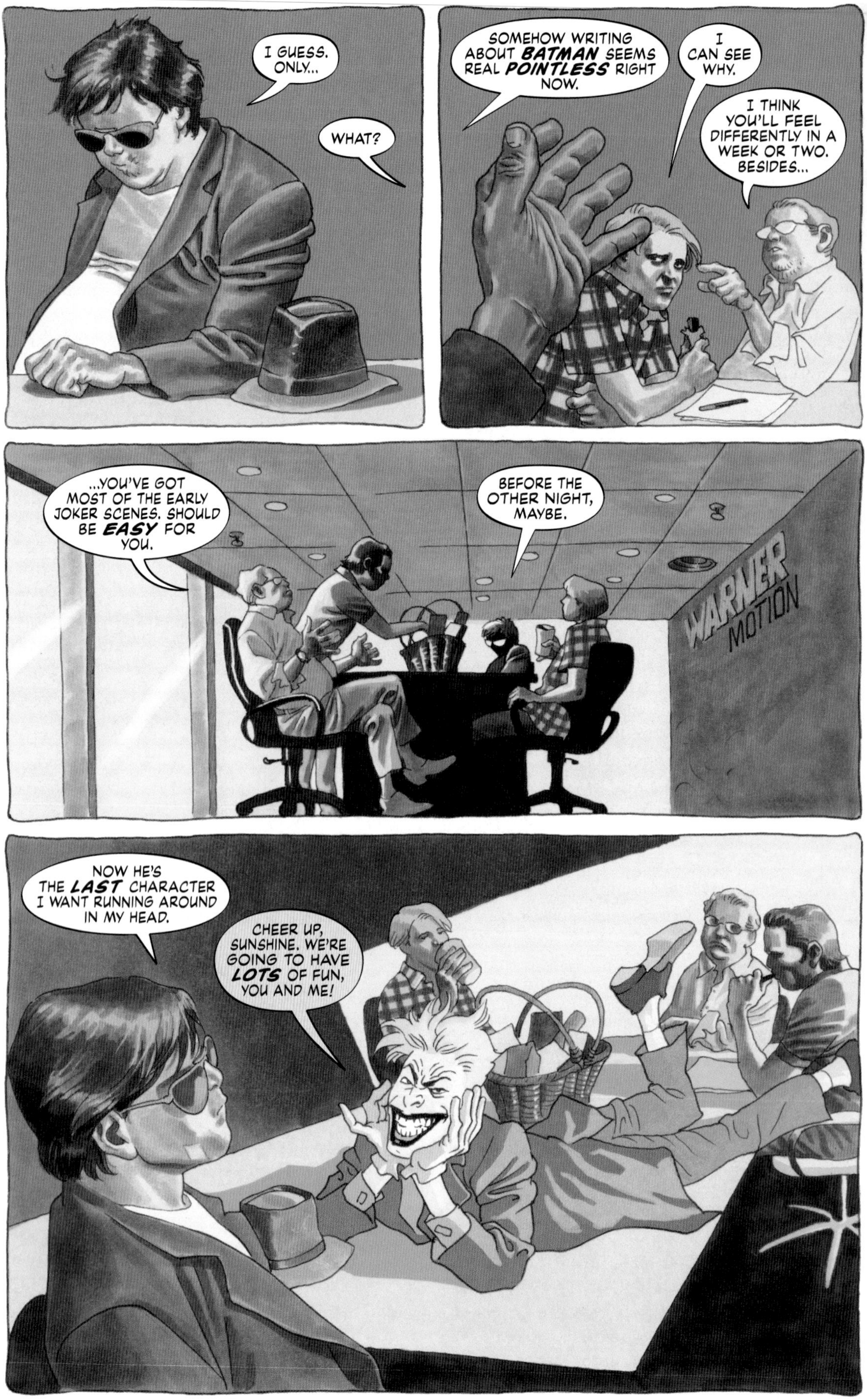

I GUESS. ONLY...
WHAT?
SOMEHOW WRITING ABOUT **BATMAN** SEEMS REAL **POINTLESS** RIGHT NOW.
I CAN SEE WHY.
I THINK YOU'LL FEEL DIFFERENTLY IN A WEEK OR TWO. BESIDES...
...YOU'VE GOT MOST OF THE EARLY JOKER SCENES. SHOULD BE **EASY** FOR YOU.
BEFORE THE OTHER NIGHT, MAYBE.
WARNER
MOTION
NOW HE'S THE **LAST** CHARACTER I WANT RUNNING AROUND IN MY HEAD.
CHEER UP, SUNSHINE. WE'RE GOING TO HAVE **LOTS** OF FUN, YOU AND ME!

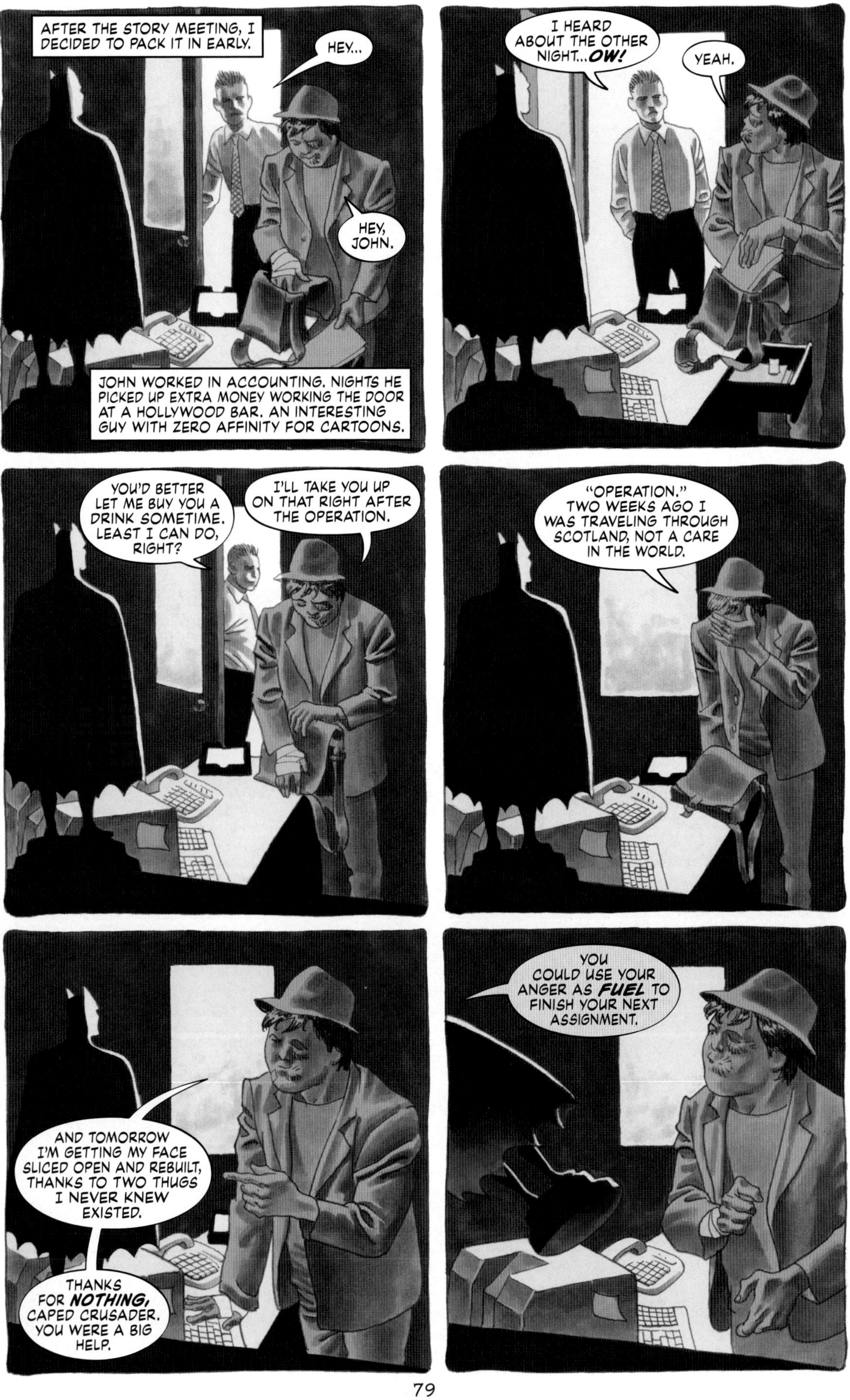
AFTER THE STORY MEETING, I DECIDED TO PACK IT IN EARLY.
HEY...
HEY, JOHN.
JOHN WORKED IN ACCOUNTING. NIGHTS HE PICKED UP EXTRA MONEY WORKING THE DOOR AT A HOLLYWOOD BAR. AN INTERESTING GUY WITH ZERO AFFINITY FOR CARTOONS.
I HEARD ABOUT THE OTHER NIGHT...**OW!**
YEAH.
YOU'D BETTER LET ME BUY YOU A DRINK SOMETIME. LEAST I CAN DO, RIGHT?
I'LL TAKE YOU UP ON THAT RIGHT AFTER THE OPERATION.
"OPERATION." TWO WEEKS AGO I WAS TRAVELING THROUGH SCOTLAND, NOT A CARE IN THE WORLD.
AND TOMORROW I'M GETTING MY FACE SLICED OPEN AND REBUILT, THANKS TO TWO THUGS I NEVER KNEW EXISTED.
THANKS FOR **NOTHING,** CAPED CRUSADER. YOU WERE A BIG HELP.
YOU COULD USE YOUR ANGER AS **FUEL** TO FINISH YOUR NEXT ASSIGNMENT.

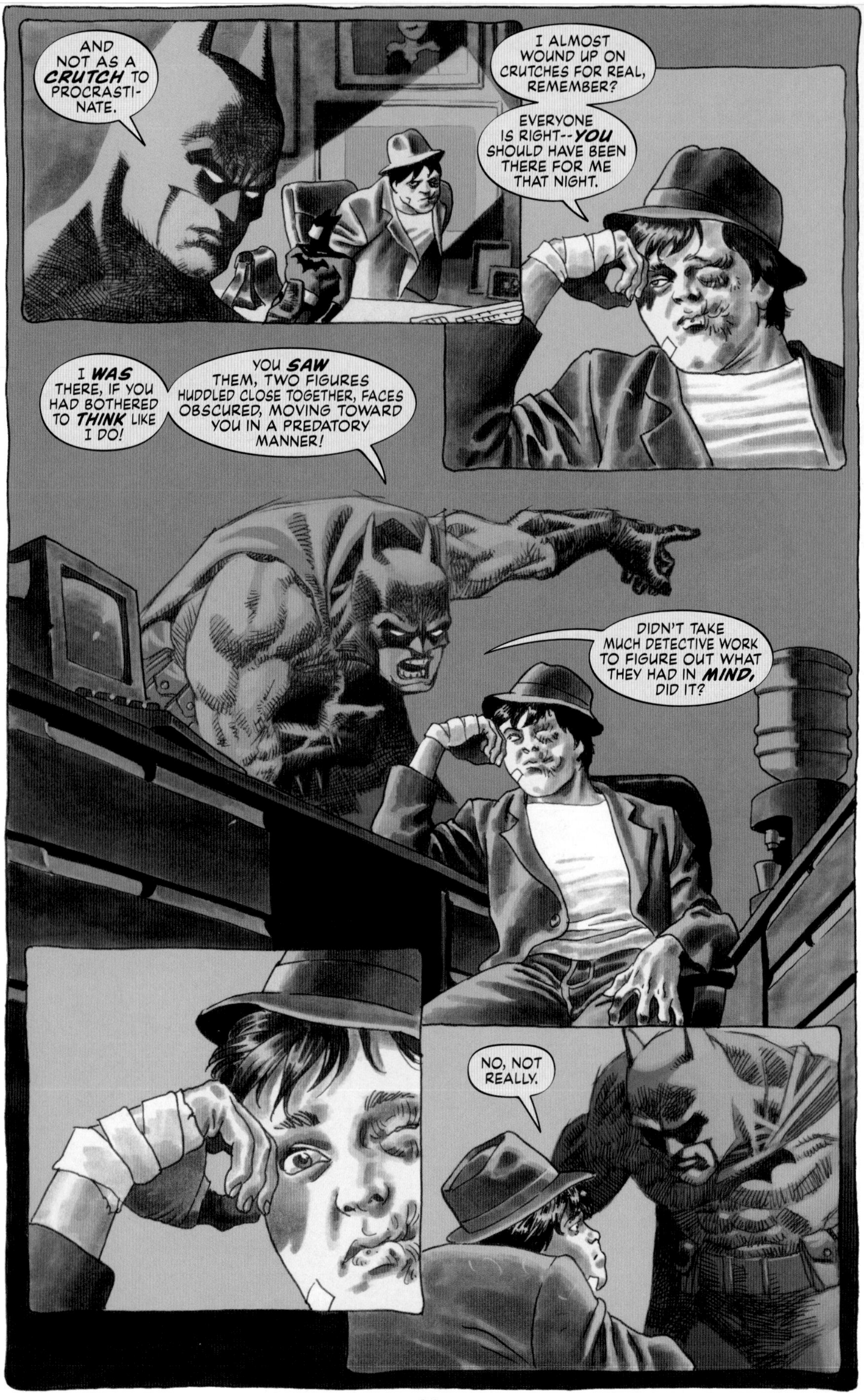
AND NOT AS A **CRUTCH** TO PROCRASTI-NATE.
I ALMOST WOUND UP ON CRUTCHES FOR REAL, REMEMBER?
EVERYONE IS RIGHT--**YOU** SHOULD HAVE BEEN THERE FOR ME THAT NIGHT.
I **WAS** THERE, IF YOU HAD BOTHERED TO **THINK** LIKE I DO!
YOU **SAW** THEM, TWO FIGURES HUDDLED CLOSE TOGETHER, FACES OBSCURED, MOVING TOWARD YOU IN A PREDATORY MANNER!
DIDN'T TAKE MUCH DETECTIVE WORK TO FIGURE OUT WHAT THEY HAD IN **MIND,** DID IT?
NO, NOT REALLY.

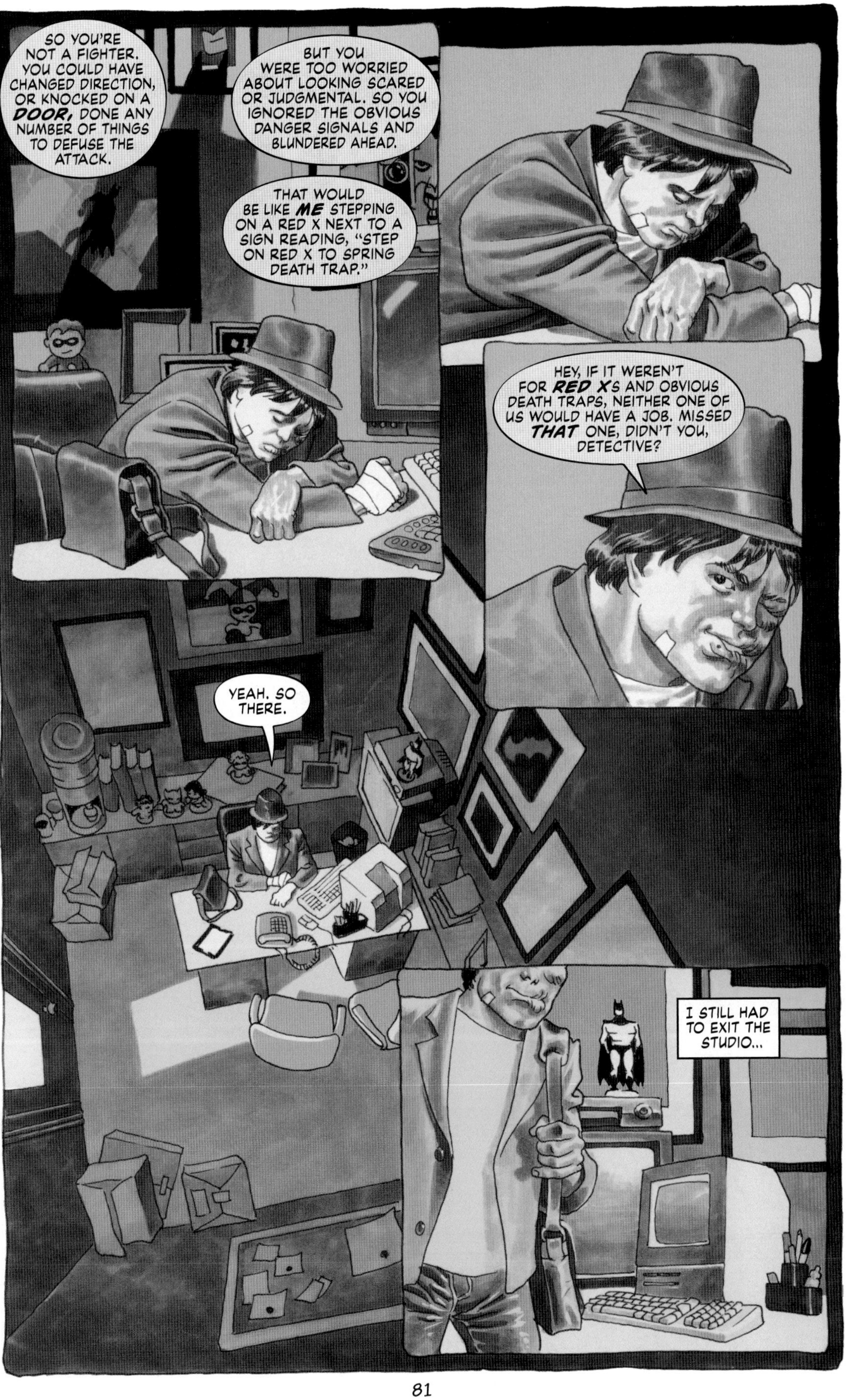
SO YOU'RE NOT A FIGHTER. YOU COULD HAVE CHANGED DIRECTION, OR KNOCKED ON A DOOR, DONE ANY NUMBER OF THINGS TO DEFUSE THE ATTACK.
BUT YOU WERE TOO WORRIED ABOUT LOOKING SCARED OR JUDGMENTAL. SO YOU IGNORED THE OBVIOUS DANGER SIGNALS AND BLUNDERED AHEAD.
THAT WOULD BE LIKE ME STEPPING ON A RED X NEXT TO A SIGN READING, "STEP ON RED X TO SPRING DEATH TRAP."
HEY, IF IT WEREN'T FOR RED XS AND OBVIOUS DEATH TRAPS, NEITHER ONE OF US WOULD HAVE A JOB. MISSED THAT ONE, DIDN'T YOU, DETECTIVE?
YEAH. SO THERE.
I STILL HAD TO EXIT THE STUDIO...

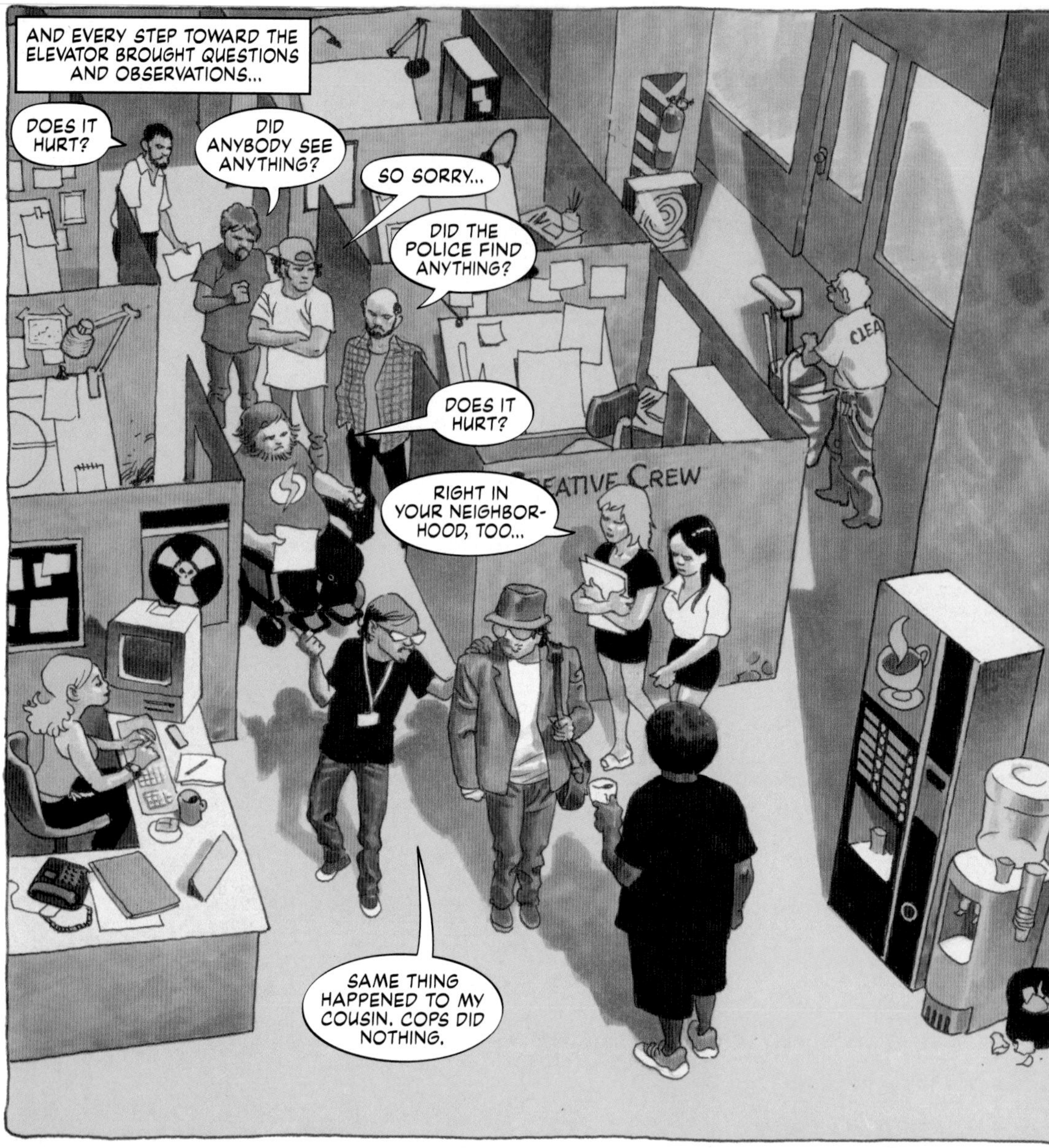
AND EVERY STEP TOWARD THE ELEVATOR BROUGHT QUESTIONS AND OBSERVATIONS...
DOES IT HURT?
DID ANYBODY SEE ANYTHING?
SO SORRY...
DID THE POLICE FIND ANYTHING?
DOES IT HURT?
RIGHT IN YOUR NEIGHBOR-HOOD, TOO...
SAME THING HAPPENED TO MY COUSIN. COPS DID NOTHING.
CREATIVE CREW

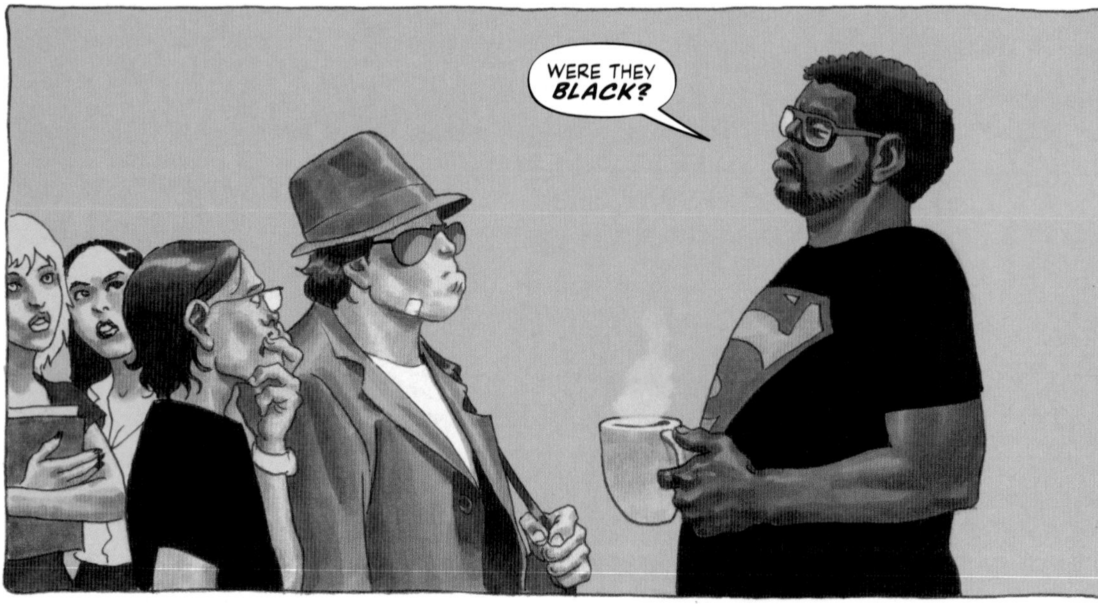
WERE THEY *BLACK?*

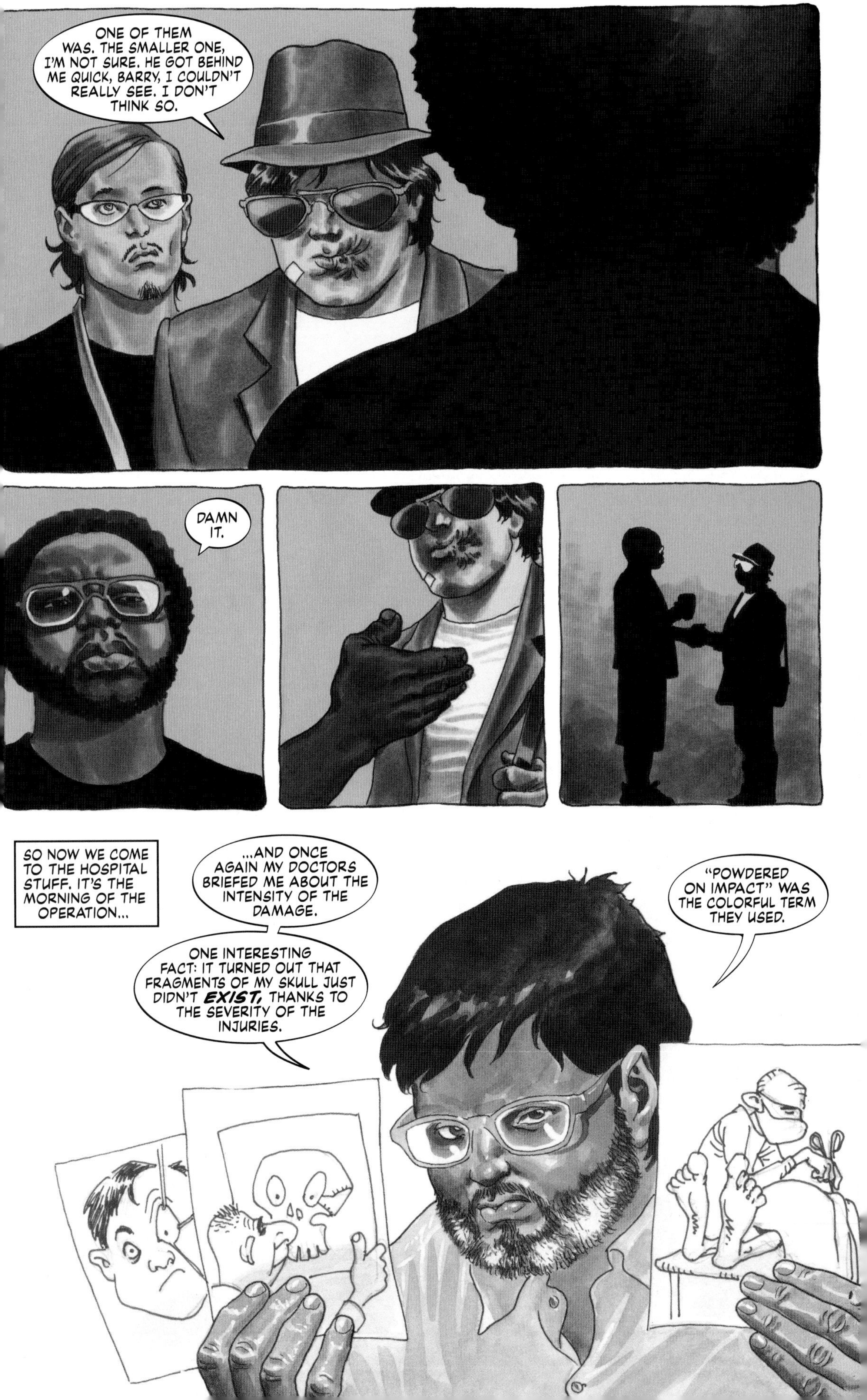

ONE OF THEM WAS. THE SMALLER ONE, I'M NOT SURE. HE GOT BEHIND ME QUICK, BARRY, I COULDN'T REALLY SEE. I DON'T THINK SO.
DAMN IT.
SO NOW WE COME TO THE HOSPITAL STUFF. IT'S THE MORNING OF THE OPERATION...
...AND ONCE AGAIN MY DOCTORS BRIEFED ME ABOUT THE INTENSITY OF THE DAMAGE.
ONE INTERESTING FACT: IT TURNED OUT THAT FRAGMENTS OF MY SKULL JUST DIDN'T ***EXIST,*** THANKS TO THE SEVERITY OF THE INJURIES.
"POWDERED ON IMPACT" WAS THE COLORFUL TERM THEY USED.

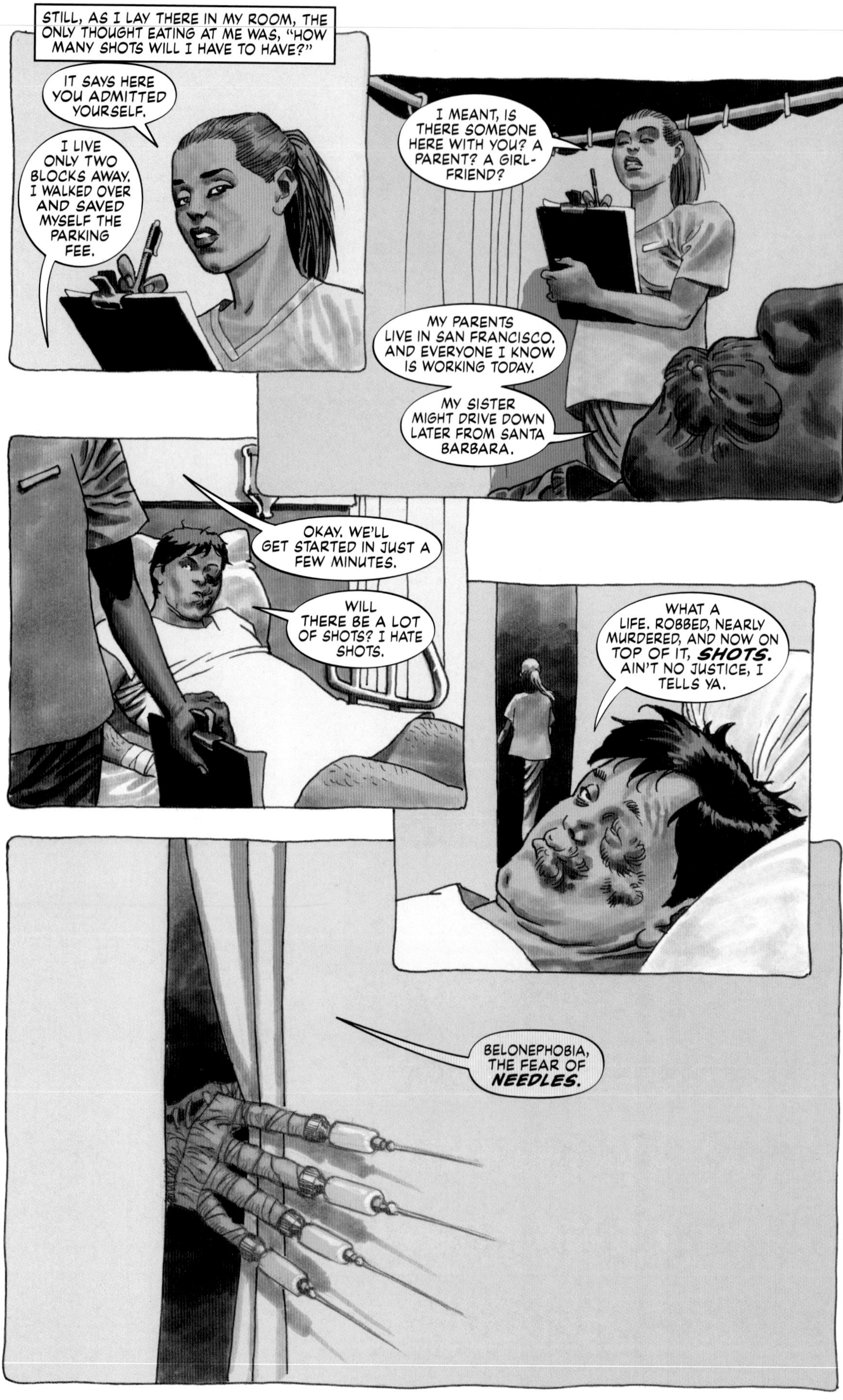
STILL, AS I LAY THERE IN MY ROOM, THE ONLY THOUGHT EATING AT ME WAS, "HOW MANY SHOTS WILL I HAVE TO HAVE?"
IT SAYS HERE YOU ADMITTED YOURSELF.
I LIVE ONLY TWO BLOCKS AWAY. I WALKED OVER AND SAVED MYSELF THE PARKING FEE.
I MEANT, IS THERE SOMEONE HERE WITH YOU? A PARENT? A GIRL-FRIEND?
MY PARENTS LIVE IN SAN FRANCISCO. AND EVERYONE I KNOW IS WORKING TODAY.
MY SISTER MIGHT DRIVE DOWN LATER FROM SANTA BARBARA.
OKAY. WE'LL GET STARTED IN JUST A FEW MINUTES.
WILL THERE BE A LOT OF SHOTS? I HATE SHOTS.
WHAT A LIFE. ROBBED, NEARLY MURDERED, AND NOW ON TOP OF IT, SHOTS. AIN'T NO JUSTICE, I TELLS YA.
BELONEPHOBIA, THE FEAR OF NEEDLES.

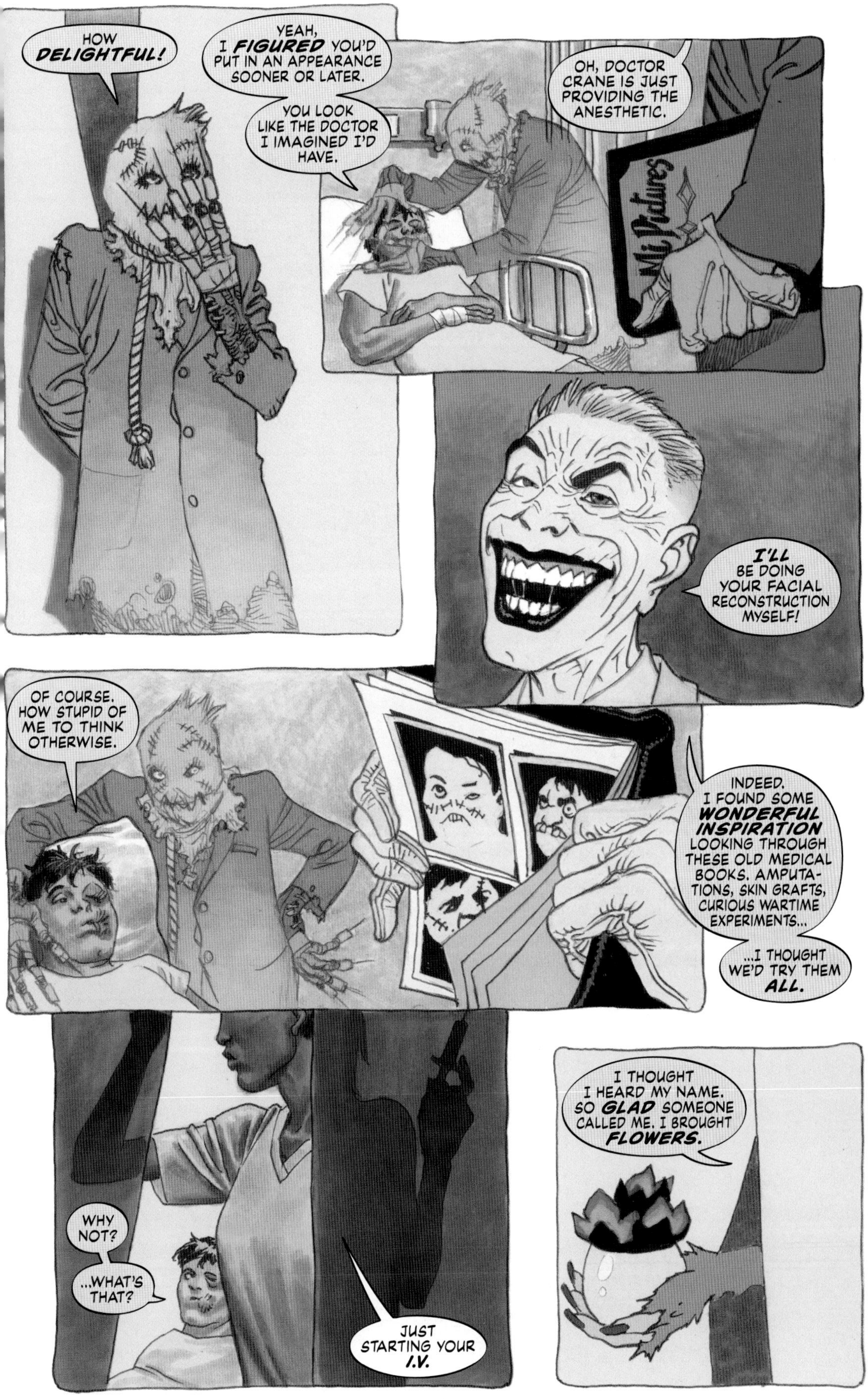
HOW DELIGHTFUL!
YEAH, I FIGURED YOU'D PUT IN AN APPEARANCE SOONER OR LATER.
YOU LOOK LIKE THE DOCTOR I IMAGINED I'D HAVE.
OH, DOCTOR CRANE IS JUST PROVIDING THE ANESTHETIC.
My Pictures
I'LL BE DOING YOUR FACIAL RECONSTRUCTION MYSELF!
OF COURSE. HOW STUPID OF ME TO THINK OTHERWISE.
INDEED. I FOUND SOME WONDERFUL INSPIRATION LOOKING THROUGH THESE OLD MEDICAL BOOKS. AMPUTATIONS, SKIN GRAFTS, CURIOUS WARTIME EXPERIMENTS...
...I THOUGHT WE'D TRY THEM ALL.
WHY NOT?
...WHAT'S THAT?
JUST STARTING YOUR I.V.
I THOUGHT I HEARD MY NAME. SO GLAD SOMEONE CALLED ME. I BROUGHT FLOWERS.

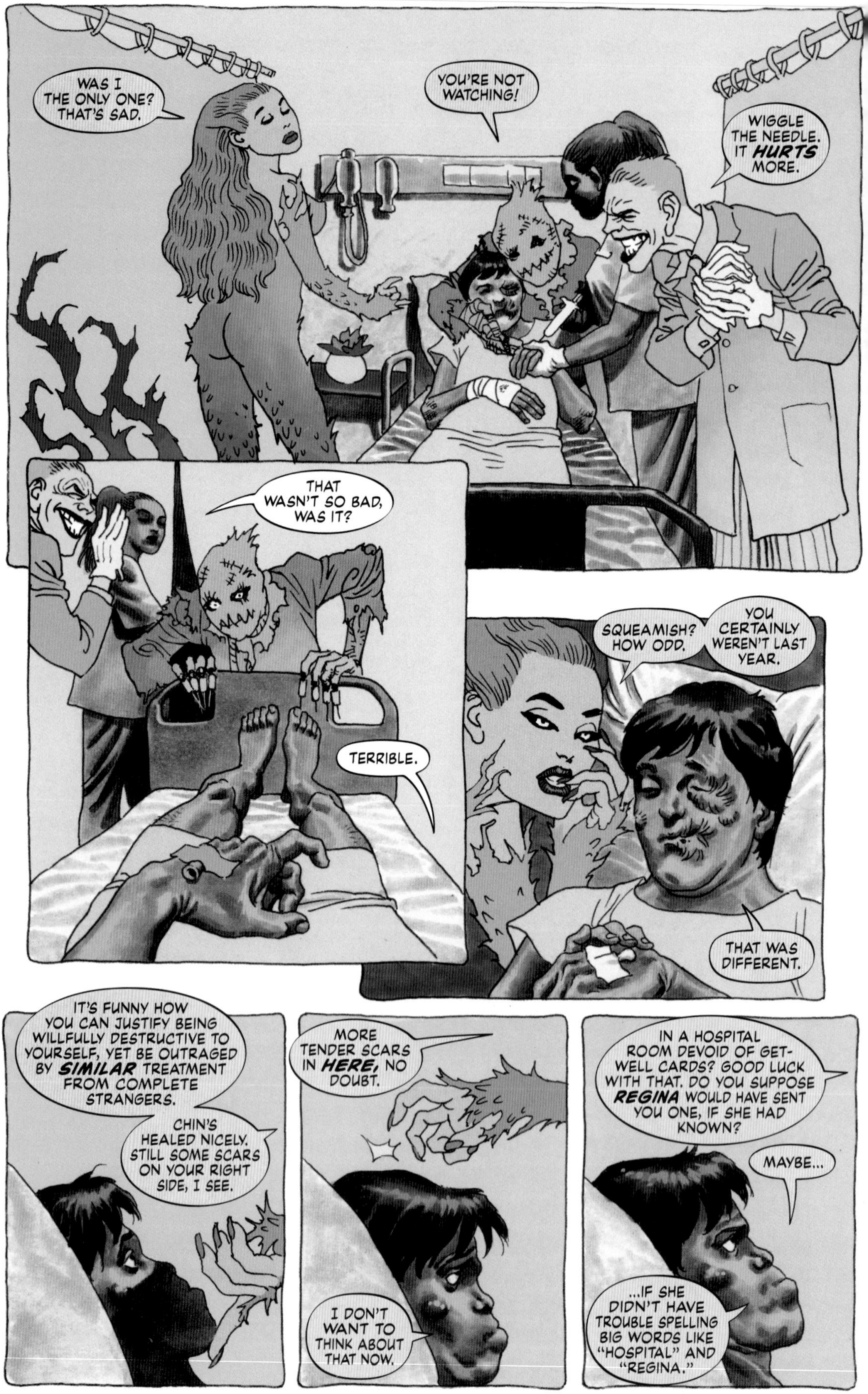

WAS I THE ONLY ONE? THAT'S SAD.
YOU'RE NOT WATCHING!
WIGGLE THE NEEDLE. IT HURTS MORE.
THAT WASN'T SO BAD, WAS IT?
TERRIBLE.
SQUEAMISH? HOW ODD.
YOU CERTAINLY WEREN'T LAST YEAR.
THAT WAS DIFFERENT.
IT'S FUNNY HOW YOU CAN JUSTIFY BEING WILLFULLY DESTRUCTIVE TO YOURSELF, YET BE OUTRAGED BY SIMILAR TREATMENT FROM COMPLETE STRANGERS.
CHIN'S HEALED NICELY. STILL SOME SCARS ON YOUR RIGHT SIDE, I SEE.
MORE TENDER SCARS IN HERE, NO DOUBT.
I DON'T WANT TO THINK ABOUT THAT NOW.
IN A HOSPITAL ROOM DEVOID OF GET-WELL CARDS? GOOD LUCK WITH THAT. DO YOU SUPPOSE REGINA WOULD HAVE SENT YOU ONE, IF SHE HAD KNOWN?
MAYBE...
...IF SHE DIDN'T HAVE TROUBLE SPELLING BIG WORDS LIKE "HOSPITAL" AND "REGINA."

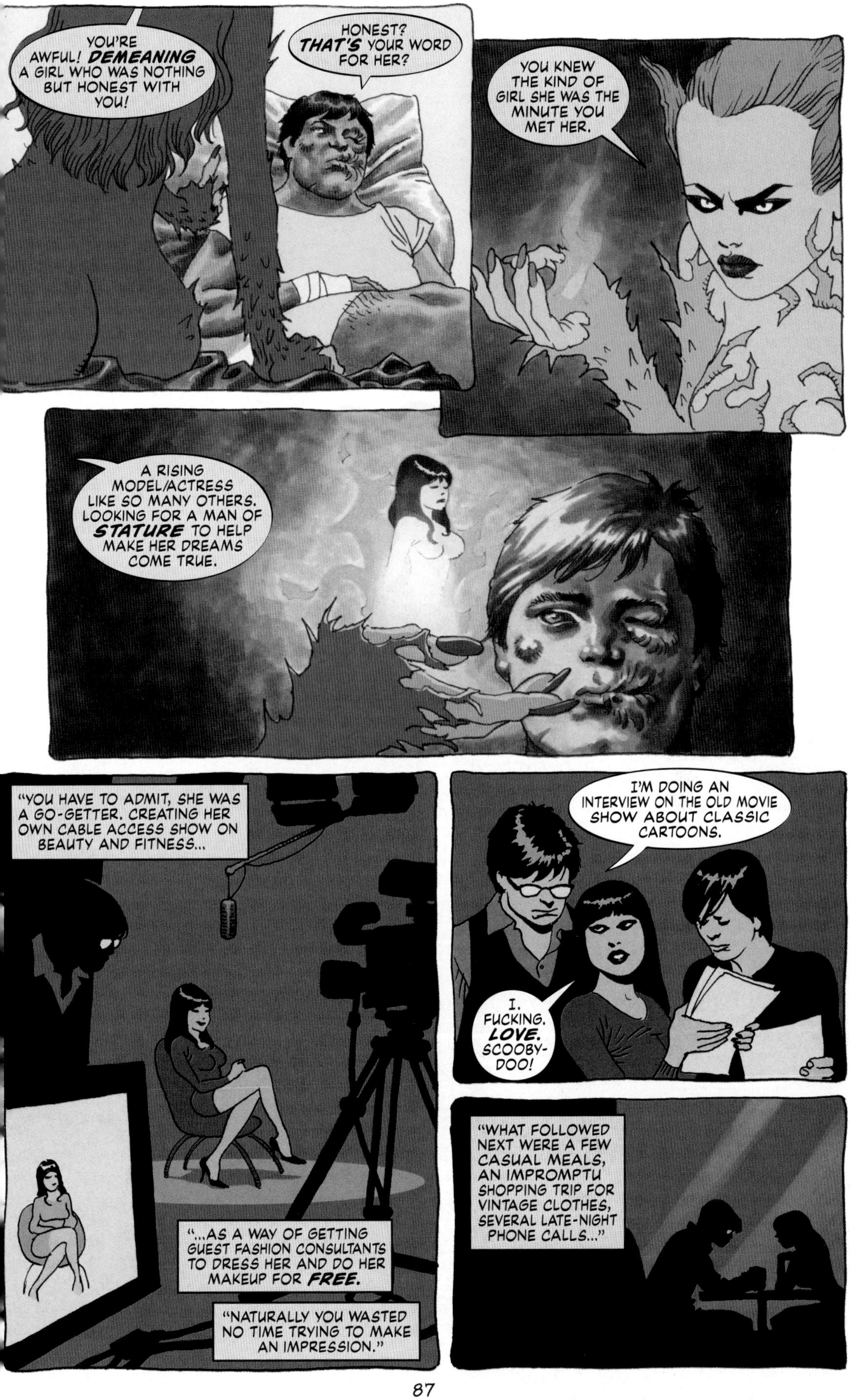
YOU'RE AWFUL! DEMEANING A GIRL WHO WAS NOTHING BUT HONEST WITH YOU!
HONEST? THAT'S YOUR WORD FOR HER?
YOU KNEW THE KIND OF GIRL SHE WAS THE MINUTE YOU MET HER.
A RISING MODEL/ACTRESS LIKE SO MANY OTHERS. LOOKING FOR A MAN OF STATURE TO HELP MAKE HER DREAMS COME TRUE.
"YOU HAVE TO ADMIT, SHE WAS A GO-GETTER. CREATING HER OWN CABLE ACCESS SHOW ON BEAUTY AND FITNESS...
"...AS A WAY OF GETTING GUEST FASHION CONSULTANTS TO DRESS HER AND DO HER MAKEUP FOR FREE.
"NATURALLY YOU WASTED NO TIME TRYING TO MAKE AN IMPRESSION."
I'M DOING AN INTERVIEW ON THE OLD MOVIE SHOW ABOUT CLASSIC CARTOONS.
I. FUCKING. LOVE. SCOOBY-DOO!
"WHAT FOLLOWED NEXT WERE A FEW CASUAL MEALS, AN IMPROMPTU SHOPPING TRIP FOR VINTAGE CLOTHES, SEVERAL LATE-NIGHT PHONE CALLS..."

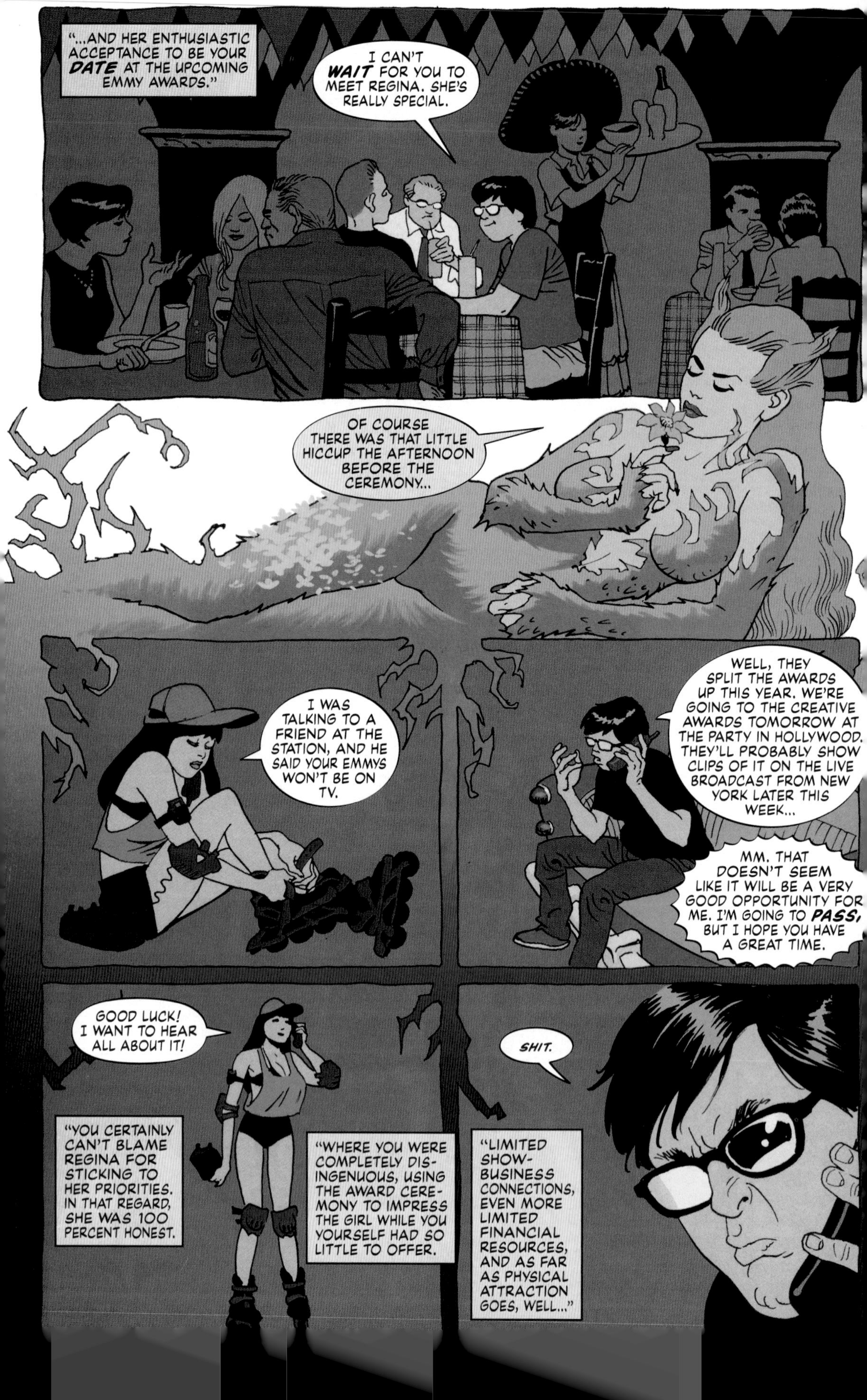
"...AND HER ENTHUSIASTIC ACCEPTANCE TO BE YOUR DATE AT THE UPCOMING EMMY AWARDS."
I CAN'T WAIT FOR YOU TO MEET REGINA. SHE'S REALLY SPECIAL.
OF COURSE THERE WAS THAT LITTLE HICCUP THE AFTERNOON BEFORE THE CEREMONY...
I WAS TALKING TO A FRIEND AT THE STATION, AND HE SAID YOUR EMMYS WON'T BE ON TV.
WELL, THEY SPLIT THE AWARDS UP THIS YEAR. WE'RE GOING TO THE CREATIVE AWARDS TOMORROW AT THE PARTY IN HOLLYWOOD. THEY'LL PROBABLY SHOW CLIPS OF IT ON THE LIVE BROADCAST FROM NEW YORK LATER THIS WEEK...
MM. THAT DOESN'T SEEM LIKE IT WILL BE A VERY GOOD OPPORTUNITY FOR ME. I'M GOING TO PASS, BUT I HOPE YOU HAVE A GREAT TIME.
GOOD LUCK! I WANT TO HEAR ALL ABOUT IT!
"YOU CERTAINLY CAN'T BLAME REGINA FOR STICKING TO HER PRIORITIES. IN THAT REGARD, SHE WAS 100 PERCENT HONEST.
"WHERE YOU WERE COMPLETELY DIS-INGENUOUS, USING THE AWARD CERE-MONY TO IMPRESS THE GIRL WHILE YOU YOURSELF HAD SO LITTLE TO OFFER.
SHIT.
"LIMITED SHOW-BUSINESS CONNECTIONS, EVEN MORE LIMITED FINANCIAL RESOURCES, AND AS FAR AS PHYSICAL ATTRACTION GOES, WELL..."

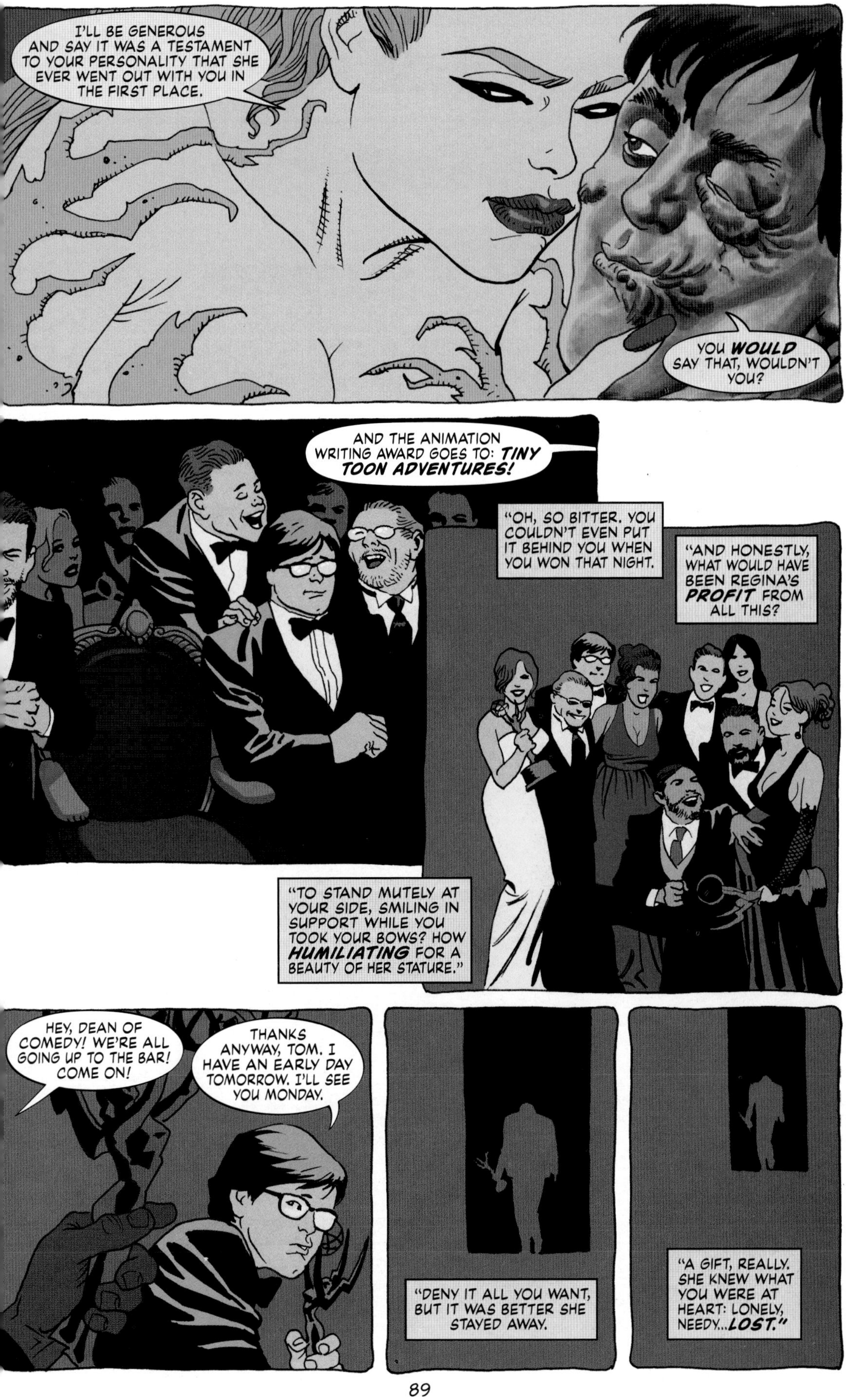
I'LL BE GENEROUS AND SAY IT WAS A TESTAMENT TO YOUR PERSONALITY THAT SHE EVER WENT OUT WITH YOU IN THE FIRST PLACE.
YOU WOULD SAY THAT, WOULDN'T YOU?
AND THE ANIMATION WRITING AWARD GOES TO: TINY TOON ADVENTURES!
"OH, SO BITTER. YOU COULDN'T EVEN PUT IT BEHIND YOU WHEN YOU WON THAT NIGHT.
"AND HONESTLY, WHAT WOULD HAVE BEEN REGINA'S PROFIT FROM ALL THIS?
"TO STAND MUTELY AT YOUR SIDE, SMILING IN SUPPORT WHILE YOU TOOK YOUR BOWS? HOW HUMILIATING FOR A BEAUTY OF HER STATURE."
HEY, DEAN OF COMEDY! WE'RE ALL GOING UP TO THE BAR! COME ON!
THANKS ANYWAY, TOM. I HAVE AN EARLY DAY TOMORROW. I'LL SEE YOU MONDAY.
"DENY IT ALL YOU WANT, BUT IT WAS BETTER SHE STAYED AWAY.
"A GIFT, REALLY. SHE KNEW WHAT YOU WERE AT HEART: LONELY, NEEDY...LOST."

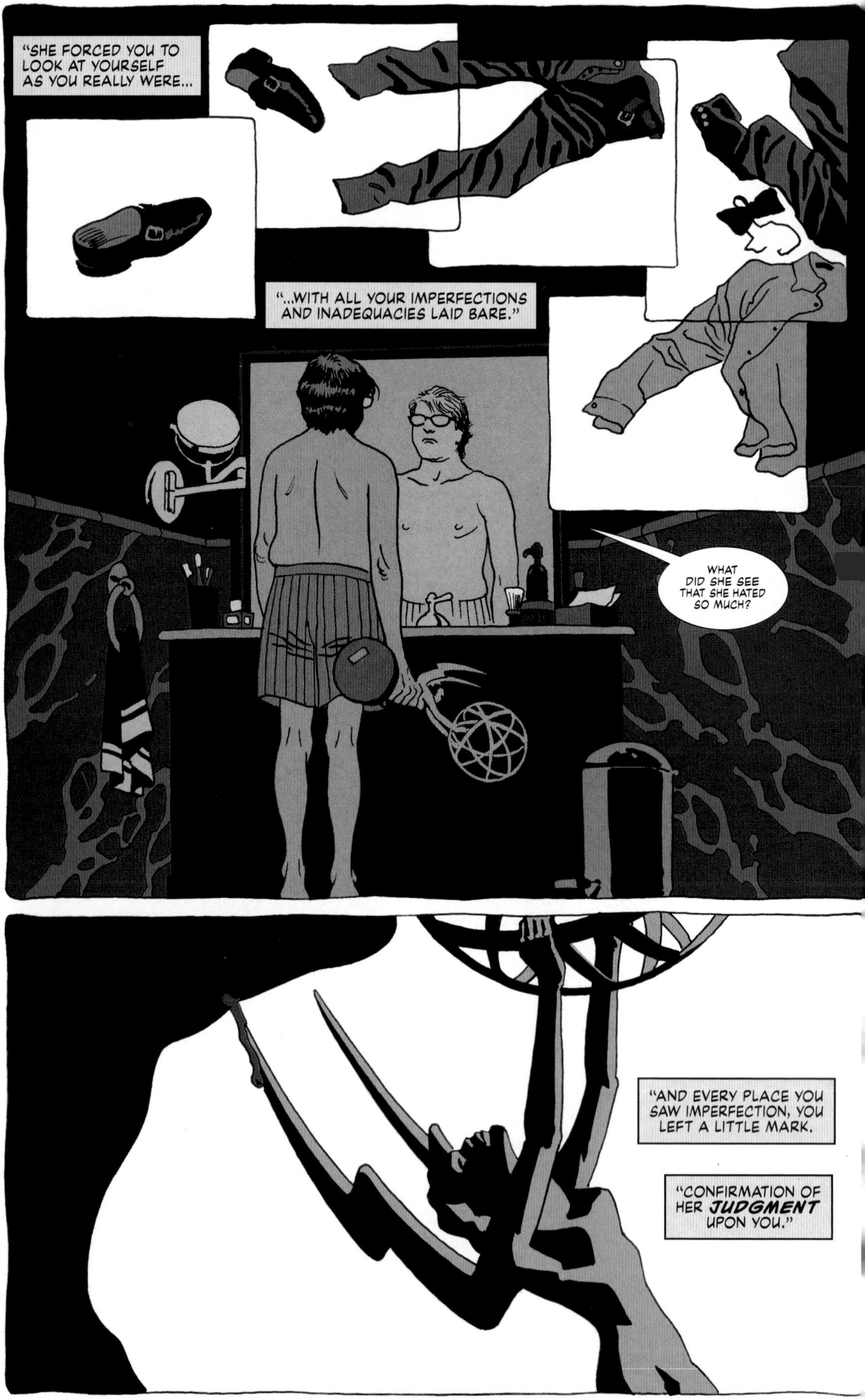
"SHE FORCED YOU TO LOOK AT YOURSELF AS YOU REALLY WERE...
"...WITH ALL YOUR IMPERFECTIONS AND INADEQUACIES LAID BARE."
WHAT DID SHE SEE THAT SHE HATED SO MUCH?
"AND EVERY PLACE YOU SAW IMPERFECTION, YOU LEFT A LITTLE MARK.
"CONFIRMATION OF HER *JUDGMENT* UPON YOU."

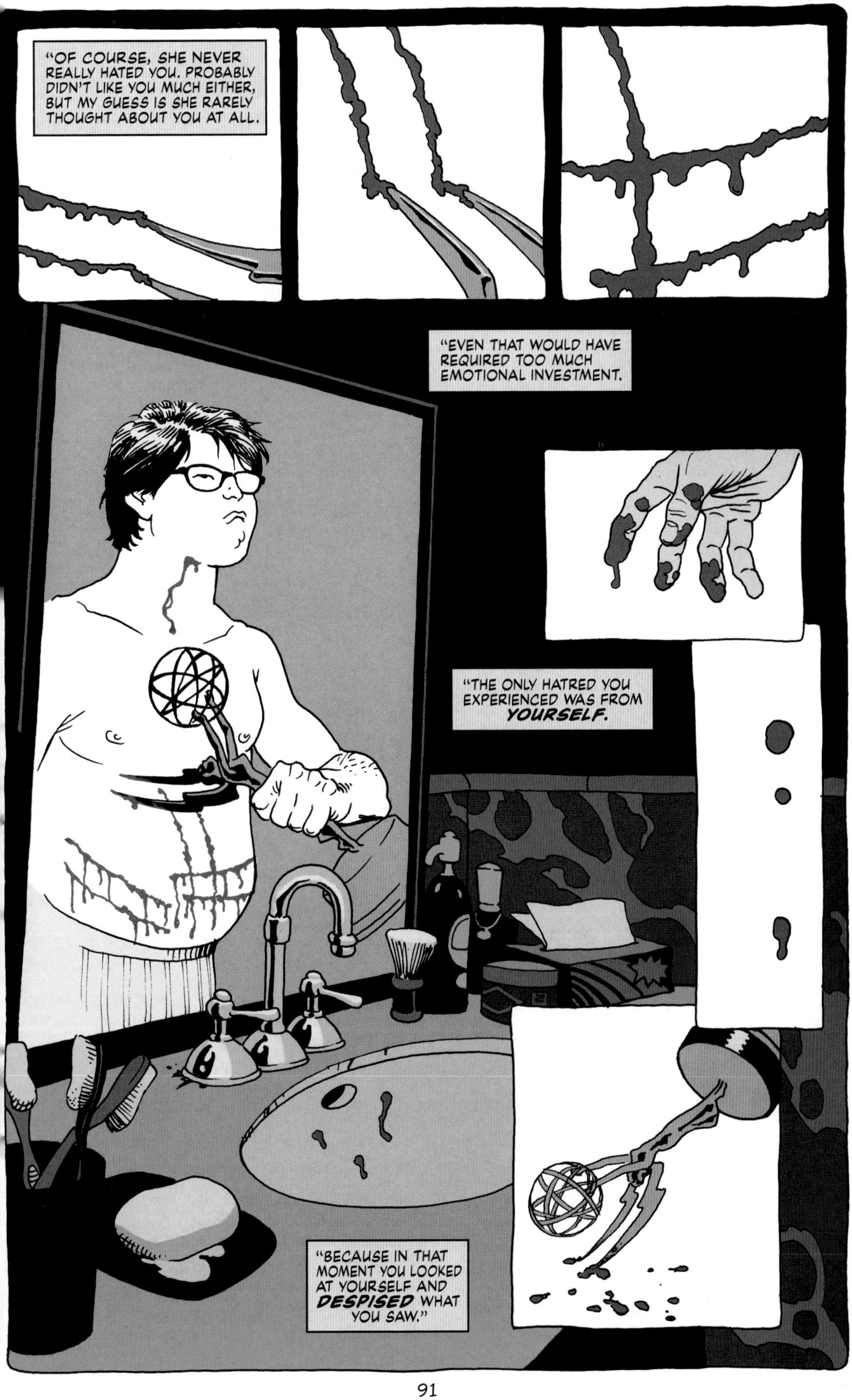
"OF COURSE, SHE NEVER REALLY HATED YOU. PROBABLY DIDN'T LIKE YOU MUCH EITHER, BUT MY GUESS IS SHE RARELY THOUGHT ABOUT YOU AT ALL.
"EVEN THAT WOULD HAVE REQUIRED TOO MUCH EMOTIONAL INVESTMENT.
"THE ONLY HATRED YOU EXPERIENCED WAS FROM *YOURSELF*.
"BECAUSE IN THAT MOMENT YOU LOOKED AT YOURSELF AND *DESPISED* WHAT YOU SAW."

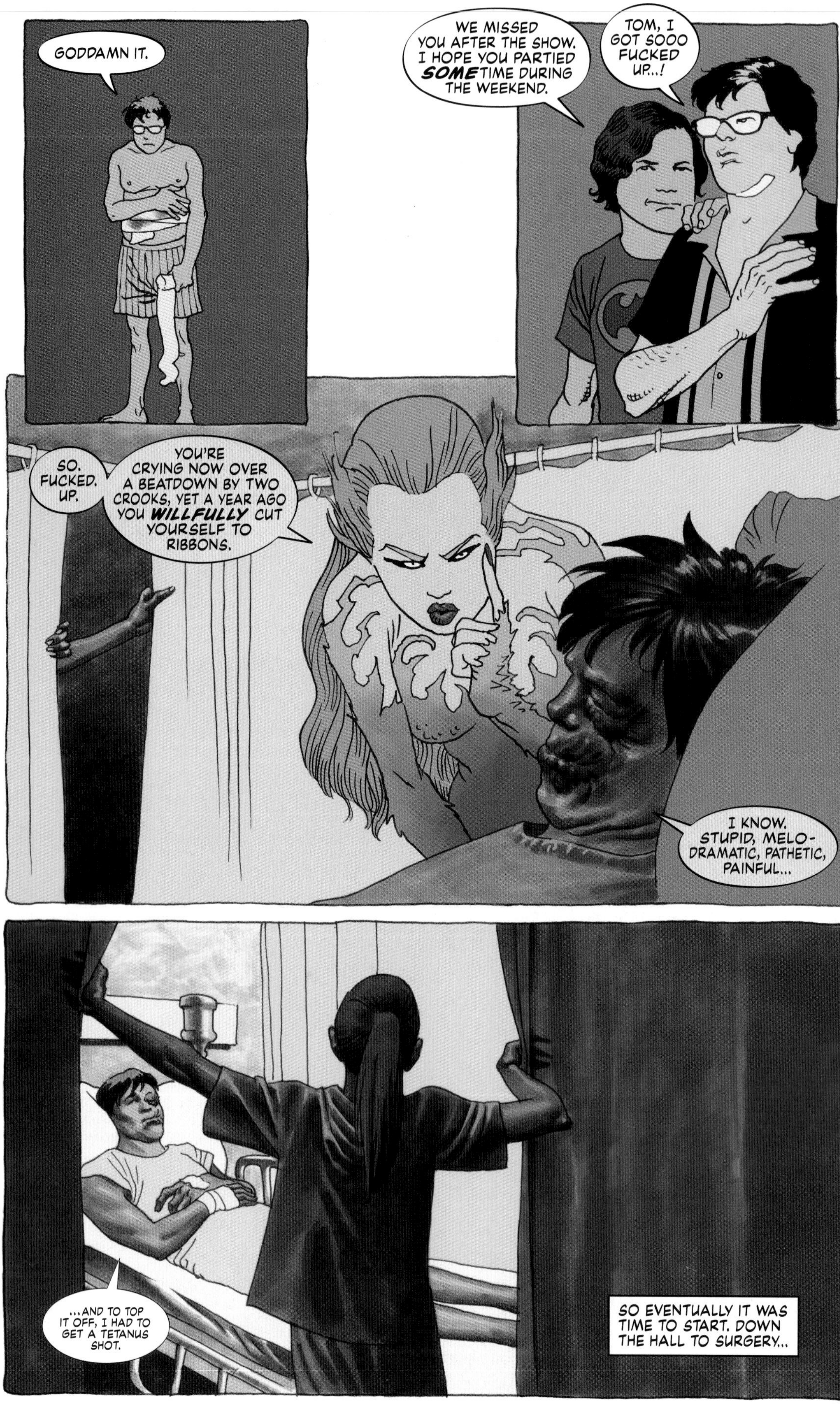
GODDAMN IT.
WE MISSED YOU AFTER THE SHOW. I HOPE YOU PARTIED SOMETIME DURING THE WEEKEND.
TOM, I GOT SOOO FUCKED UP...!
SO. FUCKED. UP.
YOU'RE CRYING NOW OVER A BEATDOWN BY TWO CROOKS, YET A YEAR AGO YOU WILLFULLY CUT YOURSELF TO RIBBONS.
I KNOW. STUPID, MELO-DRAMATIC, PATHETIC, PAINFUL...
...AND TO TOP IT OFF, I HAD TO GET A TETANUS SHOT.
SO EVENTUALLY IT WAS TIME TO START. DOWN THE HALL TO SURGERY...

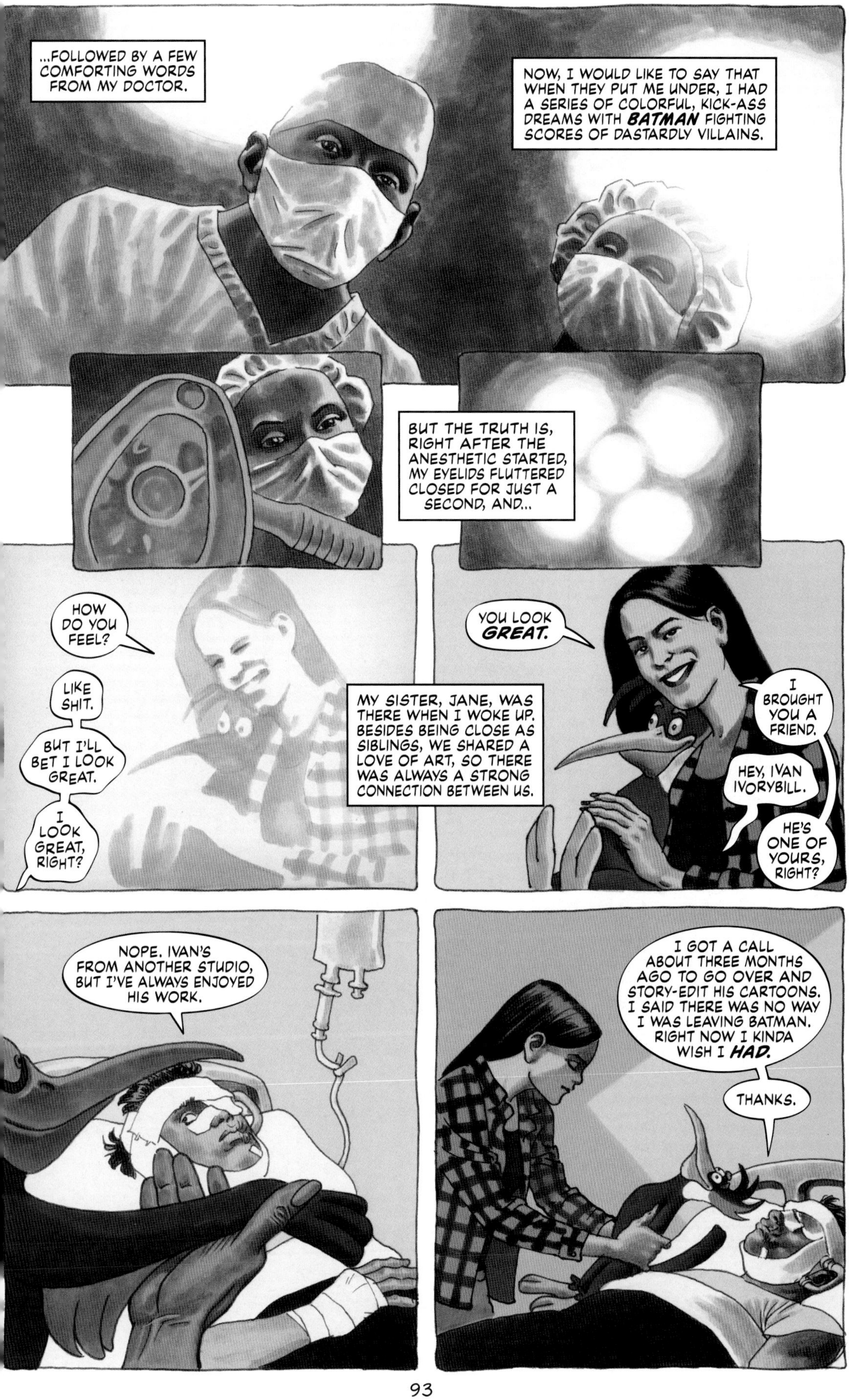

...FOLLOWED BY A FEW COMFORTING WORDS FROM MY DOCTOR.
NOW, I WOULD LIKE TO SAY THAT WHEN THEY PUT ME UNDER, I HAD A SERIES OF COLORFUL, KICK-ASS DREAMS WITH BATMAN FIGHTING SCORES OF DASTARDLY VILLAINS.
BUT THE TRUTH IS, RIGHT AFTER THE ANESTHETIC STARTED, MY EYELIDS FLUTTERED CLOSED FOR JUST A SECOND, AND...
HOW DO YOU FEEL?
LIKE SHIT.
BUT I'LL BET I LOOK GREAT.
I LOOK GREAT, RIGHT?
MY SISTER, JANE, WAS THERE WHEN I WOKE UP. BESIDES BEING CLOSE AS SIBLINGS, WE SHARED A LOVE OF ART, SO THERE WAS ALWAYS A STRONG CONNECTION BETWEEN US.
YOU LOOK GREAT.
I BROUGHT YOU A FRIEND.
HEY, IVAN IVORYBILL.
HE'S ONE OF YOURS, RIGHT?
NOPE. IVAN'S FROM ANOTHER STUDIO, BUT I'VE ALWAYS ENJOYED HIS WORK.
I GOT A CALL ABOUT THREE MONTHS AGO TO GO OVER AND STORY-EDIT HIS CARTOONS. I SAID THERE WAS NO WAY I WAS LEAVING BATMAN. RIGHT NOW I KINDA WISH I HAD.
THANKS.

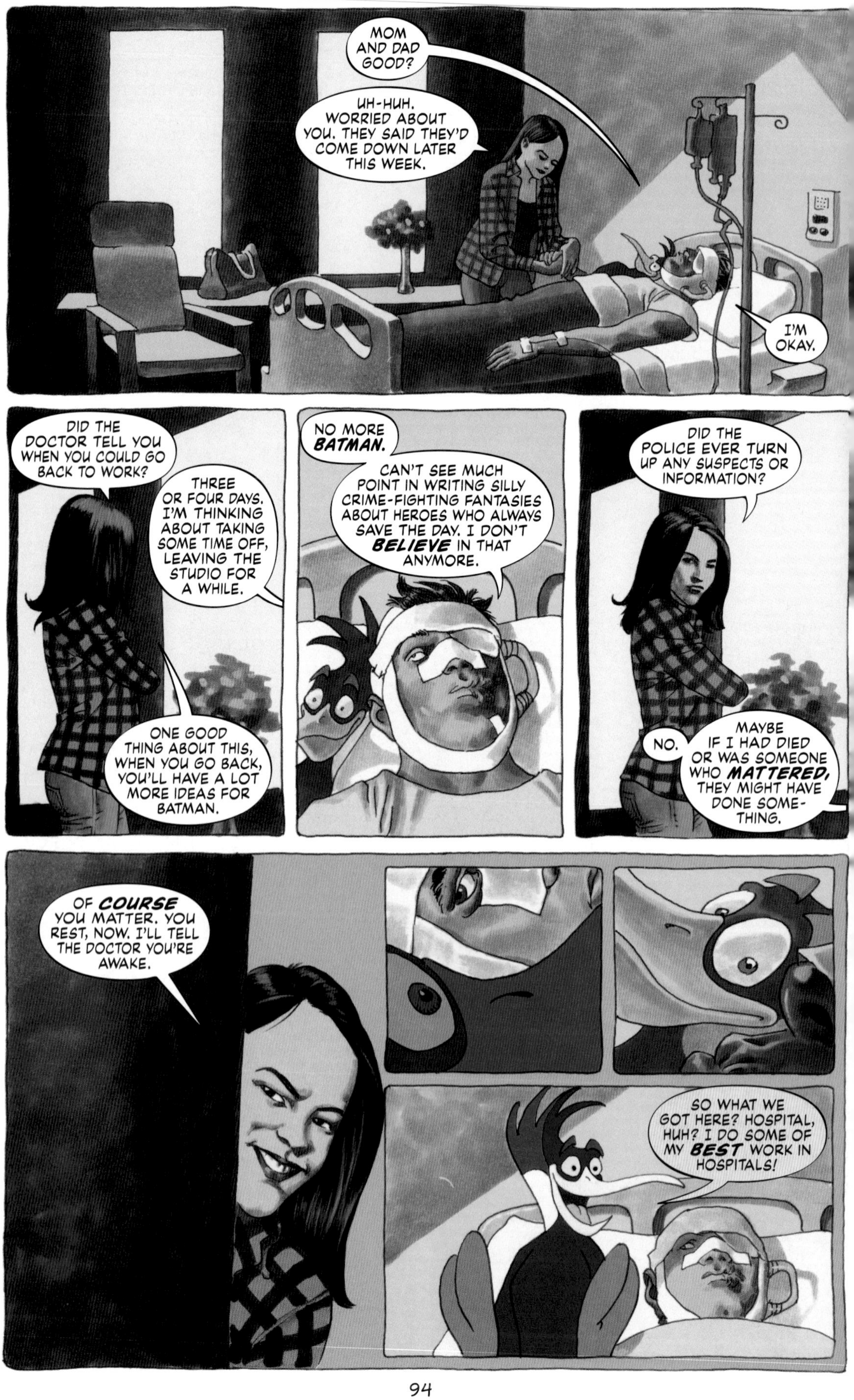
MOM AND DAD GOOD?
UH-HUH. WORRIED ABOUT YOU. THEY SAID THEY'D COME DOWN LATER THIS WEEK.
I'M OKAY.
DID THE DOCTOR TELL YOU WHEN YOU COULD GO BACK TO WORK?
THREE OR FOUR DAYS. I'M THINKING ABOUT TAKING SOME TIME OFF, LEAVING THE STUDIO FOR A WHILE.
ONE GOOD THING ABOUT THIS, WHEN YOU GO BACK, YOU'LL HAVE A LOT MORE IDEAS FOR BATMAN.
NO MORE **BATMAN.**
CAN'T SEE MUCH POINT IN WRITING SILLY CRIME-FIGHTING FANTASIES ABOUT HEROES WHO ALWAYS SAVE THE DAY. I DON'T **BELIEVE** IN THAT ANYMORE.
DID THE POLICE EVER TURN UP ANY SUSPECTS OR INFORMATION?
NO.
MAYBE IF I HAD DIED OR WAS SOMEONE WHO **MATTERED,** THEY MIGHT HAVE DONE SOME-THING.
OF **COURSE** YOU MATTER. YOU REST, NOW. I'LL TELL THE DOCTOR YOU'RE AWAKE.
SO WHAT WE GOT HERE? HOSPITAL, HUH? I DO SOME OF MY **BEST** WORK IN HOSPITALS!

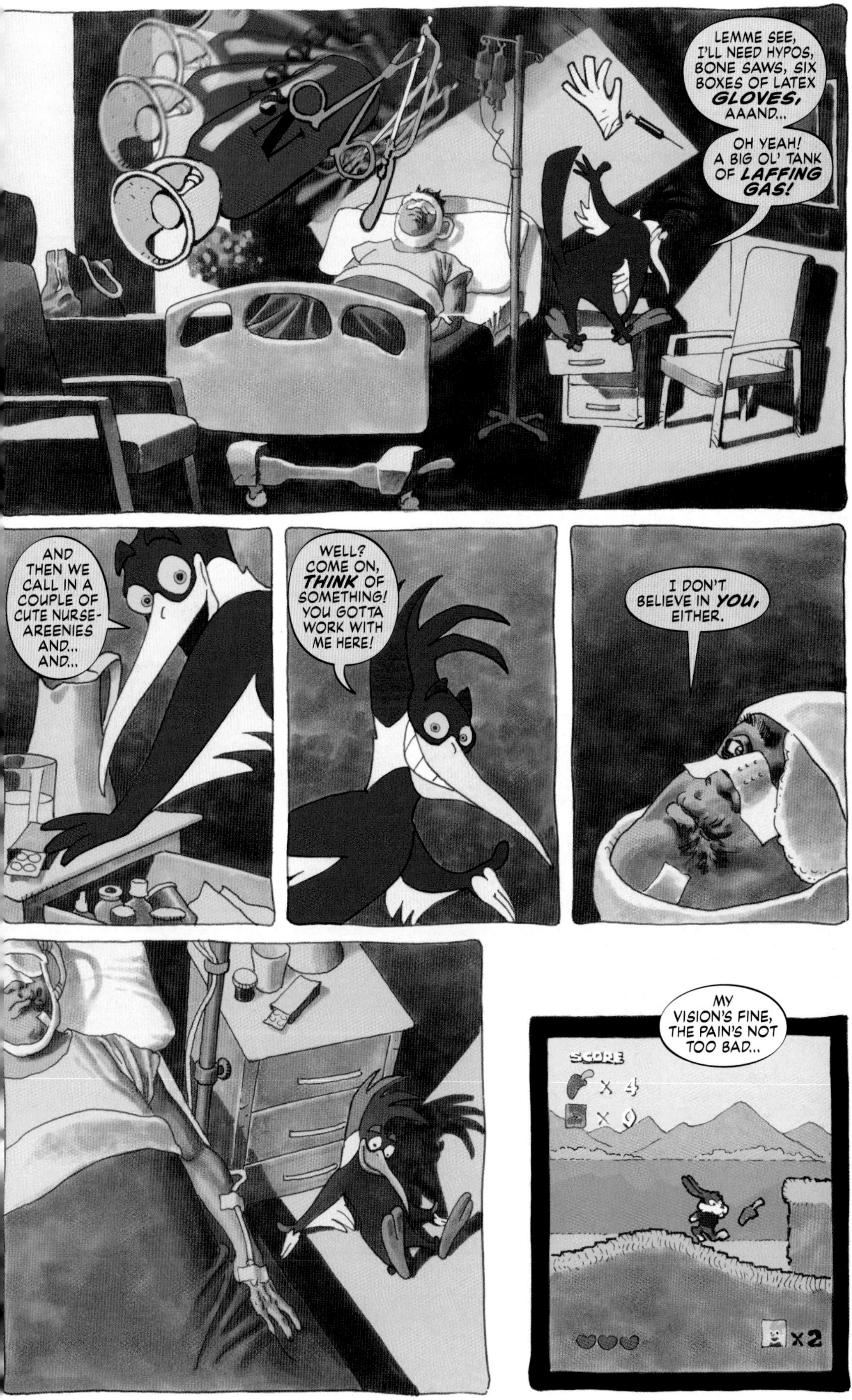
LEMME SEE, I'LL NEED HYPOS, BONE SAWS, SIX BOXES OF LATEX GLOVES, AAAND...
OH YEAH! A BIG OL' TANK OF LAFFING GAS!
AND THEN WE CALL IN A COUPLE OF CUTE NURSE-AREENIES AND... AND...
WELL? COME ON, THINK OF SOMETHING! YOU GOTTA WORK WITH ME HERE!
I DON'T BELIEVE IN YOU, EITHER.
MY VISION'S FINE, THE PAIN'S NOT TOO BAD...
SCORE
X 4
X 0
X2

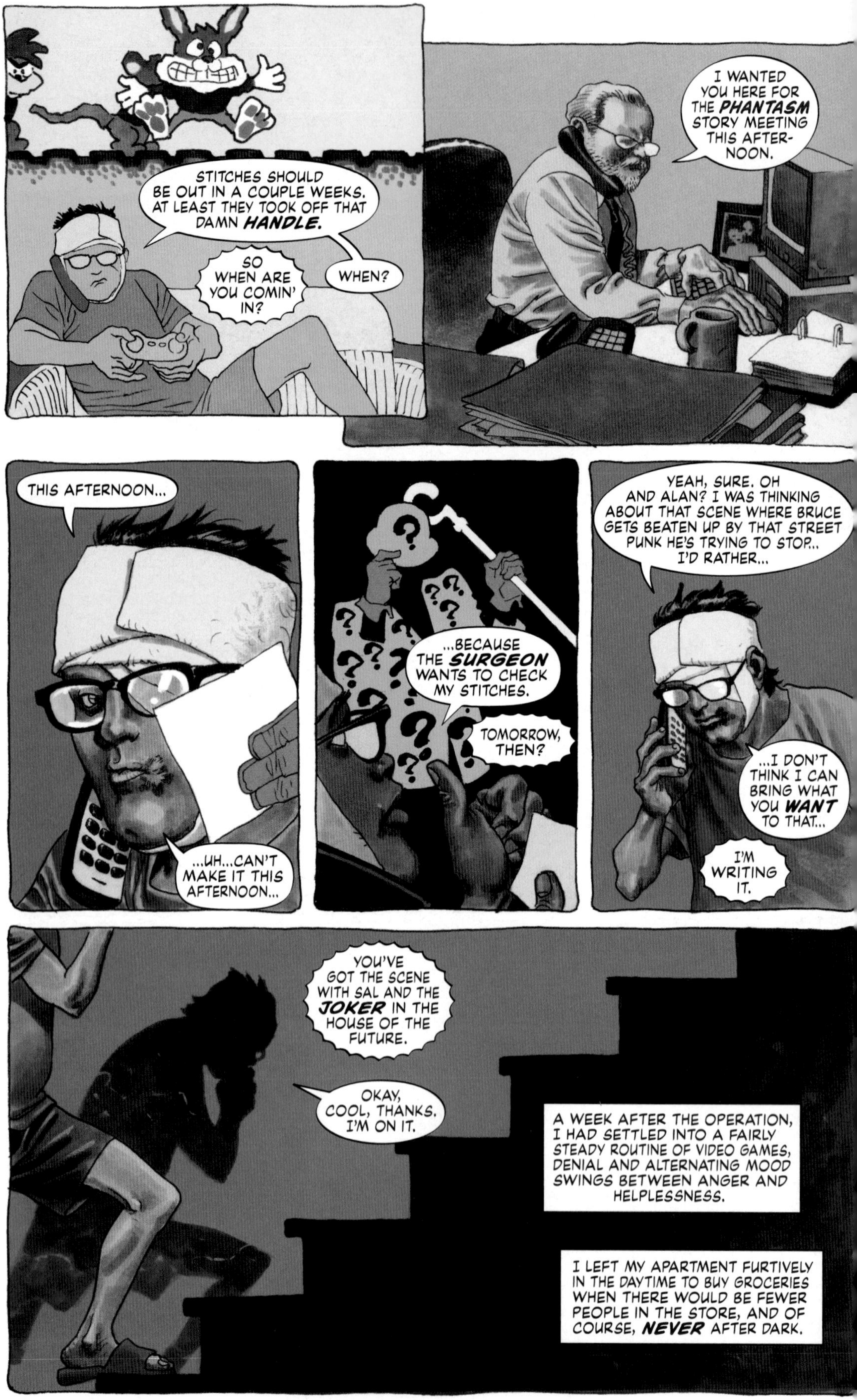
STITCHES SHOULD BE OUT IN A COUPLE WEEKS. AT LEAST THEY TOOK OFF THAT DAMN *HANDLE.*
SO WHEN ARE YOU COMIN' IN?
WHEN?
I WANTED YOU HERE FOR THE *PHANTASM* STORY MEETING THIS AFTER-NOON.
THIS AFTERNOON...
...UH...CAN'T MAKE IT THIS AFTERNOON...
...BECAUSE THE *SURGEON* WANTS TO CHECK MY STITCHES.
TOMORROW, THEN?
YEAH, SURE. OH AND ALAN? I WAS THINKING ABOUT THAT SCENE WHERE BRUCE GETS BEATEN UP BY THAT STREET PUNK HE'S TRYING TO STOP.. I'D RATHER...
...I DON'T THINK I CAN BRING WHAT YOU *WANT* TO THAT...
I'M WRITING IT.
YOU'VE GOT THE SCENE WITH SAL AND THE *JOKER* IN THE HOUSE OF THE FUTURE.
OKAY, COOL, THANKS. I'M ON IT.
A WEEK AFTER THE OPERATION, I HAD SETTLED INTO A FAIRLY STEADY ROUTINE OF VIDEO GAMES, DENIAL AND ALTERNATING MOOD SWINGS BETWEEN ANGER AND HELPLESSNESS.
I LEFT MY APARTMENT FURTIVELY IN THE DAYTIME TO BUY GROCERIES WHEN THERE WOULD BE FEWER PEOPLE IN THE STORE, AND OF COURSE, *NEVER* AFTER DARK.

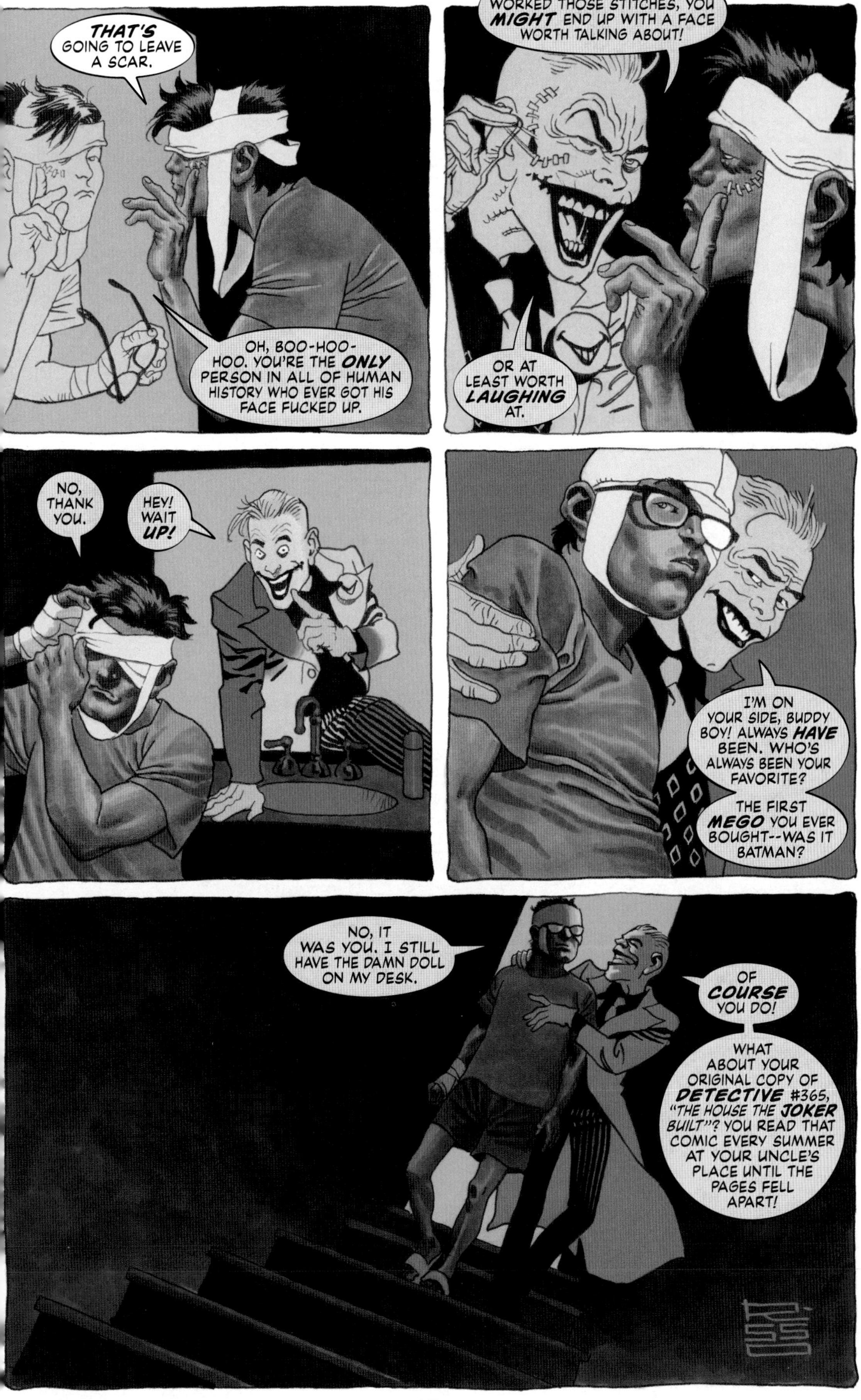
THAT'S GOING TO LEAVE A SCAR.
OH, BOO-HOO-HOO. YOU'RE THE ONLY PERSON IN ALL OF HUMAN HISTORY WHO EVER GOT HIS FACE FUCKED UP.
NOW IF YOU REALLY WORKED THOSE STITCHES, YOU MIGHT END UP WITH A FACE WORTH TALKING ABOUT!
OR AT LEAST WORTH LAUGHING AT.
NO, THANK YOU.
HEY! WAIT UP!
I'M ON YOUR SIDE, BUDDY BOY! ALWAYS HAVE BEEN. WHO'S ALWAYS BEEN YOUR FAVORITE?
THE FIRST MEGO YOU EVER BOUGHT--WAS IT BATMAN?
NO, IT WAS YOU. I STILL HAVE THE DAMN DOLL ON MY DESK.
OF COURSE YOU DO!
WHAT ABOUT YOUR ORIGINAL COPY OF DETECTIVE #365, "THE HOUSE THE JOKER BUILT"? YOU READ THAT COMIC EVERY SUMMER AT YOUR UNCLE'S PLACE UNTIL THE PAGES FELL APART!

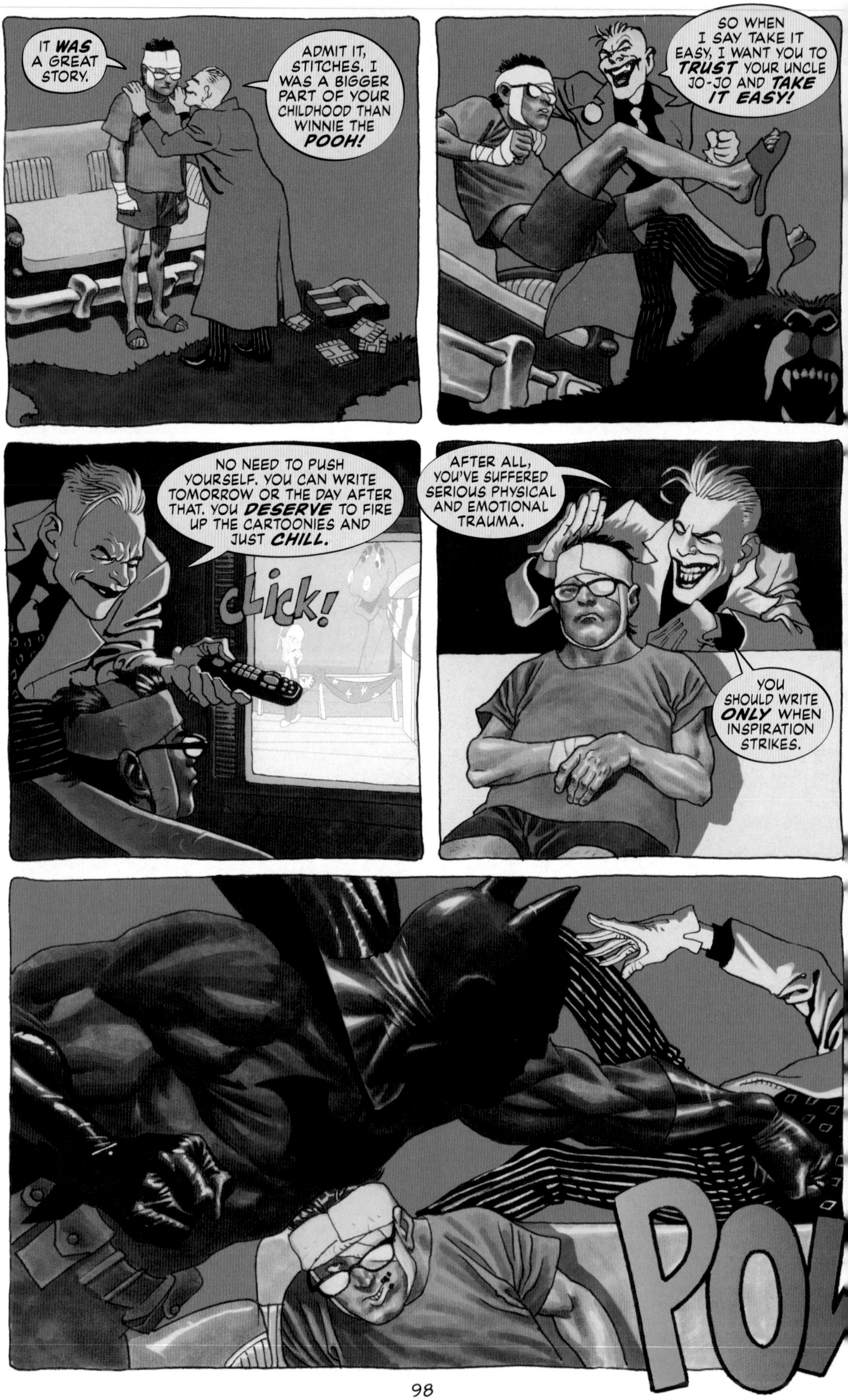
IT WAS A GREAT STORY.
ADMIT IT, STITCHES. I WAS A BIGGER PART OF YOUR CHILDHOOD THAN WINNIE THE POOH!
SO WHEN I SAY TAKE IT EASY, I WANT YOU TO TRUST YOUR UNCLE JO-JO AND TAKE IT EASY!
NO NEED TO PUSH YOURSELF. YOU CAN WRITE TOMORROW OR THE DAY AFTER THAT. YOU DESERVE TO FIRE UP THE CARTOONIES AND JUST CHILL.
CLICK!
AFTER ALL, YOU'VE SUFFERED SERIOUS PHYSICAL AND EMOTIONAL TRAUMA.
YOU SHOULD WRITE ONLY WHEN INSPIRATION STRIKES.
POW

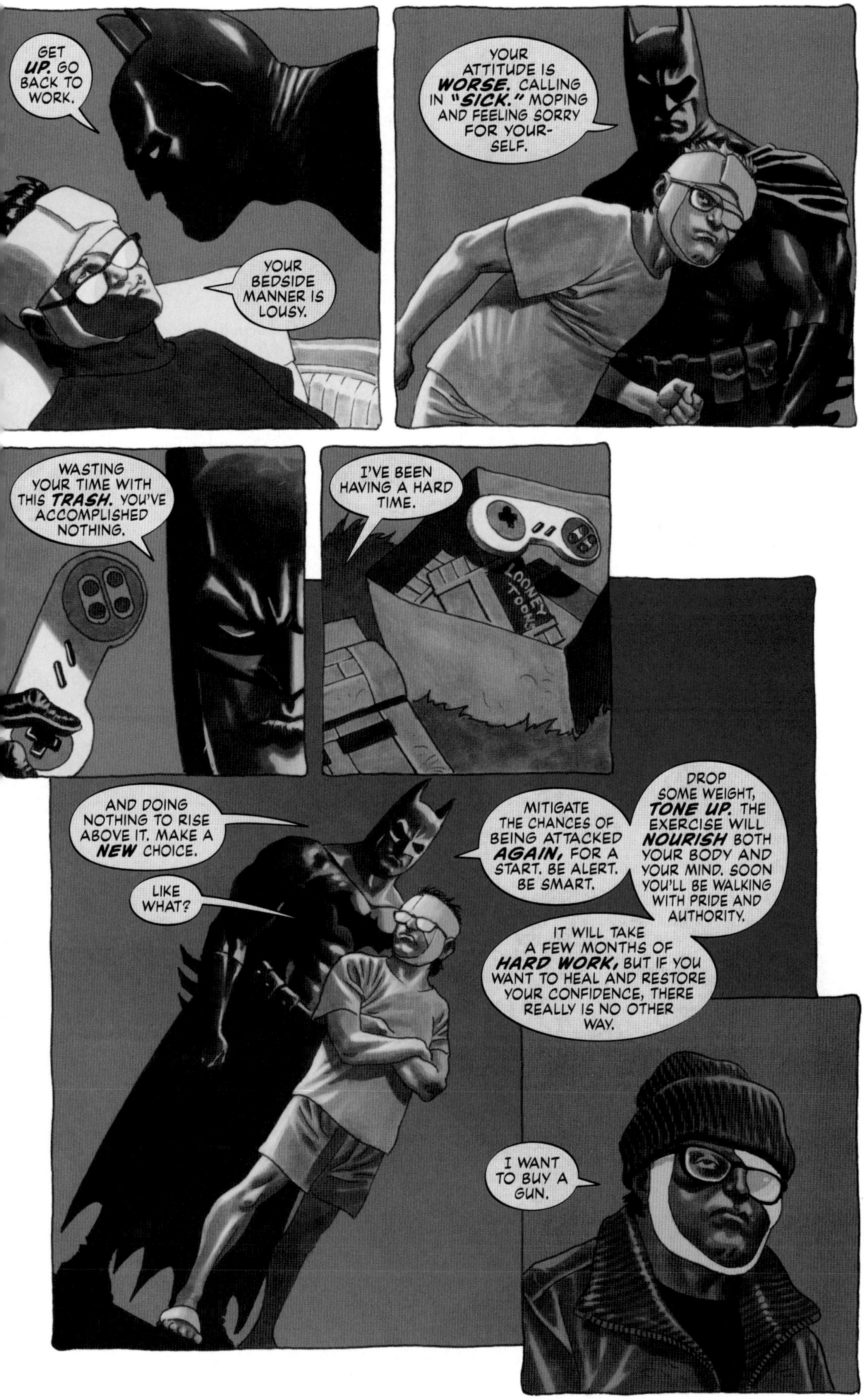
GET UP. GO BACK TO WORK.
YOUR BEDSIDE MANNER IS LOUSY.
YOUR ATTITUDE IS WORSE. CALLING IN "SICK." MOPING AND FEELING SORRY FOR YOURSELF.
WASTING YOUR TIME WITH THIS TRASH. YOU'VE ACCOMPLISHED NOTHING.
I'VE BEEN HAVING A HARD TIME.
LOONEY TOONS
AND DOING NOTHING TO RISE ABOVE IT. MAKE A NEW CHOICE.
LIKE WHAT?
MITIGATE THE CHANCES OF BEING ATTACKED AGAIN, FOR A START. BE ALERT. BE SMART.
DROP SOME WEIGHT, TONE UP. THE EXERCISE WILL NOURISH BOTH YOUR BODY AND YOUR MIND. SOON YOU'LL BE WALKING WITH PRIDE AND AUTHORITY.
IT WILL TAKE A FEW MONTHS OF HARD WORK, BUT IF YOU WANT TO HEAL AND RESTORE YOUR CONFIDENCE, THERE REALLY IS NO OTHER WAY.
I WANT TO BUY A GUN.

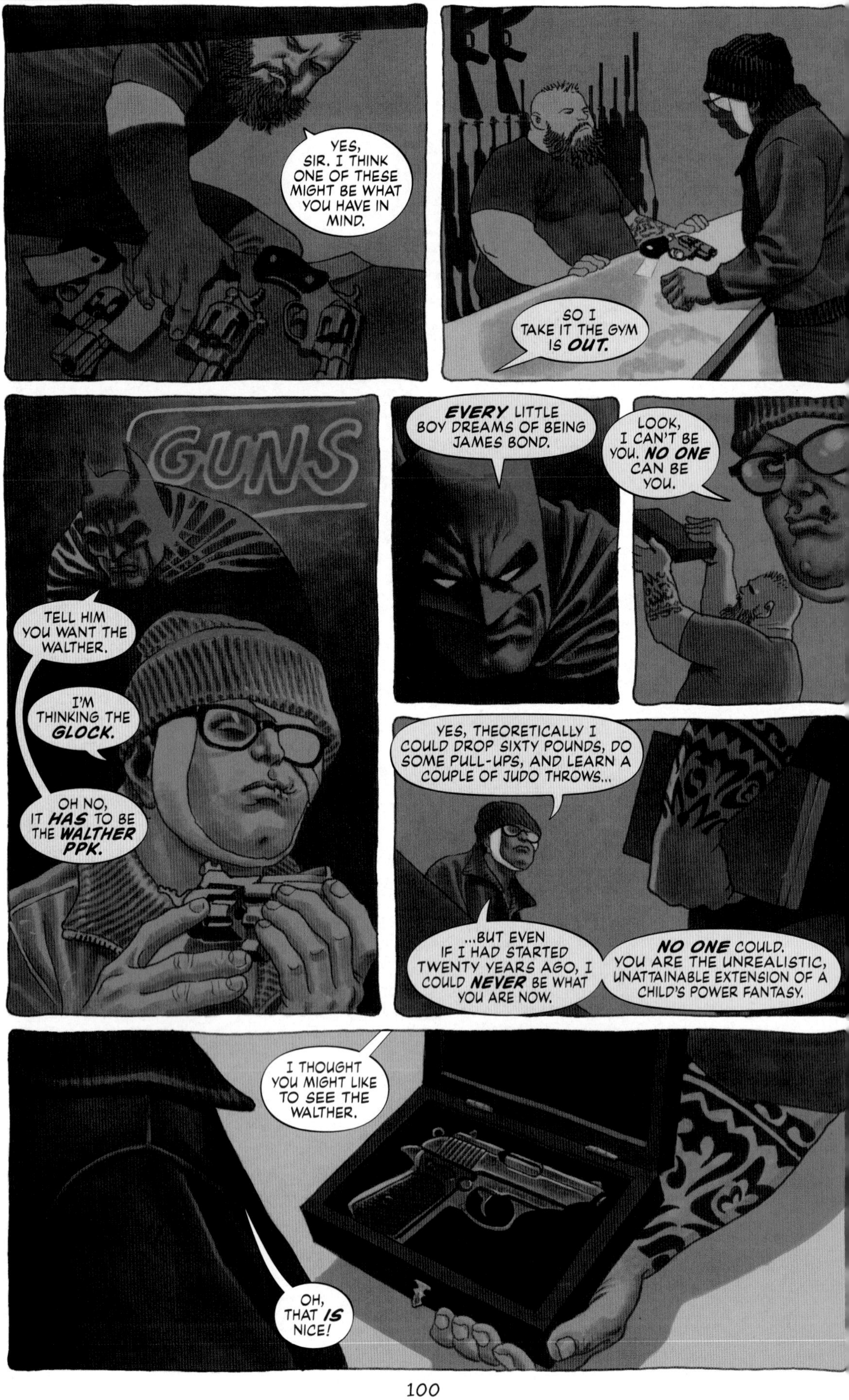

YES, SIR. I THINK ONE OF THESE MIGHT BE WHAT YOU HAVE IN MIND.
SO I TAKE IT THE GYM IS **OUT.**
TELL HIM YOU WANT THE WALTHER.
I'M THINKING THE **GLOCK.**
OH NO, IT **HAS** TO BE THE **WALTHER PPK.**
GUNS
EVERY LITTLE BOY DREAMS OF BEING JAMES BOND.
LOOK, I CAN'T BE YOU. **NO ONE** CAN BE YOU.
YES, THEORETICALLY I COULD DROP SIXTY POUNDS, DO SOME PULL-UPS, AND LEARN A COUPLE OF JUDO THROWS...
...BUT EVEN IF I HAD STARTED TWENTY YEARS AGO, I COULD **NEVER** BE WHAT YOU ARE NOW.
NO ONE COULD. YOU ARE THE UNREALISTIC, UNATTAINABLE EXTENSION OF A CHILD'S POWER FANTASY.
I THOUGHT YOU MIGHT LIKE TO SEE THE WALTHER.
OH, THAT **IS** NICE!

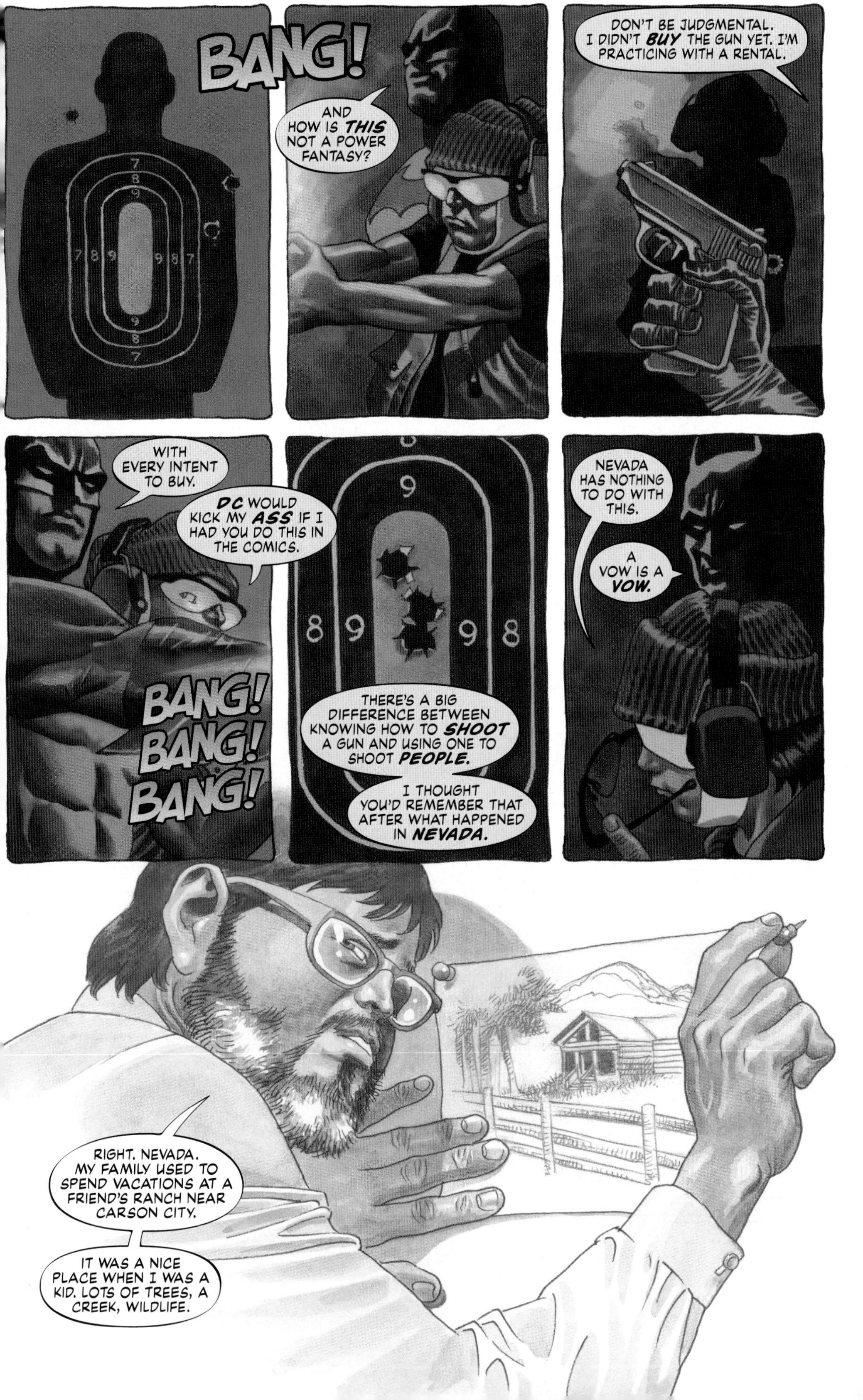
BANG!
AND HOW IS THIS NOT A POWER FANTASY?
DON'T BE JUDGMENTAL. I DIDN'T BUY THE GUN YET. I'M PRACTICING WITH A RENTAL.
WITH EVERY INTENT TO BUY.
DC WOULD KICK MY ASS IF I HAD YOU DO THIS IN THE COMICS.
BANG! BANG! BANG!
THERE'S A BIG DIFFERENCE BETWEEN KNOWING HOW TO SHOOT A GUN AND USING ONE TO SHOOT PEOPLE.
I THOUGHT YOU'D REMEMBER THAT AFTER WHAT HAPPENED IN NEVADA.
NEVADA HAS NOTHING TO DO WITH THIS.
A VOW IS A VOW.
RIGHT. NEVADA. MY FAMILY USED TO SPEND VACATIONS AT A FRIEND'S RANCH NEAR CARSON CITY.
IT WAS A NICE PLACE WHEN I WAS A KID. LOTS OF TREES, A CREEK, WILDLIFE.

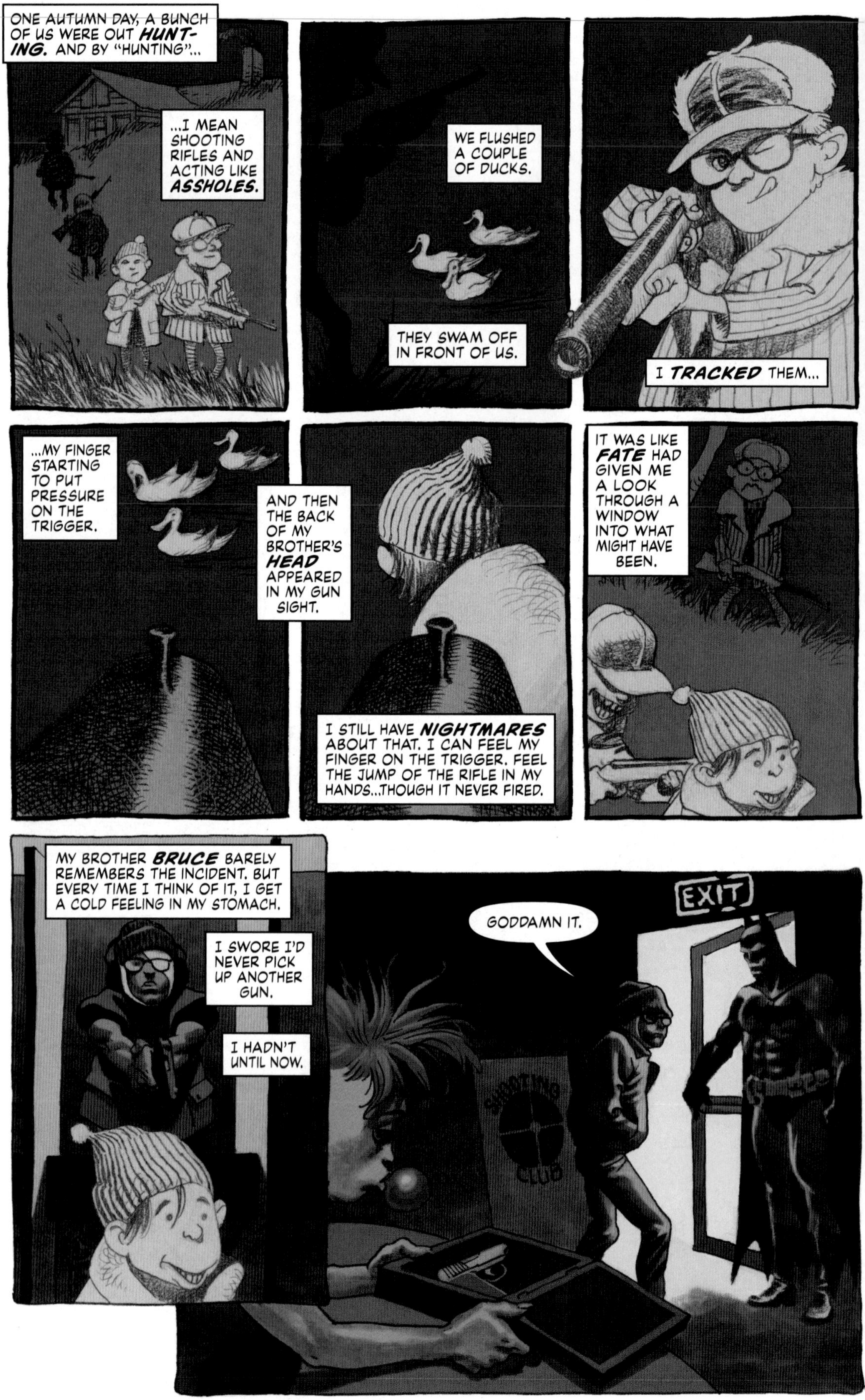
ONE AUTUMN DAY, A BUNCH OF US WERE OUT HUNT-ING. AND BY "HUNTING"...
...I MEAN SHOOTING RIFLES AND ACTING LIKE ASSHOLES.
WE FLUSHED A COUPLE OF DUCKS.
THEY SWAM OFF IN FRONT OF US.
I TRACKED THEM...
...MY FINGER STARTING TO PUT PRESSURE ON THE TRIGGER.
AND THEN THE BACK OF MY BROTHER'S HEAD APPEARED IN MY GUN SIGHT.
I STILL HAVE NIGHTMARES ABOUT THAT. I CAN FEEL MY FINGER ON THE TRIGGER. FEEL THE JUMP OF THE RIFLE IN MY HANDS...THOUGH IT NEVER FIRED.
IT WAS LIKE FATE HAD GIVEN ME A LOOK THROUGH A WINDOW INTO WHAT MIGHT HAVE BEEN.
MY BROTHER BRUCE BARELY REMEMBERS THE INCIDENT. BUT EVERY TIME I THINK OF IT, I GET A COLD FEELING IN MY STOMACH.
I SWORE I'D NEVER PICK UP ANOTHER GUN.
I HADN'T UNTIL NOW.
GODDAMN IT.
EXIT
SHOOTING CLUB

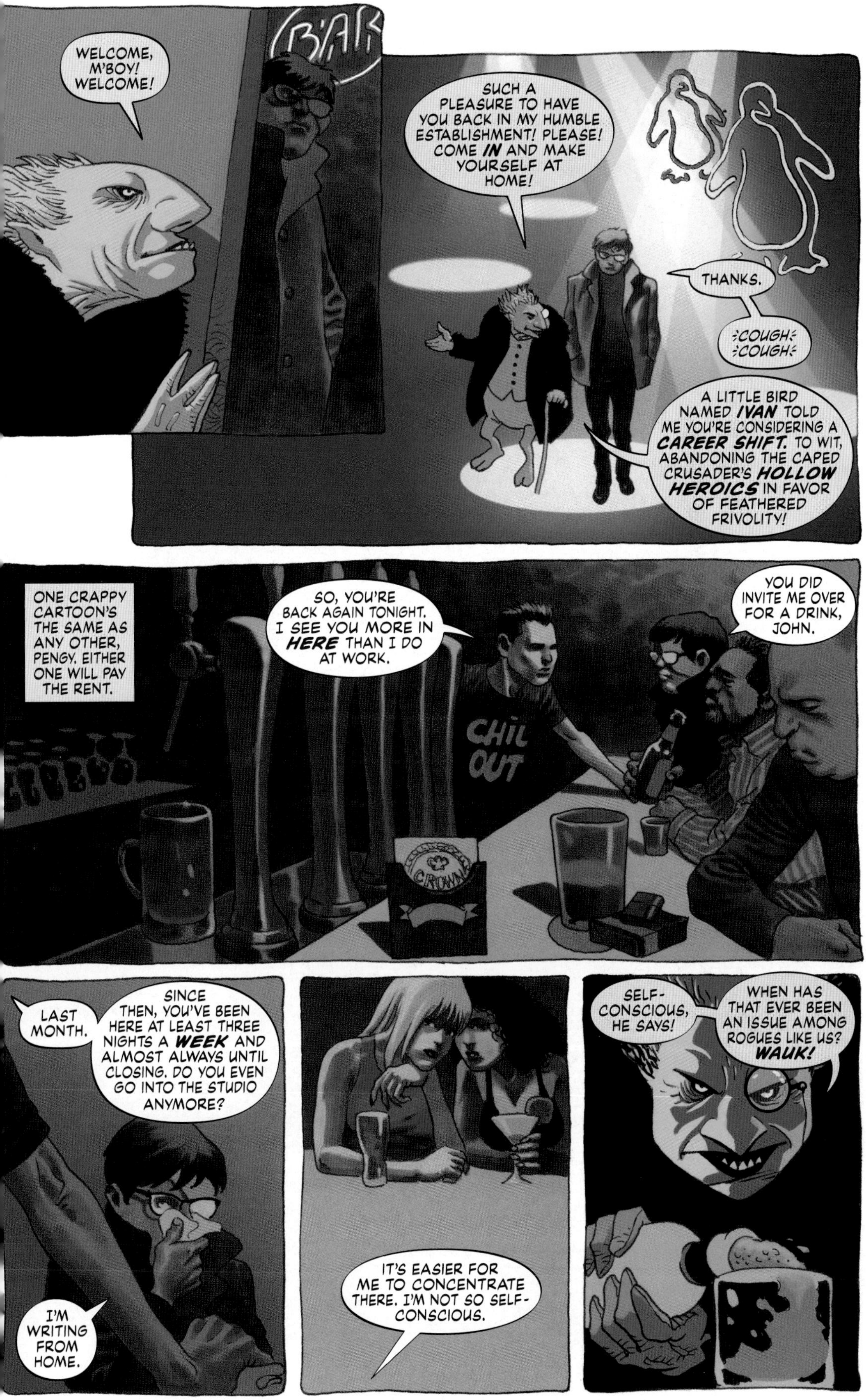
BAR
WELCOME, M'BOY! WELCOME!
SUCH A PLEASURE TO HAVE YOU BACK IN MY HUMBLE ESTABLISHMENT! PLEASE! COME IN AND MAKE YOURSELF AT HOME!
THANKS.
COUGH COUGH
A LITTLE BIRD NAMED IVAN TOLD ME YOU'RE CONSIDERING A CAREER SHIFT. TO WIT, ABANDONING THE CAPED CRUSADER'S HOLLOW HEROICS IN FAVOR OF FEATHERED FRIVOLITY!
ONE CRAPPY CARTOON'S THE SAME AS ANY OTHER, PENGY. EITHER ONE WILL PAY THE RENT.
SO, YOU'RE BACK AGAIN TONIGHT. I SEE YOU MORE IN HERE THAN I DO AT WORK.
YOU DID INVITE ME OVER FOR A DRINK, JOHN.
CHILL OUT
CROWN
LAST MONTH.
SINCE THEN, YOU'VE BEEN HERE AT LEAST THREE NIGHTS A WEEK AND ALMOST ALWAYS UNTIL CLOSING. DO YOU EVEN GO INTO THE STUDIO ANYMORE?
I'M WRITING FROM HOME.
IT'S EASIER FOR ME TO CONCENTRATE THERE. I'M NOT SO SELF-CONSCIOUS.
SELF-CONSCIOUS, HE SAYS!
WHEN HAS THAT EVER BEEN AN ISSUE AMONG ROGUES LIKE US? WAUK!

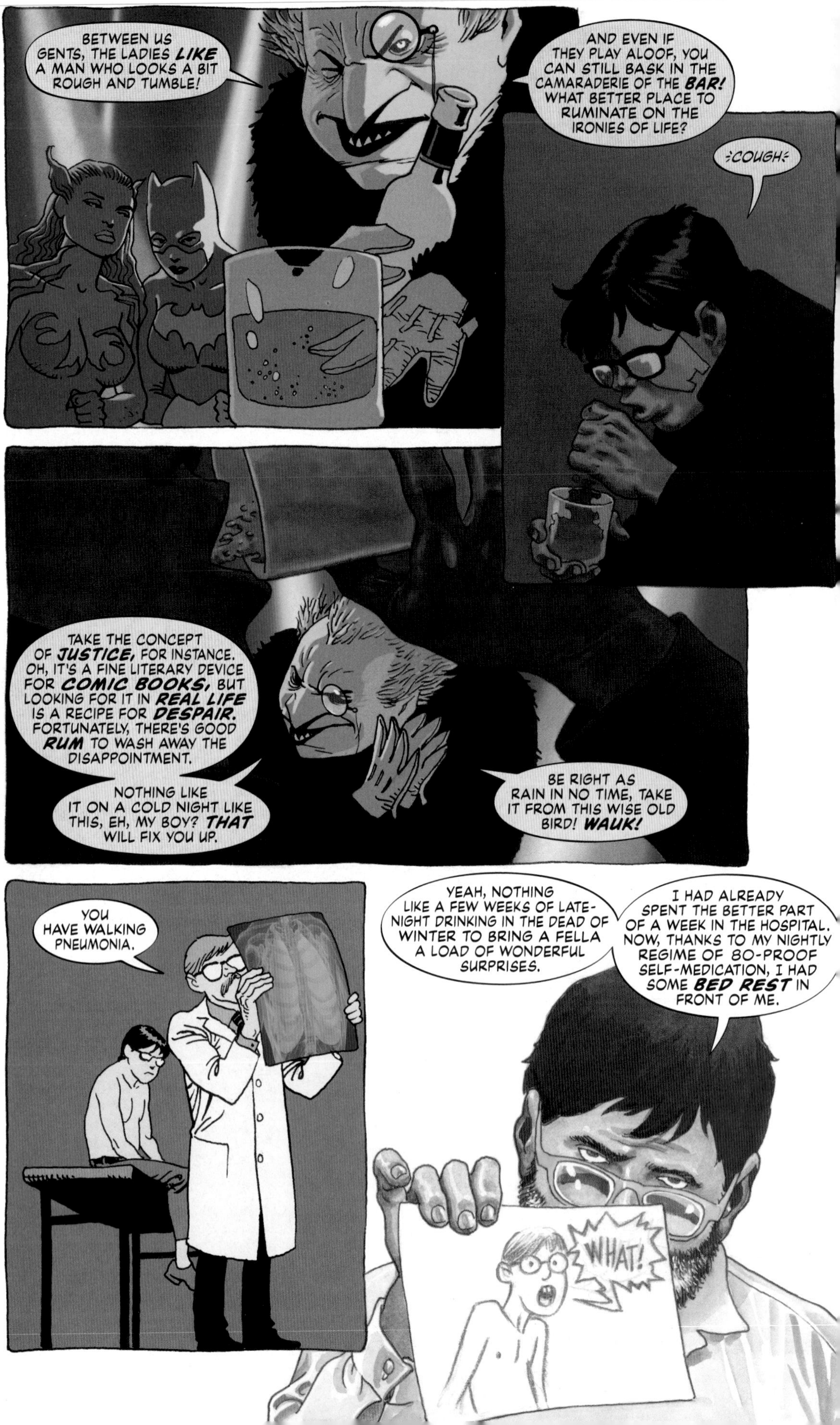
BETWEEN US GENTS, THE LADIES LIKE A MAN WHO LOOKS A BIT ROUGH AND TUMBLE!
AND EVEN IF THEY PLAY ALOOF, YOU CAN STILL BASK IN THE CAMARADERIE OF THE BAR! WHAT BETTER PLACE TO RUMINATE ON THE IRONIES OF LIFE?
COUGH
TAKE THE CONCEPT OF JUSTICE, FOR INSTANCE. OH, IT'S A FINE LITERARY DEVICE FOR COMIC BOOKS, BUT LOOKING FOR IT IN REAL LIFE IS A RECIPE FOR DESPAIR. FORTUNATELY, THERE'S GOOD RUM TO WASH AWAY THE DISAPPOINTMENT.
NOTHING LIKE IT ON A COLD NIGHT LIKE THIS, EH, MY BOY? THAT WILL FIX YOU UP.
BE RIGHT AS RAIN IN NO TIME, TAKE IT FROM THIS WISE OLD BIRD! WAUK!
YOU HAVE WALKING PNEUMONIA.
YEAH, NOTHING LIKE A FEW WEEKS OF LATE-NIGHT DRINKING IN THE DEAD OF WINTER TO BRING A FELLA A LOAD OF WONDERFUL SURPRISES.
I HAD ALREADY SPENT THE BETTER PART OF A WEEK IN THE HOSPITAL. NOW, THANKS TO MY NIGHTLY REGIME OF 80-PROOF SELF-MEDICATION, I HAD SOME BED REST IN FRONT OF ME.
WHAT!

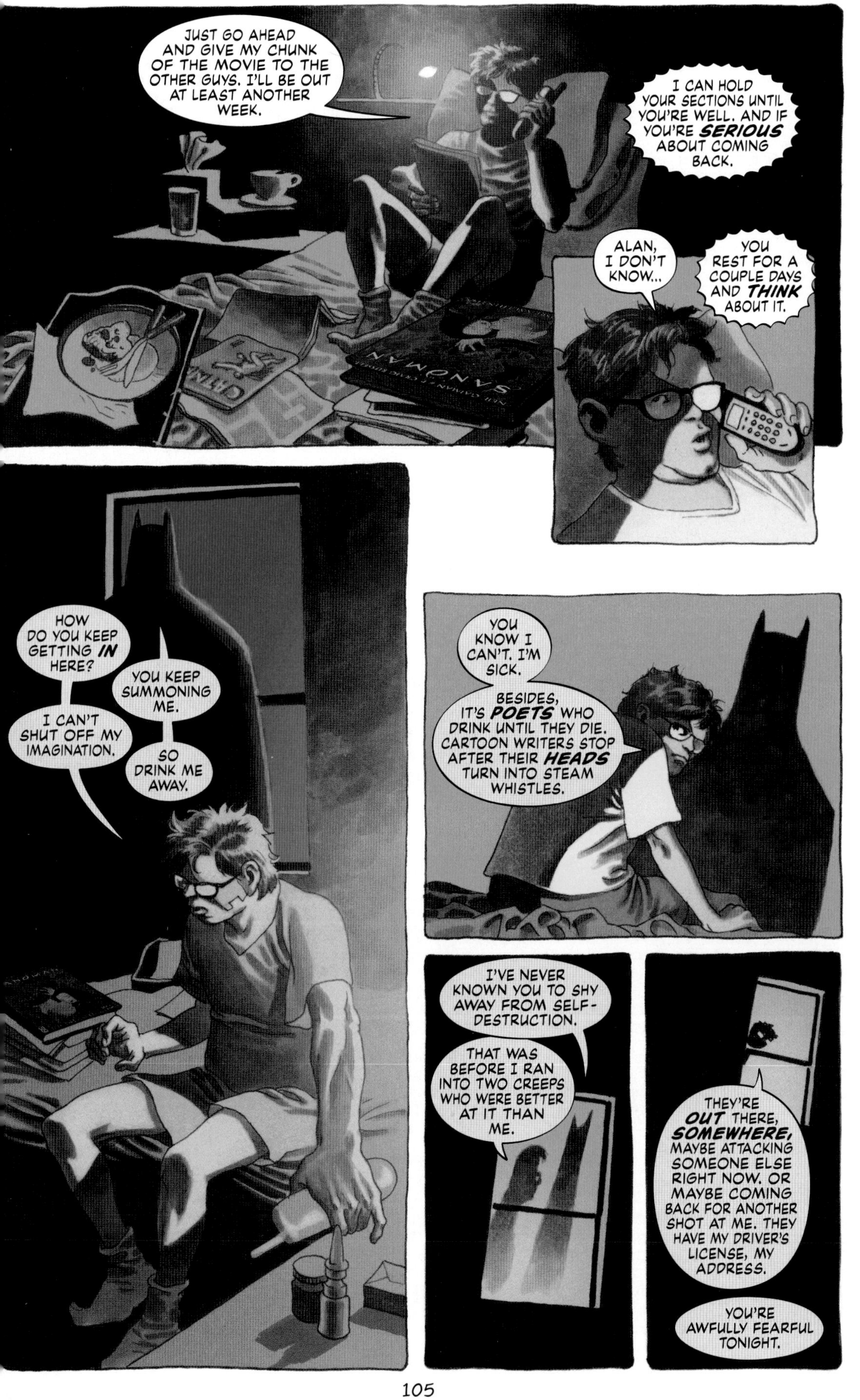
JUST GO AHEAD AND GIVE MY CHUNK OF THE MOVIE TO THE OTHER GUYS. I'LL BE OUT AT LEAST ANOTHER WEEK.
I CAN HOLD YOUR SECTIONS UNTIL YOU'RE WELL. AND IF YOU'RE SERIOUS ABOUT COMING BACK.
ALAN, I DON'T KNOW...
YOU REST FOR A COUPLE DAYS AND THINK ABOUT IT.
HOW DO YOU KEEP GETTING IN HERE?
YOU KEEP SUMMONING ME.
I CAN'T SHUT OFF MY IMAGINATION.
SO DRINK ME AWAY.
YOU KNOW I CAN'T. I'M SICK.
BESIDES, IT'S POETS WHO DRINK UNTIL THEY DIE. CARTOON WRITERS STOP AFTER THEIR HEADS TURN INTO STEAM WHISTLES.
I'VE NEVER KNOWN YOU TO SHY AWAY FROM SELF-DESTRUCTION.
THAT WAS BEFORE I RAN INTO TWO CREEPS WHO WERE BETTER AT IT THAN ME.
THEY'RE OUT THERE, SOMEWHERE, MAYBE ATTACKING SOMEONE ELSE RIGHT NOW. OR MAYBE COMING BACK FOR ANOTHER SHOT AT ME. THEY HAVE MY DRIVER'S LICENSE, MY ADDRESS.
YOU'RE AWFULLY FEARFUL TONIGHT.

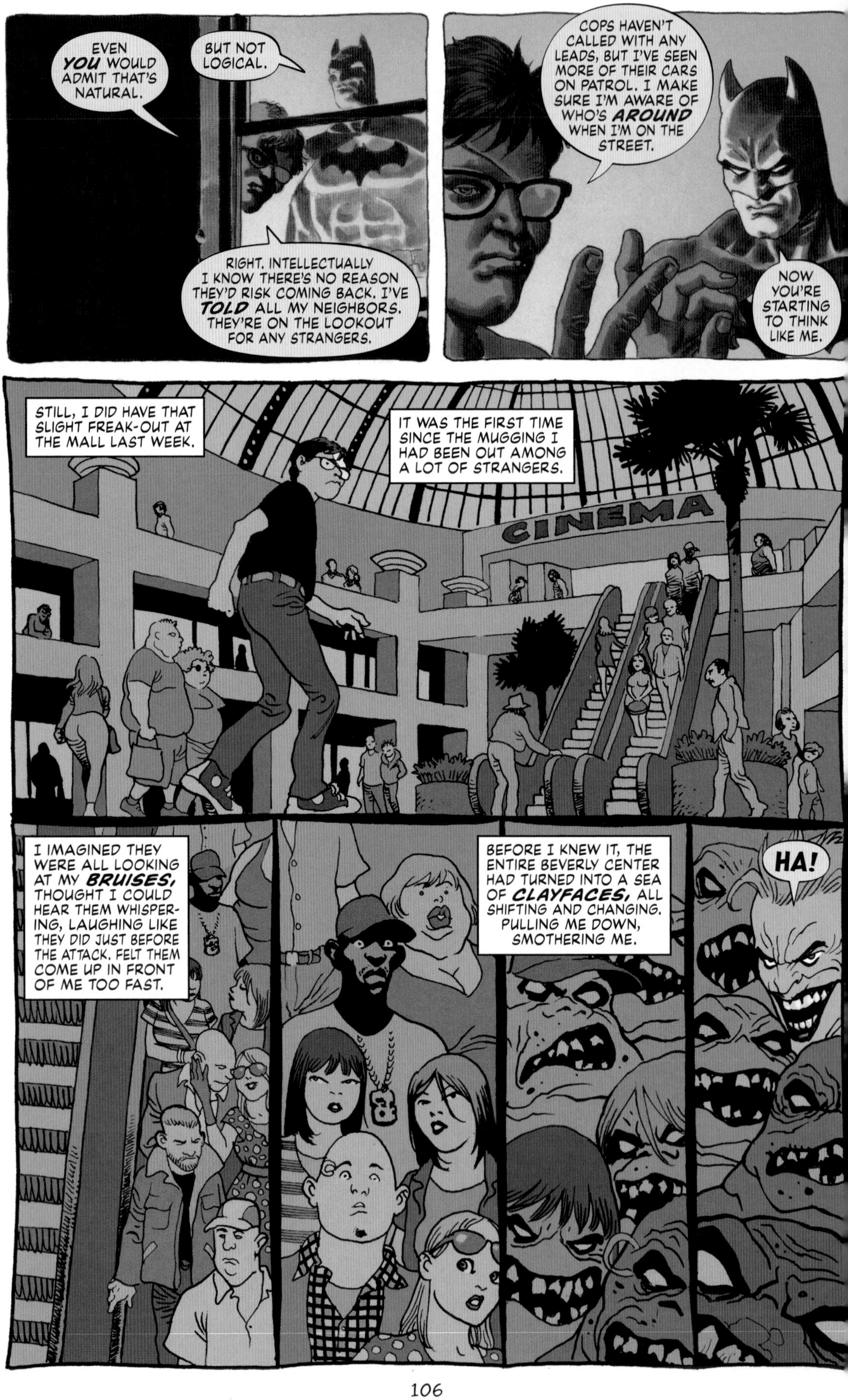
EVEN YOU WOULD ADMIT THAT'S NATURAL.
BUT NOT LOGICAL.
RIGHT. INTELLECTUALLY I KNOW THERE'S NO REASON THEY'D RISK COMING BACK. I'VE TOLD ALL MY NEIGHBORS. THEY'RE ON THE LOOKOUT FOR ANY STRANGERS.
COPS HAVEN'T CALLED WITH ANY LEADS, BUT I'VE SEEN MORE OF THEIR CARS ON PATROL. I MAKE SURE I'M AWARE OF WHO'S AROUND WHEN I'M ON THE STREET.
NOW YOU'RE STARTING TO THINK LIKE ME.
STILL, I DID HAVE THAT SLIGHT FREAK-OUT AT THE MALL LAST WEEK.
IT WAS THE FIRST TIME SINCE THE MUGGING I HAD BEEN OUT AMONG A LOT OF STRANGERS.
CINEMA
I IMAGINED THEY WERE ALL LOOKING AT MY BRUISES, THOUGHT I COULD HEAR THEM WHISPERING, LAUGHING LIKE THEY DID JUST BEFORE THE ATTACK. FELT THEM COME UP IN FRONT OF ME TOO FAST.
BEFORE I KNEW IT, THE ENTIRE BEVERLY CENTER HAD TURNED INTO A SEA OF CLAYFACES, ALL SHIFTING AND CHANGING. PULLING ME DOWN, SMOTHERING ME.
HA!

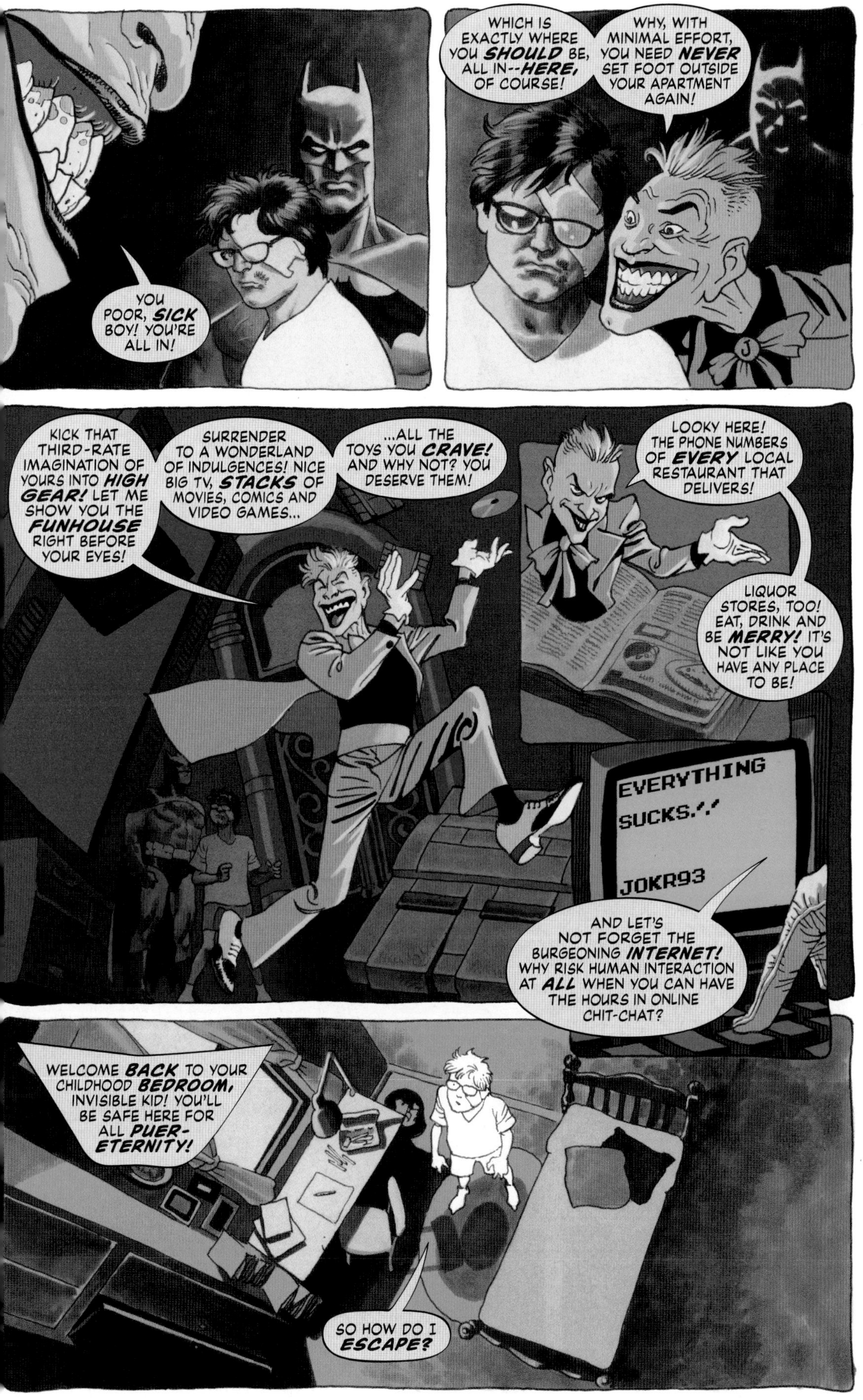
YOU POOR, SICK BOY! YOU'RE ALL IN!
WHICH IS EXACTLY WHERE YOU SHOULD BE, ALL IN--HERE, OF COURSE!
WHY, WITH MINIMAL EFFORT, YOU NEED NEVER SET FOOT OUTSIDE YOUR APARTMENT AGAIN!
KICK THAT THIRD-RATE IMAGINATION OF YOURS INTO HIGH GEAR! LET ME SHOW YOU THE FUNHOUSE RIGHT BEFORE YOUR EYES!
SURRENDER TO A WONDERLAND OF INDULGENCES! NICE BIG TV, STACKS OF MOVIES, COMICS AND VIDEO GAMES...
...ALL THE TOYS YOU CRAVE! AND WHY NOT? YOU DESERVE THEM!
LOOKY HERE! THE PHONE NUMBERS OF EVERY LOCAL RESTAURANT THAT DELIVERS!
LIQUOR STORES, TOO! EAT, DRINK AND BE MERRY! IT'S NOT LIKE YOU HAVE ANY PLACE TO BE!
EVERYTHING SUCKS.'.'
JOKR93
AND LET'S NOT FORGET THE BURGEONING INTERNET! WHY RISK HUMAN INTERACTION AT ALL WHEN YOU CAN HAVE THE HOURS IN ONLINE CHIT-CHAT?
WELCOME BACK TO YOUR CHILDHOOD BEDROOM, INVISIBLE KID! YOU'LL BE SAFE HERE FOR ALL PUER-ETERNITY!
SO HOW DO I ESCAPE?

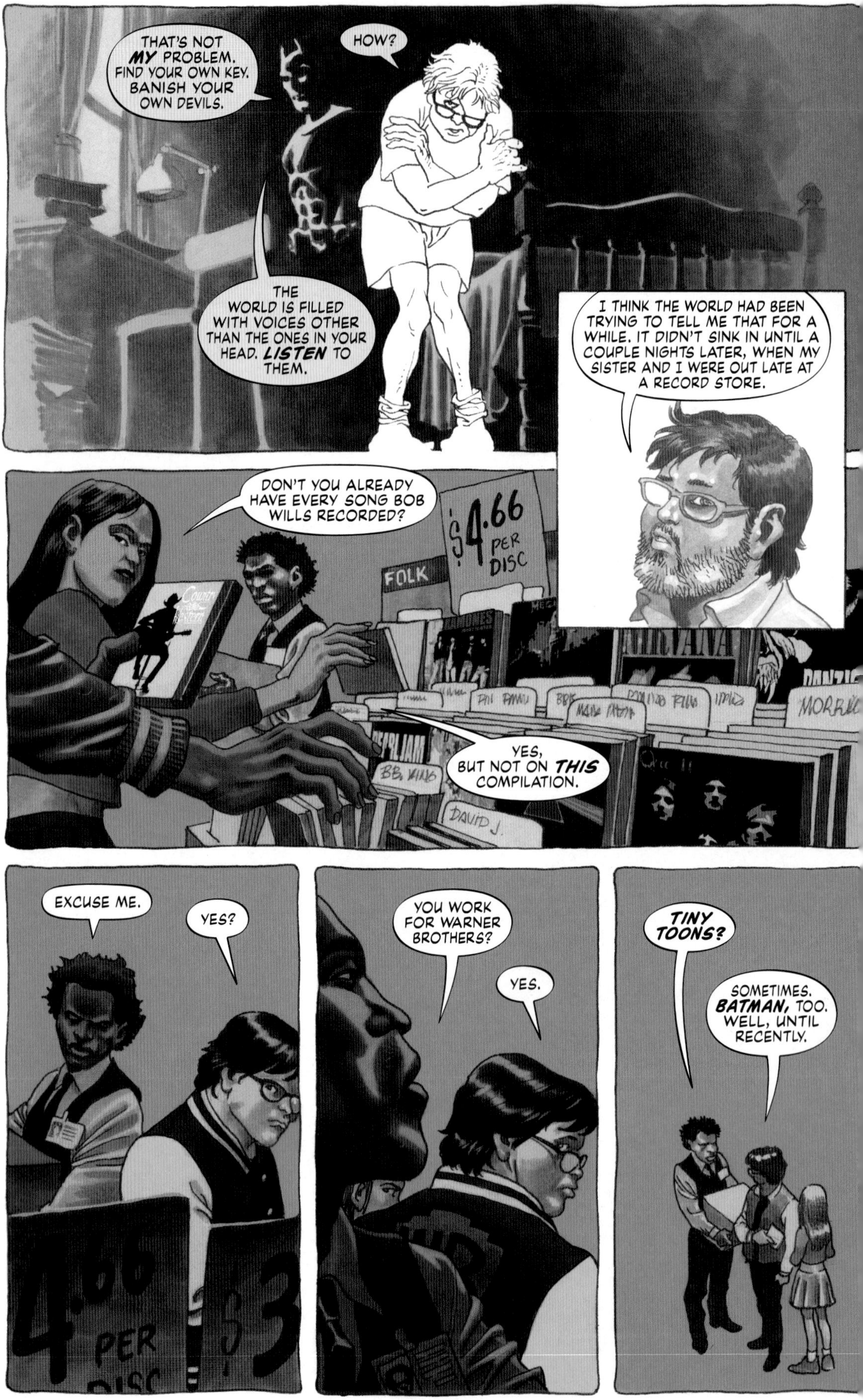
THAT'S NOT *MY* PROBLEM. FIND YOUR OWN KEY. BANISH YOUR OWN DEVILS.
HOW?
THE WORLD IS FILLED WITH VOICES OTHER THAN THE ONES IN YOUR HEAD. *LISTEN* TO THEM.
I THINK THE WORLD HAD BEEN TRYING TO TELL ME THAT FOR A WHILE. IT DIDN'T SINK IN UNTIL A COUPLE NIGHTS LATER, WHEN MY SISTER AND I WERE OUT LATE AT A RECORD STORE.
DON'T YOU ALREADY HAVE EVERY SONG BOB WILLS RECORDED?
$4.66 PER DISC
FOLK
RAMONES
NIRVANA
DANZIG
PEARL JAM
B.B. KING
DAVID J.
YES, BUT NOT ON *THIS* COMPILATION.
EXCUSE ME.
YES?
YOU WORK FOR WARNER BROTHERS?
YES.
TINY TOONS?
SOMETIMES. *BATMAN,* TOO. WELL, UNTIL RECENTLY.

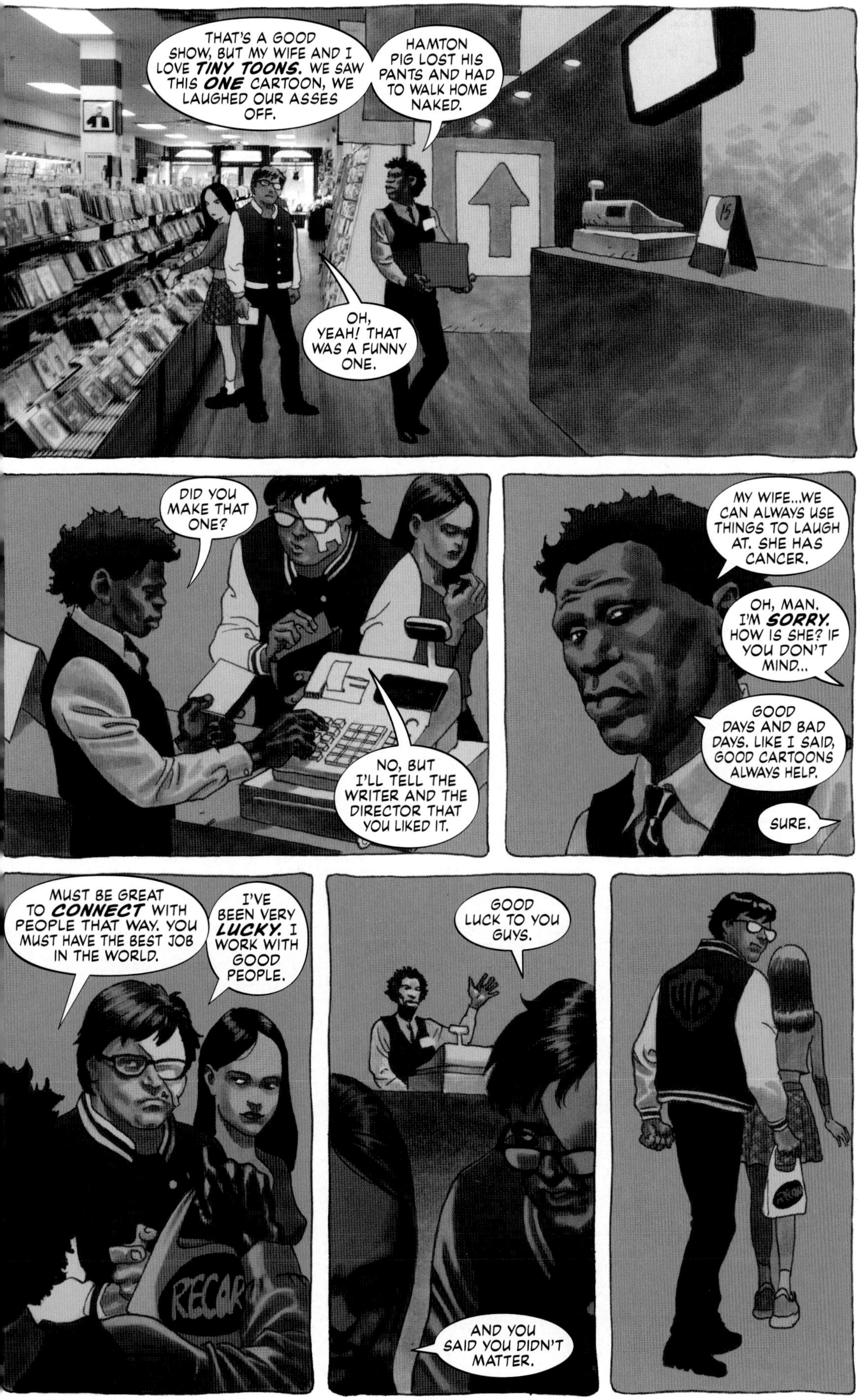
THAT'S A GOOD SHOW, BUT MY WIFE AND I LOVE TINY TOONS. WE SAW THIS ONE CARTOON, WE LAUGHED OUR ASSES OFF.
HAMTON PIG LOST HIS PANTS AND HAD TO WALK HOME NAKED.
OH, YEAH! THAT WAS A FUNNY ONE.
DID YOU MAKE THAT ONE?
NO, BUT I'LL TELL THE WRITER AND THE DIRECTOR THAT YOU LIKED IT.
MY WIFE...WE CAN ALWAYS USE THINGS TO LAUGH AT. SHE HAS CANCER.
OH, MAN. I'M SORRY. HOW IS SHE? IF YOU DON'T MIND...
GOOD DAYS AND BAD DAYS. LIKE I SAID, GOOD CARTOONS ALWAYS HELP.
SURE.
MUST BE GREAT TO CONNECT WITH PEOPLE THAT WAY. YOU MUST HAVE THE BEST JOB IN THE WORLD.
I'VE BEEN VERY LUCKY. I WORK WITH GOOD PEOPLE.
GOOD LUCK TO YOU GUYS.
AND YOU SAID YOU DIDN'T MATTER.

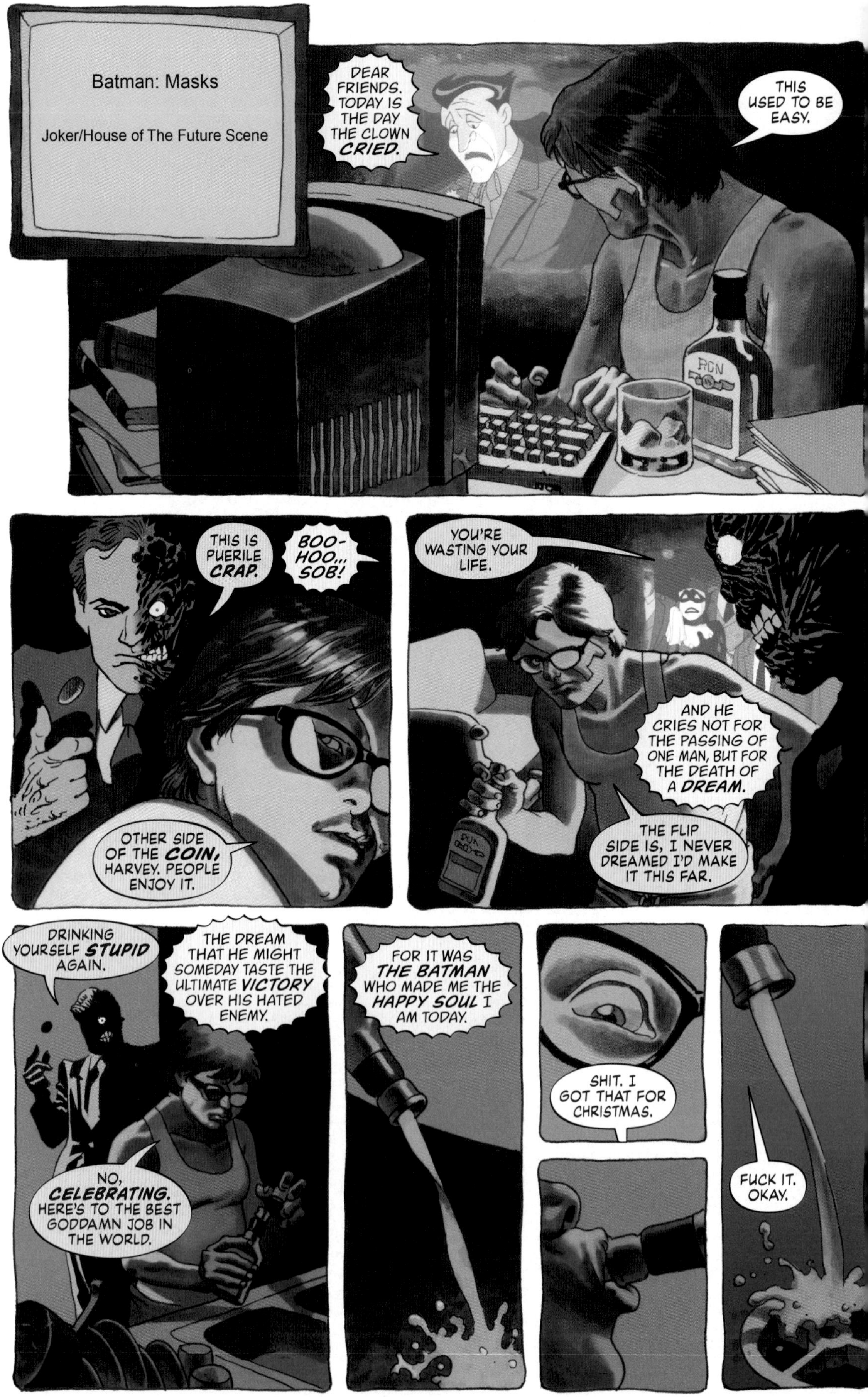
Batman: Masks
Joker/House of The Future Scene
DEAR FRIENDS. TODAY IS THE DAY THE CLOWN CRIED.
THIS USED TO BE EASY.
THIS IS PUERILE CRAP.
BOO-HOO... SOB!
OTHER SIDE OF THE COIN, HARVEY. PEOPLE ENJOY IT.
YOU'RE WASTING YOUR LIFE.
AND HE CRIES NOT FOR THE PASSING OF ONE MAN, BUT FOR THE DEATH OF A DREAM.
THE FLIP SIDE IS, I NEVER DREAMED I'D MAKE IT THIS FAR.
DRINKING YOURSELF STUPID AGAIN.
THE DREAM THAT HE MIGHT SOMEDAY TASTE THE ULTIMATE VICTORY OVER HIS HATED ENEMY.
NO, CELEBRATING. HERE'S TO THE BEST GODDAMN JOB IN THE WORLD.
FOR IT WAS THE BATMAN WHO MADE ME THE HAPPY SOUL I AM TODAY.
SHIT. I GOT THAT FOR CHRISTMAS.
FUCK IT. OKAY.

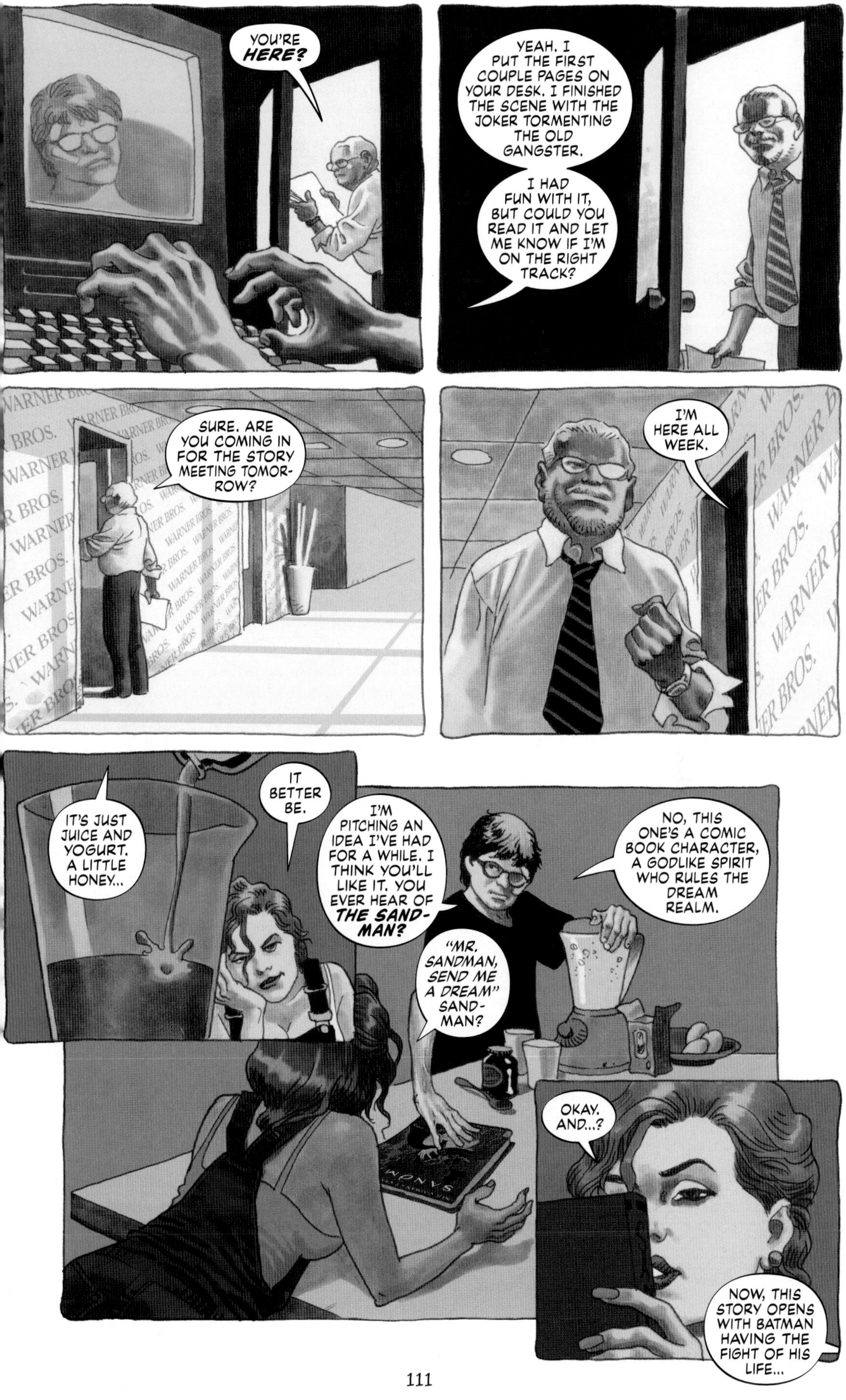

YOU'RE *HERE?*
YEAH. I PUT THE FIRST COUPLE PAGES ON YOUR DESK. I FINISHED THE SCENE WITH THE JOKER TORMENTING THE OLD GANGSTER.
I HAD FUN WITH IT, BUT COULD YOU READ IT AND LET ME KNOW IF I'M ON THE RIGHT TRACK?
SURE. ARE YOU COMING IN FOR THE STORY MEETING TOMORROW?
I'M HERE ALL WEEK.
IT'S JUST JUICE AND YOGURT. A LITTLE HONEY...
IT BETTER BE.
I'M PITCHING AN IDEA I'VE HAD FOR A WHILE. I THINK YOU'LL LIKE IT. YOU EVER HEAR OF *THE SANDMAN?*
"MR. SANDMAN, SEND ME A DREAM" SANDMAN?
NO, THIS ONE'S A COMIC BOOK CHARACTER, A GODLIKE SPIRIT WHO RULES THE DREAM REALM.
OKAY. AND...?
NOW, THIS STORY OPENS WITH BATMAN HAVING THE FIGHT OF HIS LIFE...

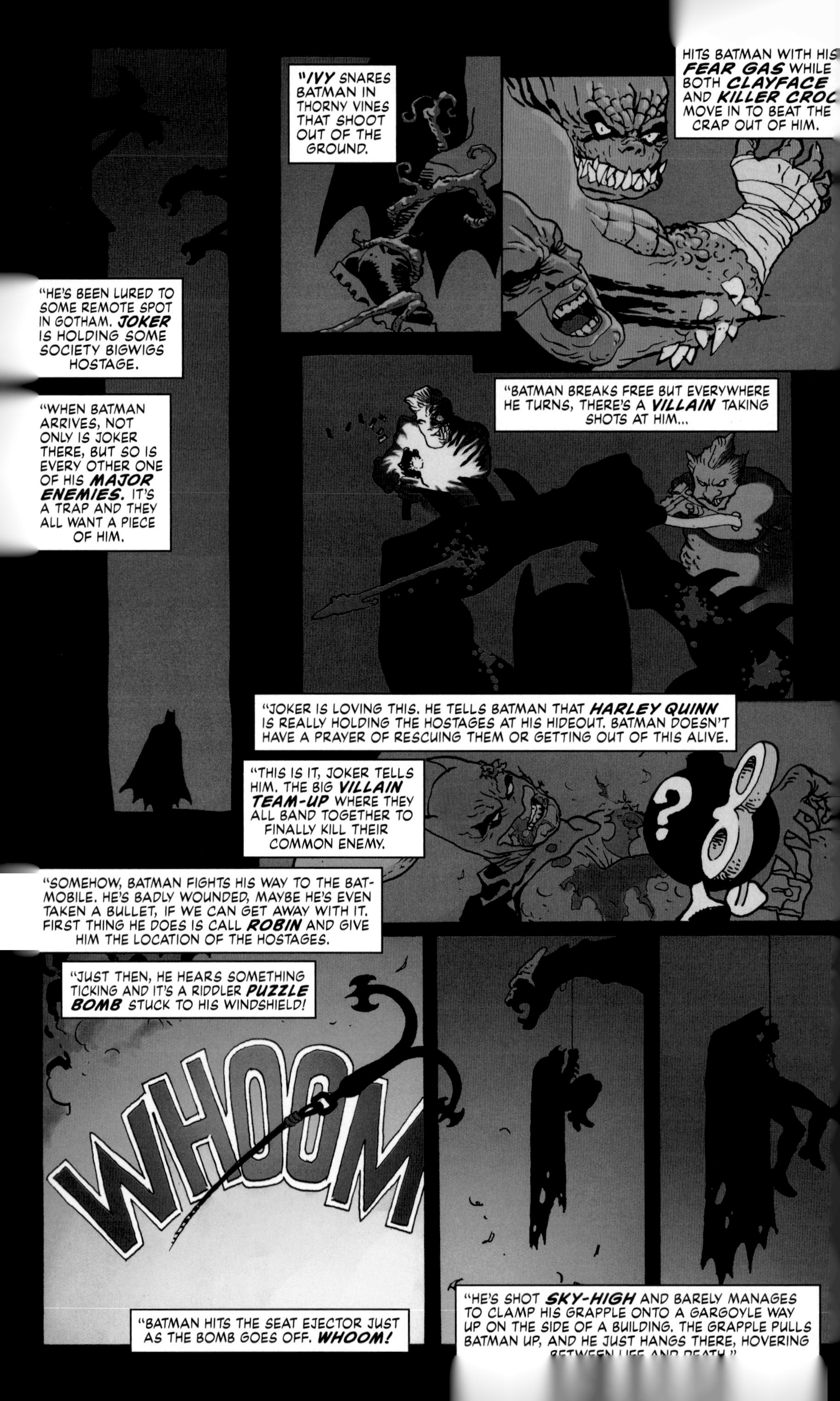
"HE'S BEEN LURED TO SOME REMOTE SPOT IN GOTHAM. JOKER IS HOLDING SOME SOCIETY BIGWIGS HOSTAGE.
"WHEN BATMAN ARRIVES, NOT ONLY IS JOKER THERE, BUT SO IS EVERY OTHER ONE OF HIS MAJOR ENEMIES. IT'S A TRAP AND THEY ALL WANT A PIECE OF HIM.
"IVY SNARES BATMAN IN THORNY VINES THAT SHOOT OUT OF THE GROUND.
HITS BATMAN WITH HIS FEAR GAS WHILE BOTH CLAYFACE AND KILLER CROC MOVE IN TO BEAT THE CRAP OUT OF HIM.
"BATMAN BREAKS FREE BUT EVERYWHERE HE TURNS, THERE'S A VILLAIN TAKING SHOTS AT HIM...
"JOKER IS LOVING THIS. HE TELLS BATMAN THAT HARLEY QUINN IS REALLY HOLDING THE HOSTAGES AT HIS HIDEOUT. BATMAN DOESN'T HAVE A PRAYER OF RESCUING THEM OR GETTING OUT OF THIS ALIVE.
"THIS IS IT, JOKER TELLS HIM. THE BIG VILLAIN TEAM-UP WHERE THEY ALL BAND TOGETHER TO FINALLY KILL THEIR COMMON ENEMY.
"SOMEHOW, BATMAN FIGHTS HIS WAY TO THE BAT-MOBILE. HE'S BADLY WOUNDED, MAYBE HE'S EVEN TAKEN A BULLET, IF WE CAN GET AWAY WITH IT. FIRST THING HE DOES IS CALL ROBIN AND GIVE HIM THE LOCATION OF THE HOSTAGES.
"JUST THEN, HE HEARS SOMETHING TICKING AND IT'S A RIDDLER PUZZLE BOMB STUCK TO HIS WINDSHIELD!
WHOOM
"BATMAN HITS THE SEAT EJECTOR JUST AS THE BOMB GOES OFF. WHOOM!
"HE'S SHOT SKY-HIGH AND BARELY MANAGES TO CLAMP HIS GRAPPLE ONTO A GARGOYLE WAY UP ON THE SIDE OF A BUILDING. THE GRAPPLE PULLS BATMAN UP, AND HE JUST HANGS THERE, HOVERING

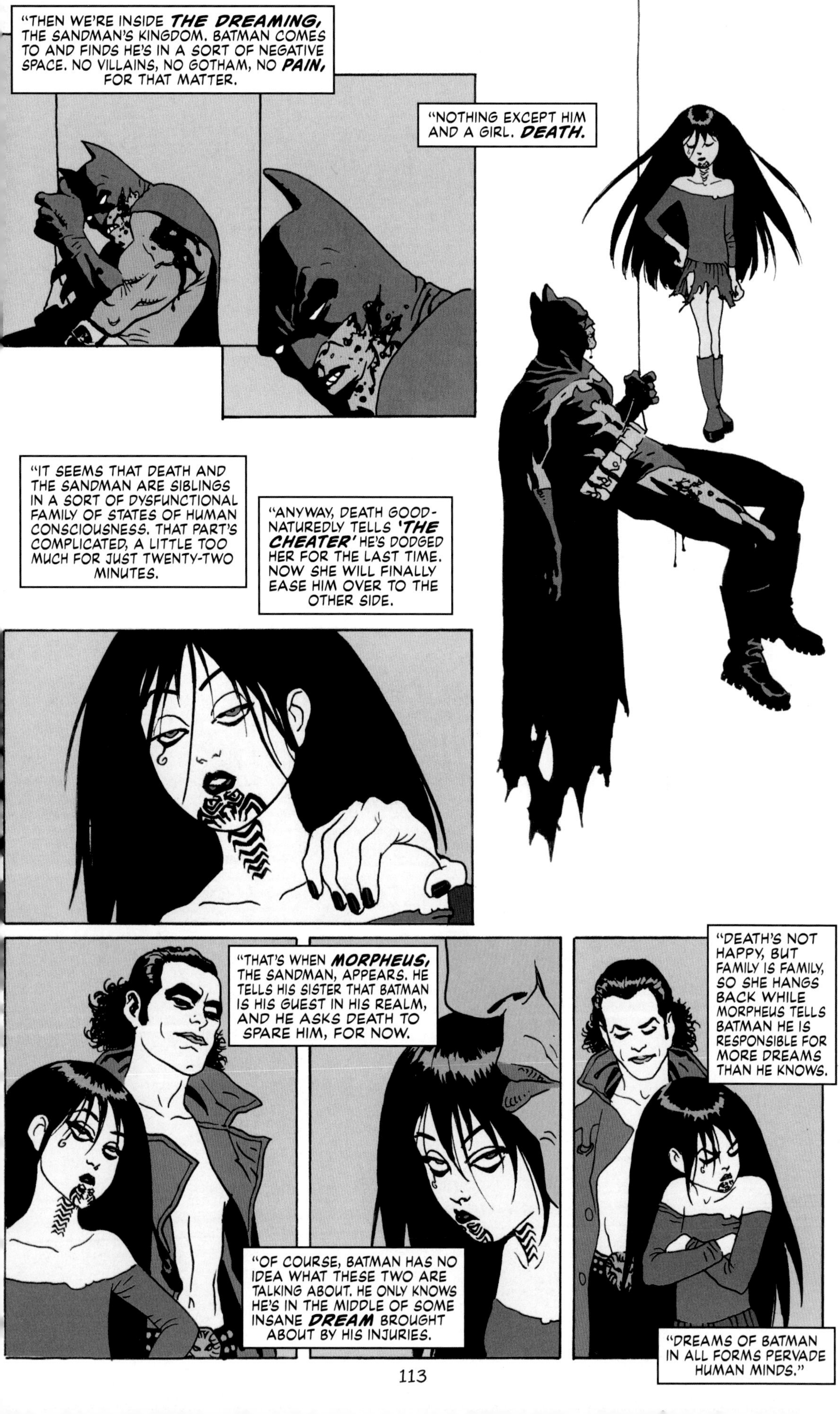
"THEN WE'RE INSIDE THE DREAMING, THE SANDMAN'S KINGDOM. BATMAN COMES TO AND FINDS HE'S IN A SORT OF NEGATIVE SPACE. NO VILLAINS, NO GOTHAM, NO PAIN, FOR THAT MATTER.
"NOTHING EXCEPT HIM AND A GIRL. DEATH.
"IT SEEMS THAT DEATH AND THE SANDMAN ARE SIBLINGS IN A SORT OF DYSFUNCTIONAL FAMILY OF STATES OF HUMAN CONSCIOUSNESS. THAT PART'S COMPLICATED, A LITTLE TOO MUCH FOR JUST TWENTY-TWO MINUTES.
"ANYWAY, DEATH GOOD-NATUREDLY TELLS 'THE CHEATER' HE'S DODGED HER FOR THE LAST TIME. NOW SHE WILL FINALLY EASE HIM OVER TO THE OTHER SIDE.
"THAT'S WHEN MORPHEUS, THE SANDMAN, APPEARS. HE TELLS HIS SISTER THAT BATMAN IS HIS GUEST IN HIS REALM, AND HE ASKS DEATH TO SPARE HIM, FOR NOW.
"OF COURSE, BATMAN HAS NO IDEA WHAT THESE TWO ARE TALKING ABOUT. HE ONLY KNOWS HE'S IN THE MIDDLE OF SOME INSANE DREAM BROUGHT ABOUT BY HIS INJURIES.
"DEATH'S NOT HAPPY, BUT FAMILY IS FAMILY, SO SHE HANGS BACK WHILE MORPHEUS TELLS BATMAN HE IS RESPONSIBLE FOR MORE DREAMS THAN HE KNOWS.
"DREAMS OF BATMAN IN ALL FORMS PERVADE HUMAN MINDS."

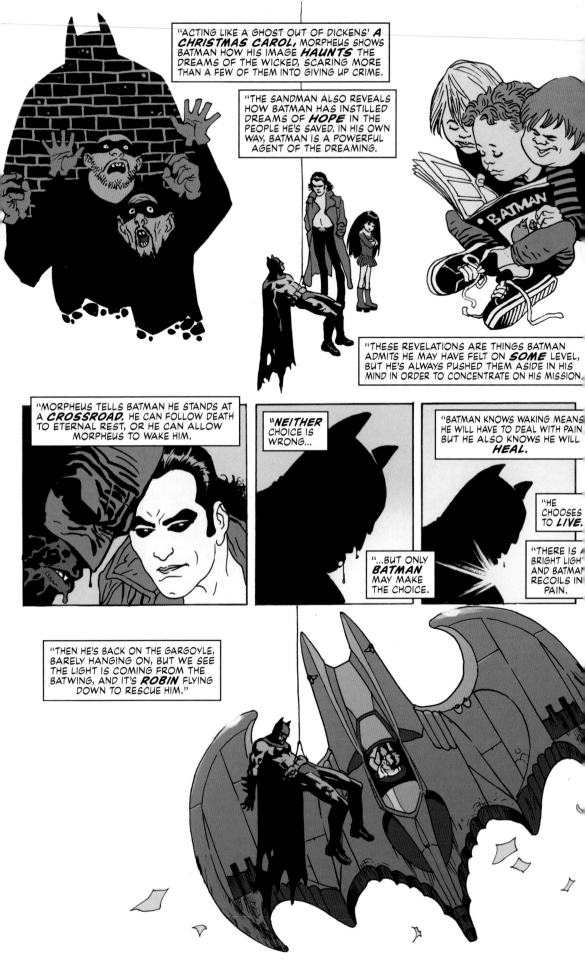

"ACTING LIKE A GHOST OUT OF DICKENS' *A CHRISTMAS CAROL,* MORPHEUS SHOWS BATMAN HOW HIS IMAGE *HAUNTS* THE DREAMS OF THE WICKED, SCARING MORE THAN A FEW OF THEM INTO GIVING UP CRIME.

"THE SANDMAN ALSO REVEALS HOW BATMAN HAS INSTILLED DREAMS OF *HOPE* IN THE PEOPLE HE'S SAVED. IN HIS OWN WAY, BATMAN IS A POWERFUL AGENT OF THE DREAMING.

"THESE REVELATIONS ARE THINGS BATMAN ADMITS HE MAY HAVE FELT ON *SOME* LEVEL, BUT HE'S ALWAYS PUSHED THEM ASIDE IN HIS MIND IN ORDER TO CONCENTRATE ON HIS MISSION.

"MORPHEUS TELLS BATMAN HE STANDS AT A *CROSSROAD.* HE CAN FOLLOW DEATH TO ETERNAL REST, OR HE CAN ALLOW MORPHEUS TO WAKE HIM.

"*NEITHER* CHOICE IS WRONG...

"...BUT ONLY *BATMAN* MAY MAKE THE CHOICE.

"BATMAN KNOWS WAKING MEANS HE WILL HAVE TO DEAL WITH PAIN, BUT HE ALSO KNOWS HE WILL *HEAL.*

"HE CHOOSES TO *LIVE.*

"THERE IS A BRIGHT LIGHT, AND BATMAN RECOILS IN PAIN.

"THEN HE'S BACK ON THE GARGOYLE, BARELY HANGING ON, BUT WE SEE THE LIGHT IS COMING FROM THE BATWING, AND IT'S *ROBIN* FLYING DOWN TO RESCUE HIM."

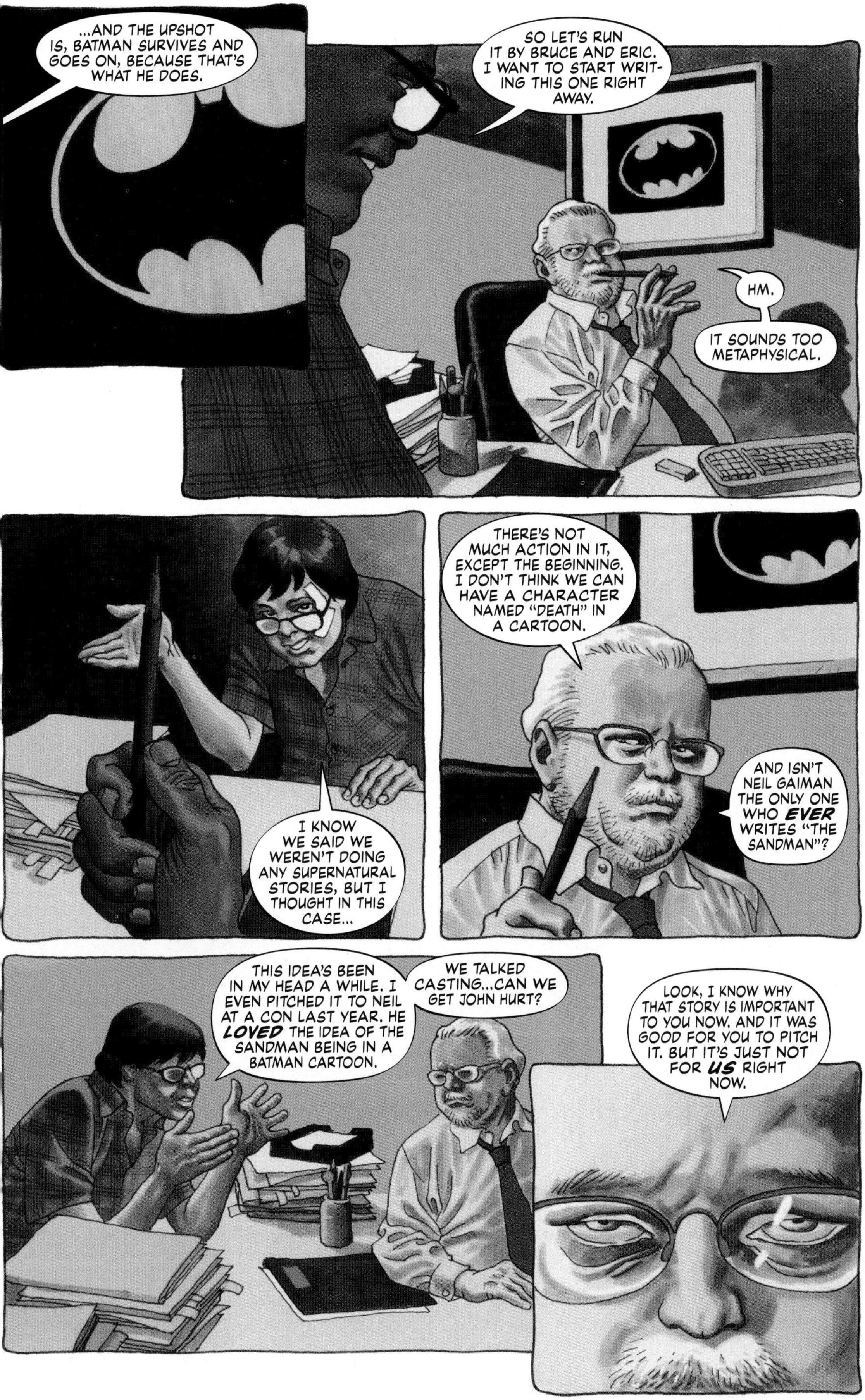
...AND THE UPSHOT IS, BATMAN SURVIVES AND GOES ON, BECAUSE THAT'S WHAT HE DOES.
SO LET'S RUN IT BY BRUCE AND ERIC. I WANT TO START WRITING THIS ONE RIGHT AWAY.
HM.
IT SOUNDS TOO METAPHYSICAL.
I KNOW WE SAID WE WEREN'T DOING ANY SUPERNATURAL STORIES, BUT I THOUGHT IN THIS CASE...
THERE'S NOT MUCH ACTION IN IT, EXCEPT THE BEGINNING. I DON'T THINK WE CAN HAVE A CHARACTER NAMED "DEATH" IN A CARTOON.
AND ISN'T NEIL GAIMAN THE ONLY ONE WHO **EVER** WRITES "THE SANDMAN"?
THIS IDEA'S BEEN IN MY HEAD A WHILE. I EVEN PITCHED IT TO NEIL AT A CON LAST YEAR. HE **LOVED** THE IDEA OF THE SANDMAN BEING IN A BATMAN CARTOON.
WE TALKED CASTING...CAN WE GET JOHN HURT?
LOOK, I KNOW WHY THAT STORY IS IMPORTANT TO YOU NOW. AND IT WAS GOOD FOR YOU TO PITCH IT. BUT IT'S JUST NOT FOR **US** RIGHT NOW.

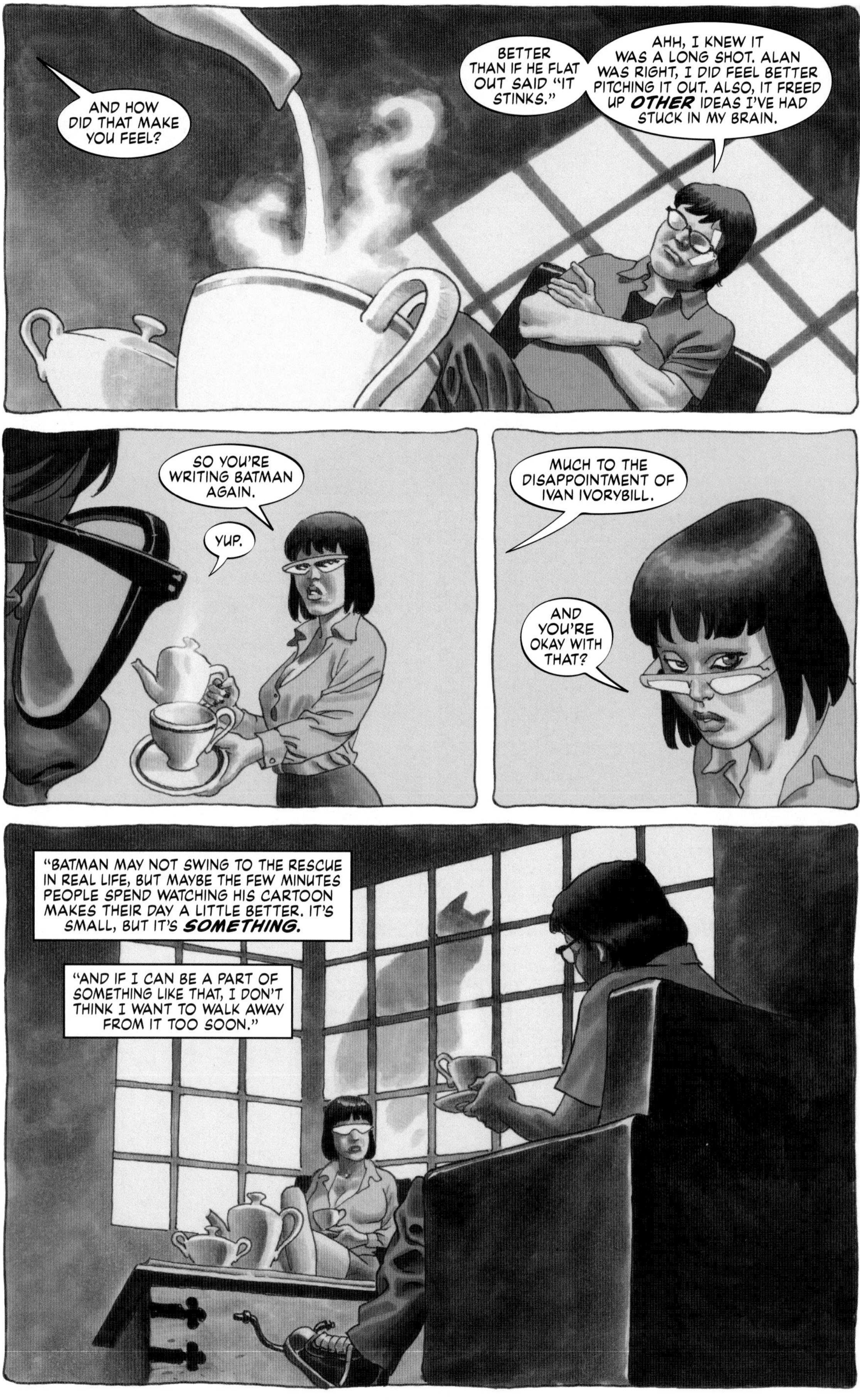
AND HOW DID THAT MAKE YOU FEEL?
BETTER THAN IF HE FLAT OUT SAID "IT STINKS."
AHH, I KNEW IT WAS A LONG SHOT. ALAN WAS RIGHT, I DID FEEL BETTER PITCHING IT OUT. ALSO, IT FREED UP **OTHER** IDEAS I'VE HAD STUCK IN MY BRAIN.
SO YOU'RE WRITING BATMAN AGAIN.
YUP.
MUCH TO THE DISAPPOINTMENT OF IVAN IVORYBILL.
AND YOU'RE OKAY WITH THAT?
"BATMAN MAY NOT SWING TO THE RESCUE IN REAL LIFE, BUT MAYBE THE FEW MINUTES PEOPLE SPEND WATCHING HIS CARTOON MAKES THEIR DAY A LITTLE BETTER. IT'S SMALL, BUT IT'S **SOMETHING.**
"AND IF I CAN BE A PART OF SOMETHING LIKE THAT, I DON'T THINK I WANT TO WALK AWAY FROM IT TOO SOON."

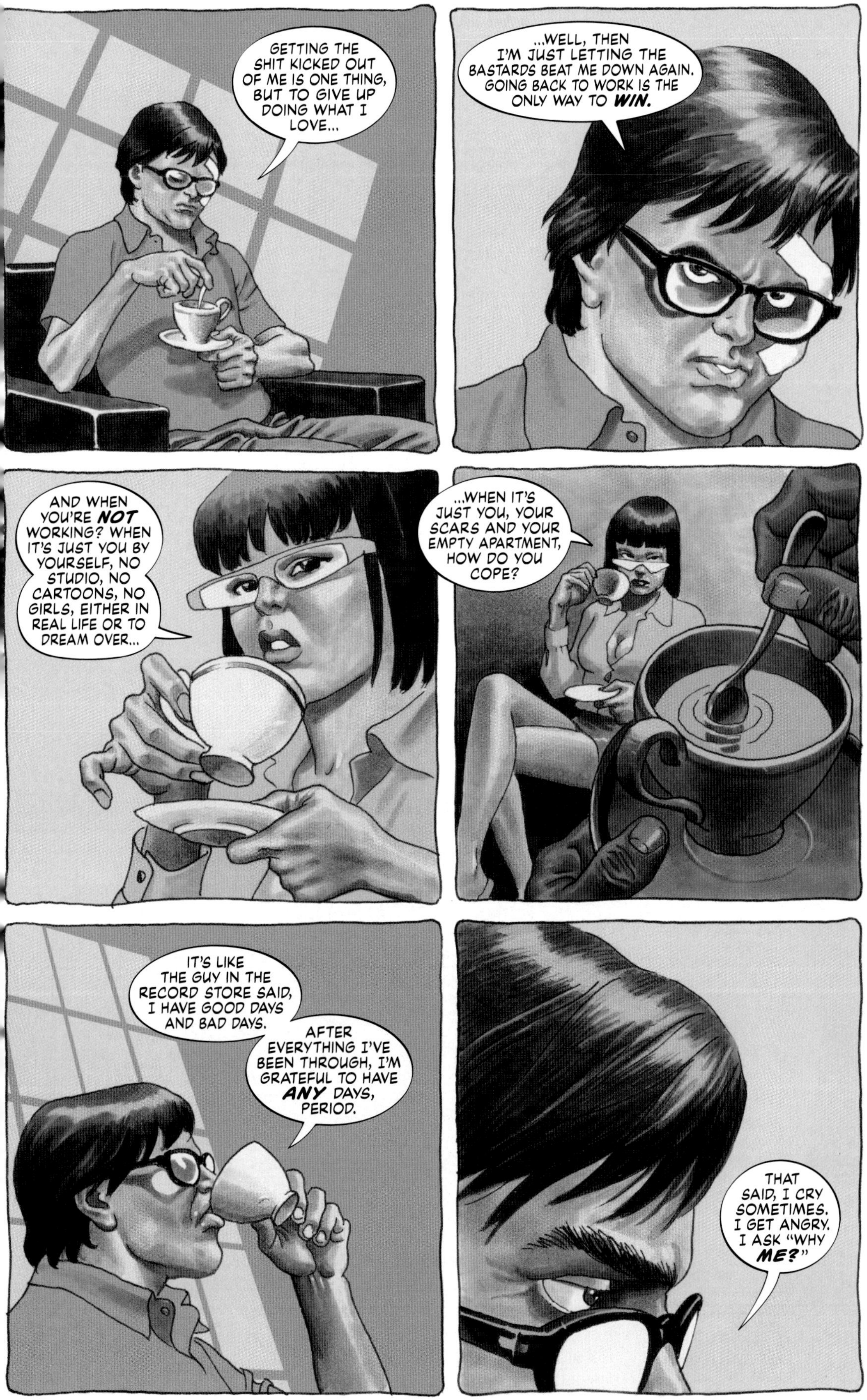
GETTING THE SHIT KICKED OUT OF ME IS ONE THING, BUT TO GIVE UP DOING WHAT I LOVE...
...WELL, THEN I'M JUST LETTING THE BASTARDS BEAT ME DOWN AGAIN. GOING BACK TO WORK IS THE ONLY WAY TO **WIN.**
AND WHEN YOU'RE **NOT** WORKING? WHEN IT'S JUST YOU BY YOURSELF, NO STUDIO, NO CARTOONS, NO GIRLS, EITHER IN REAL LIFE OR TO DREAM OVER...
...WHEN IT'S JUST YOU, YOUR SCARS AND YOUR EMPTY APARTMENT, HOW DO YOU COPE?
IT'S LIKE THE GUY IN THE RECORD STORE SAID, I HAVE GOOD DAYS AND BAD DAYS.
AFTER EVERYTHING I'VE BEEN THROUGH, I'M GRATEFUL TO HAVE **ANY** DAYS, PERIOD.
THAT SAID, I CRY SOMETIMES. I GET ANGRY. I ASK "WHY **ME?**"

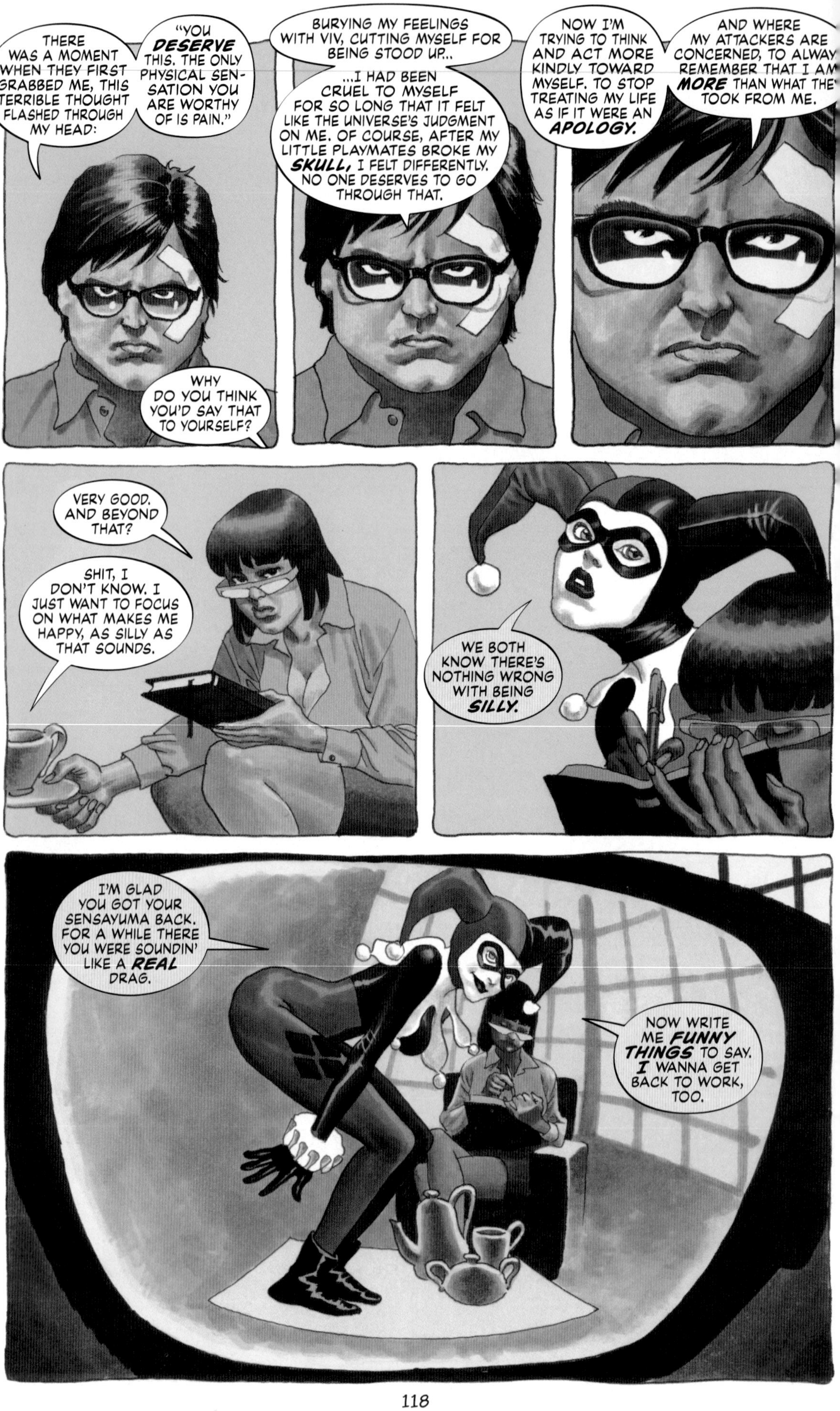

THERE WAS A MOMENT WHEN THEY FIRST GRABBED ME, THIS TERRIBLE THOUGHT FLASHED THROUGH MY HEAD:
"YOU *DESERVE* THIS. THE ONLY PHYSICAL SENSATION YOU ARE WORTHY OF IS PAIN."
WHY DO YOU THINK YOU'D SAY THAT TO YOURSELF?
BURYING MY FEELINGS WITH VIV, CUTTING MYSELF FOR BEING STOOD UP...
...I HAD BEEN CRUEL TO MYSELF FOR SO LONG THAT IT FELT LIKE THE UNIVERSE'S JUDGMENT ON ME. OF COURSE, AFTER MY LITTLE PLAYMATES BROKE MY *SKULL,* I FELT DIFFERENTLY. NO ONE DESERVES TO GO THROUGH THAT.
NOW I'M TRYING TO THINK AND ACT MORE KINDLY TOWARD MYSELF. TO STOP TREATING MY LIFE AS IF IT WERE AN *APOLOGY.*
AND WHERE MY ATTACKERS ARE CONCERNED, TO ALWAY REMEMBER THAT I AM *MORE* THAN WHAT THE TOOK FROM ME.
VERY GOOD. AND BEYOND THAT?
SHIT, I DON'T KNOW. I JUST WANT TO FOCUS ON WHAT MAKES ME HAPPY, AS SILLY AS THAT SOUNDS.
WE BOTH KNOW THERE'S NOTHING WRONG WITH BEING *SILLY.*
I'M GLAD YOU GOT YOUR SENSAYUMA BACK. FOR A WHILE THERE YOU WERE SOUNDIN' LIKE A *REAL* DRAG.
NOW WRITE ME *FUNNY THINGS* TO SAY. *I* WANNA GET BACK TO WORK, TOO.

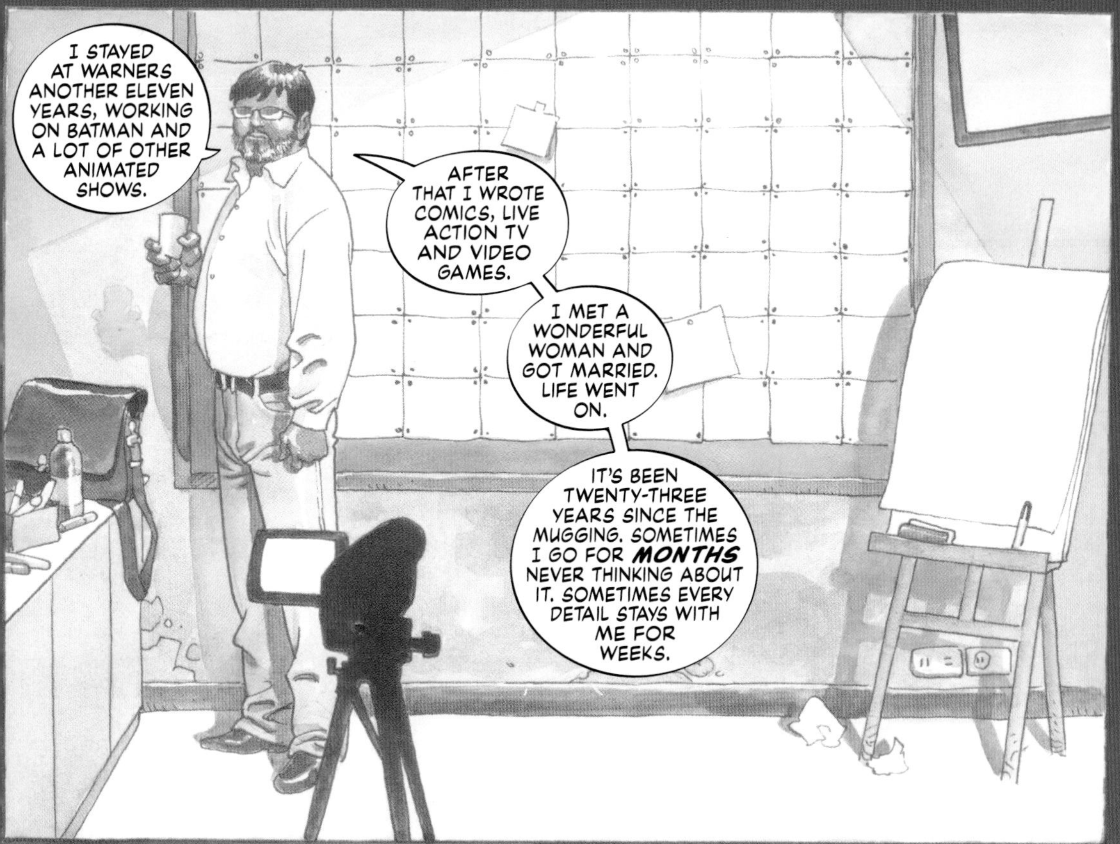
I STAYED AT WARNERS ANOTHER ELEVEN YEARS, WORKING ON BATMAN AND A LOT OF OTHER ANIMATED SHOWS.
AFTER THAT I WROTE COMICS, LIVE ACTION TV AND VIDEO GAMES.
I MET A WONDERFUL WOMAN AND GOT MARRIED. LIFE WENT ON.
IT'S BEEN TWENTY-THREE YEARS SINCE THE MUGGING. SOMETIMES I GO FOR MONTHS NEVER THINKING ABOUT IT. SOMETIMES EVERY DETAIL STAYS WITH ME FOR WEEKS.

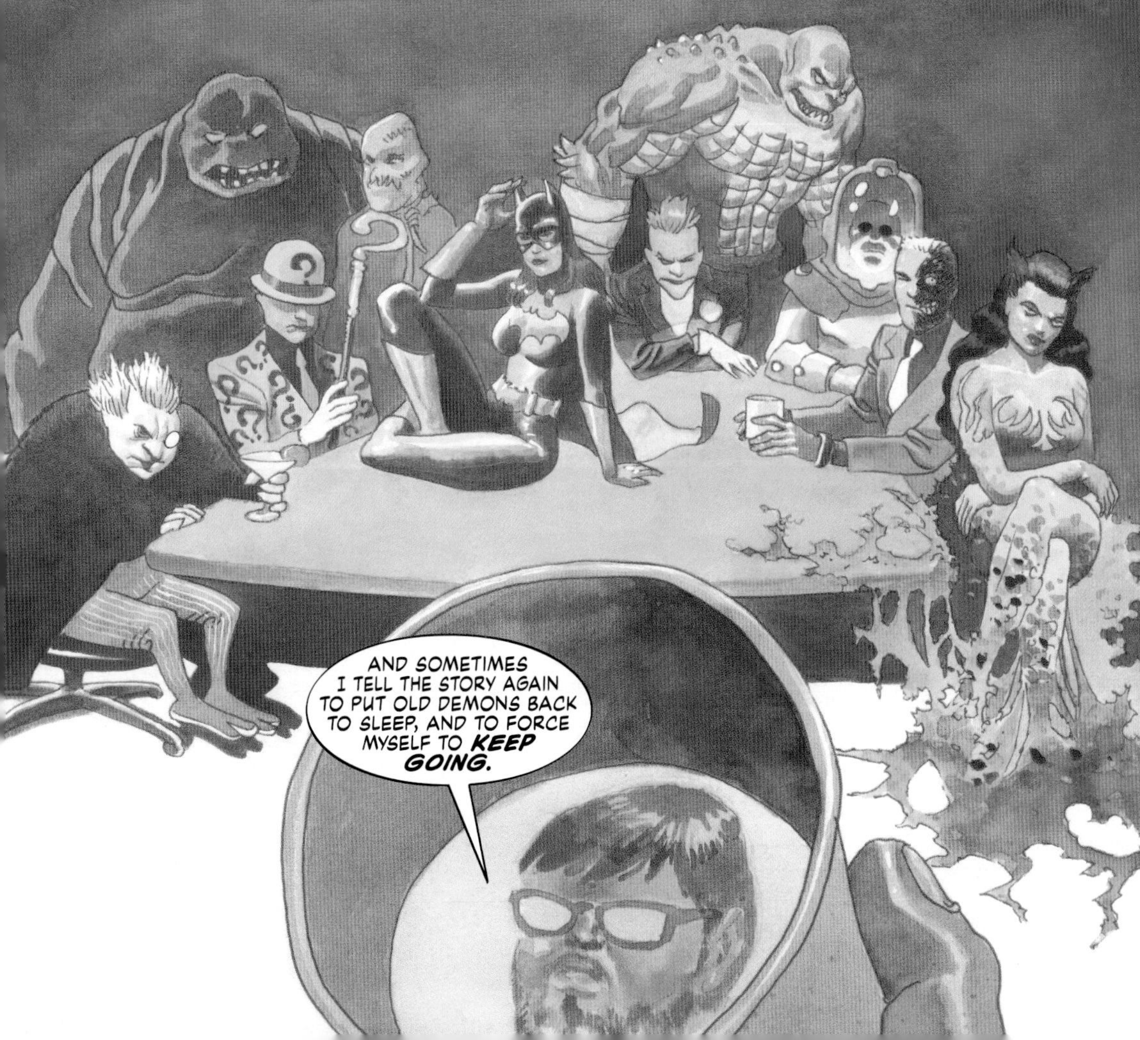
AND SOMETIMES I TELL THE STORY AGAIN TO PUT OLD DEMONS BACK TO SLEEP, AND TO FORCE MYSELF TO KEEP GOING.

SO YOUR ROSY GARDEN IS STILL FILLED WITH **THORNS**.

FROM TIME TO TIME.

BUT AT LEAST I KNOW HOW TO PRUNE THEM.

I DECIDED TO **STOP** TEARING MYSELF UP OVER SMALL DISAPPOINTMENTS.

HOW COULD I EXPECT ANYONE ELSE TO BE KIND TO ME IF I COULDN'T BE KIND TO MYSELF FIRST?

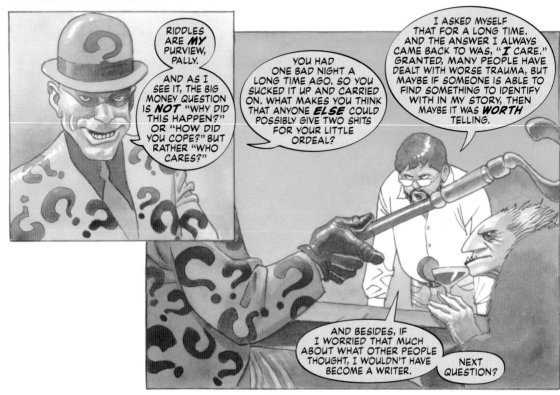

RIDDLES ARE **MY** PURVIEW, PALLY.

AND AS I SEE IT, THE BIG MONEY QUESTION IS **NOT** "WHY DID THIS HAPPEN?" OR "HOW DID YOU COPE?" BUT RATHER "WHO CARES?"

YOU HAD ONE BAD NIGHT A LONG TIME AGO. SO YOU SUCKED IT UP AND CARRIED ON. WHAT MAKES YOU THINK THAT ANYONE **ELSE** COULD POSSIBLY GIVE TWO SHITS FOR YOUR LITTLE ORDEAL?

I ASKED MYSELF THAT FOR A LONG TIME. AND THE ANSWER I ALWAYS CAME BACK TO WAS, "**I** CARE." GRANTED, MANY PEOPLE HAVE DEALT WITH WORSE TRAUMA, BUT MAYBE IF SOMEONE IS ABLE TO FIND SOMETHING TO IDENTIFY WITH IN MY STORY, THEN MAYBE IT WAS **WORTH** TELLING.

AND BESIDES, IF I WORRIED THAT MUCH ABOUT WHAT OTHER PEOPLE THOUGHT, I WOULDN'T HAVE BECOME A WRITER.

NEXT QUESTION?

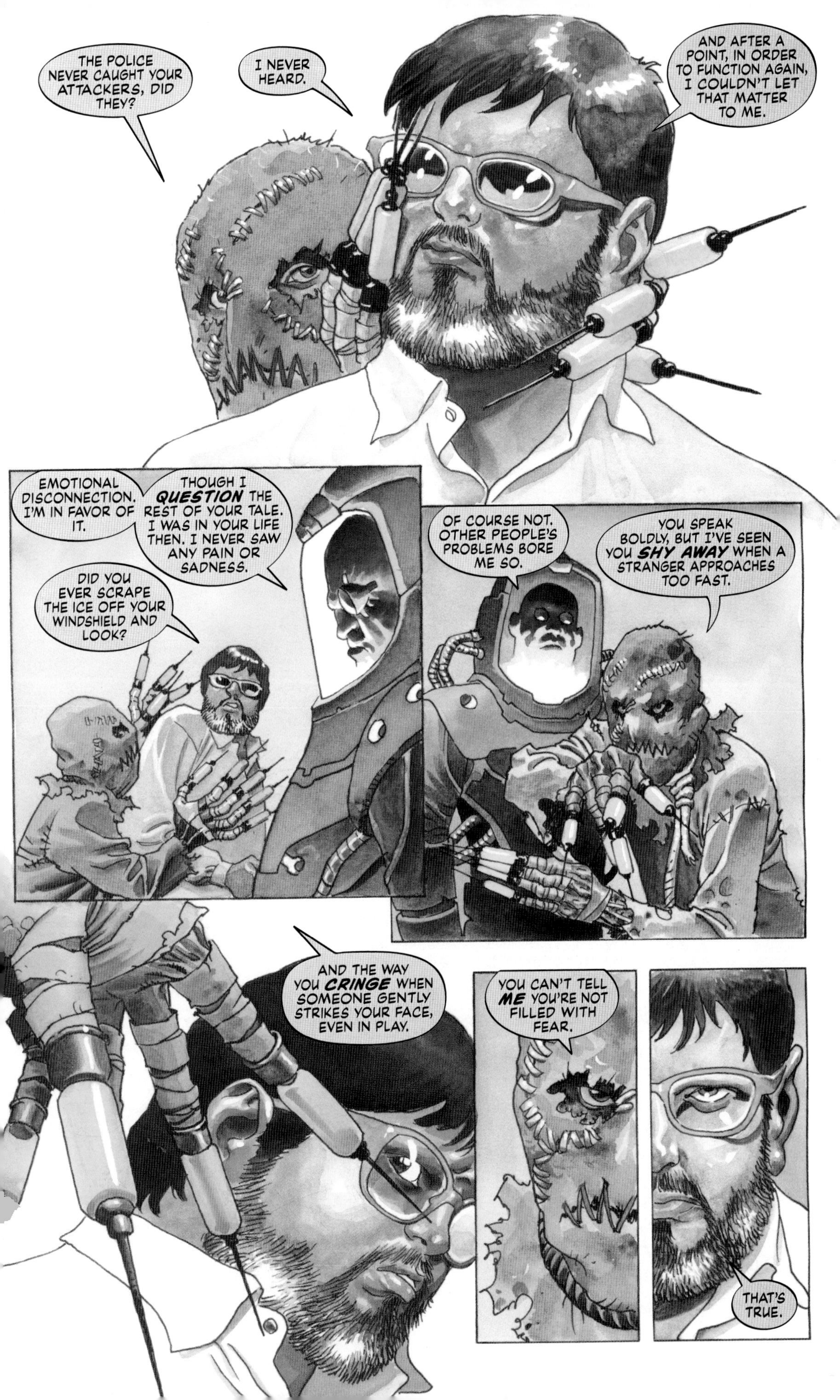

THE POLICE NEVER CAUGHT YOUR ATTACKERS, DID THEY?
I NEVER HEARD.
AND AFTER A POINT, IN ORDER TO FUNCTION AGAIN, I COULDN'T LET THAT MATTER TO ME.
EMOTIONAL DISCONNECTION. I'M IN FAVOR OF IT.
THOUGH I QUESTION THE REST OF YOUR TALE. I WAS IN YOUR LIFE THEN. I NEVER SAW ANY PAIN OR SADNESS.
DID YOU EVER SCRAPE THE ICE OFF YOUR WINDSHIELD AND LOOK?
OF COURSE NOT. OTHER PEOPLE'S PROBLEMS BORE ME SO.
YOU SPEAK BOLDLY, BUT I'VE SEEN YOU SHY AWAY WHEN A STRANGER APPROACHES TOO FAST.
AND THE WAY YOU CRINGE WHEN SOMEONE GENTLY STRIKES YOUR FACE, EVEN IN PLAY.
YOU CAN'T TELL ME YOU'RE NOT FILLED WITH FEAR.
THAT'S TRUE.

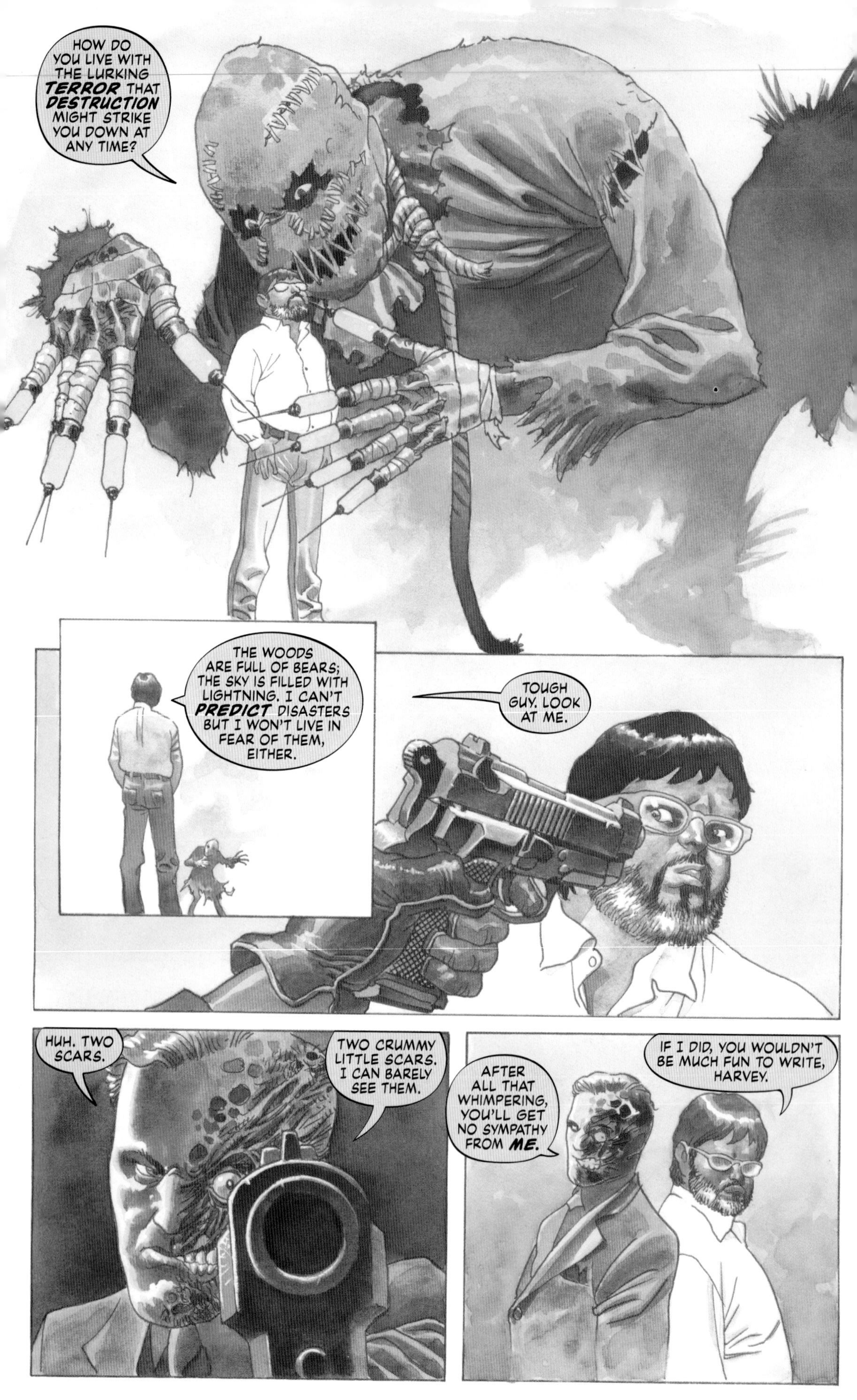

HOW DO YOU LIVE WITH THE LURKING TERROR THAT DESTRUCTION MIGHT STRIKE YOU DOWN AT ANY TIME?
THE WOODS ARE FULL OF BEARS; THE SKY IS FILLED WITH LIGHTNING. I CAN'T PREDICT DISASTERS BUT I WON'T LIVE IN FEAR OF THEM, EITHER.
TOUGH GUY. LOOK AT ME.
HUH. TWO SCARS.
TWO CRUMMY LITTLE SCARS. I CAN BARELY SEE THEM.
AFTER ALL THAT WHIMPERING, YOU'LL GET NO SYMPATHY FROM ME.
IF I DID, YOU WOULDN'T BE MUCH FUN TO WRITE, HARVEY.

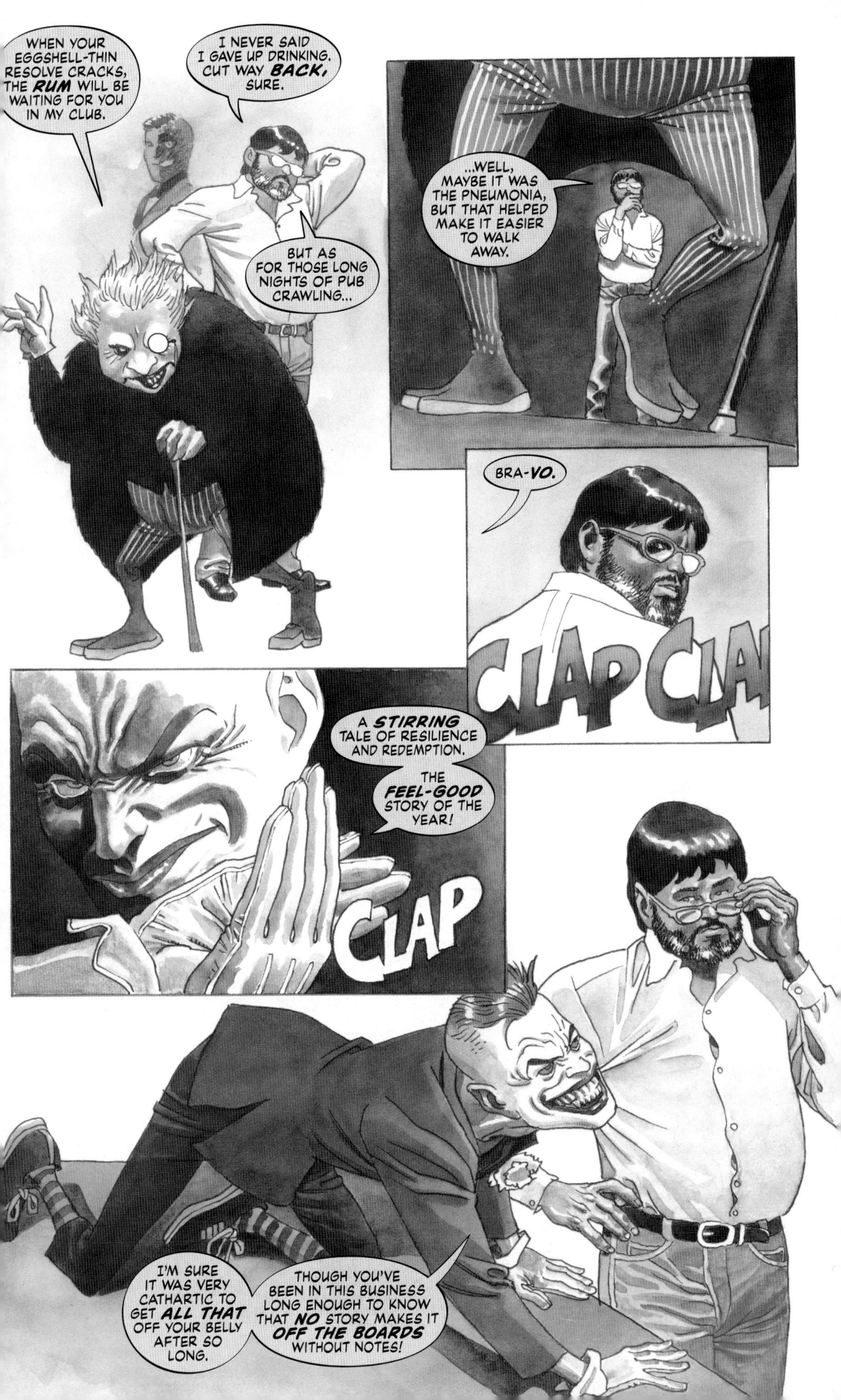

WHEN YOUR EGGSHELL-THIN RESOLVE CRACKS, THE RUM WILL BE WAITING FOR YOU IN MY CLUB.
I NEVER SAID I GAVE UP DRINKING. CUT WAY BACK, SURE.
BUT AS FOR THOSE LONG NIGHTS OF PUB CRAWLING...
...WELL, MAYBE IT WAS THE PNEUMONIA, BUT THAT HELPED MAKE IT EASIER TO WALK AWAY.
BRA-VO.
CLAP CLAP
A STIRRING TALE OF RESILIENCE AND REDEMPTION.
THE FEEL-GOOD STORY OF THE YEAR!
CLAP
I'M SURE IT WAS VERY CATHARTIC TO GET ALL THAT OFF YOUR BELLY AFTER SO LONG.
THOUGH YOU'VE BEEN IN THIS BUSINESS LONG ENOUGH TO KNOW THAT NO STORY MAKES IT OFF THE BOARDS WITHOUT NOTES!

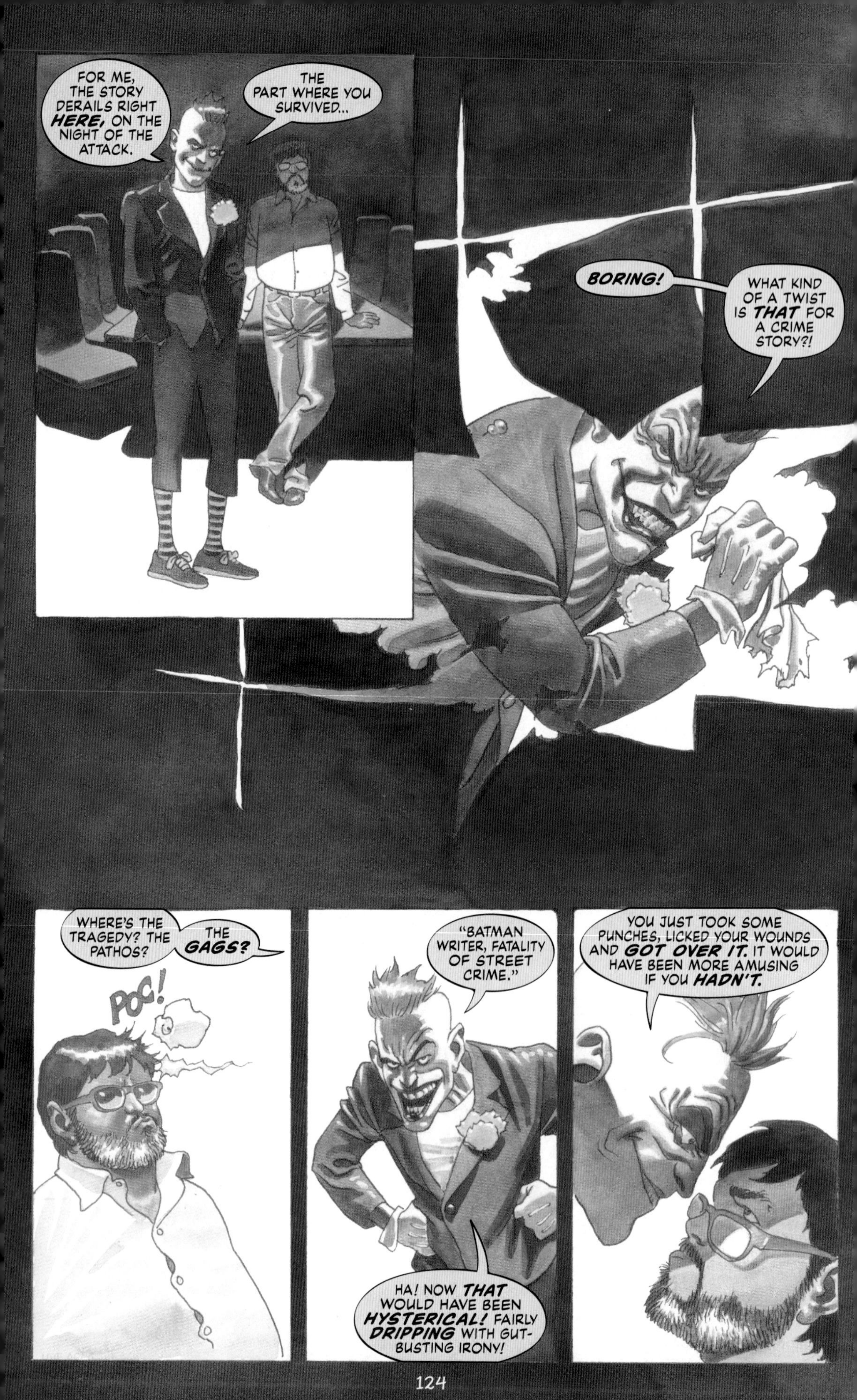
FOR ME, THE STORY DERAILS RIGHT **HERE,** ON THE NIGHT OF THE ATTACK.
THE PART WHERE YOU SURVIVED...
BORING!
WHAT KIND OF A TWIST IS **THAT** FOR A CRIME STORY?!
WHERE'S THE TRAGEDY? THE PATHOS?
THE **GAGS?**
POC!
"BATMAN WRITER, FATALITY OF STREET CRIME."
HA! NOW **THAT** WOULD HAVE BEEN **HYSTERICAL!** FAIRLY **DRIPPING** WITH GUT-BUSTING IRONY!
YOU JUST TOOK SOME PUNCHES, LICKED YOUR WOUNDS AND **GOT OVER IT.** IT WOULD HAVE BEEN MORE AMUSING IF YOU **HADN'T.**

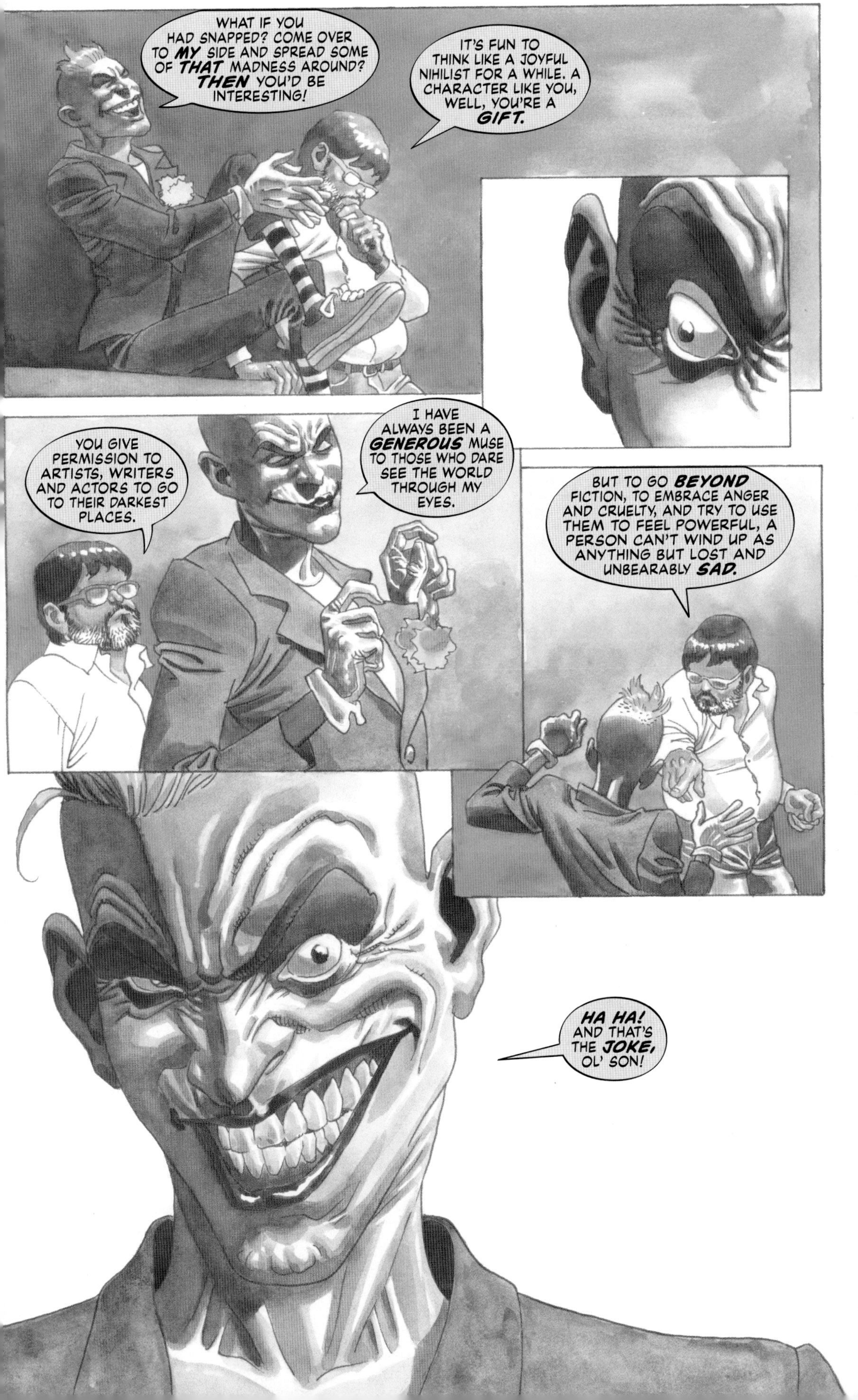
WHAT IF YOU HAD SNAPPED? COME OVER TO MY SIDE AND SPREAD SOME OF THAT MADNESS AROUND? THEN YOU'D BE INTERESTING!
IT'S FUN TO THINK LIKE A JOYFUL NIHILIST FOR A WHILE. A CHARACTER LIKE YOU, WELL, YOU'RE A GIFT.
YOU GIVE PERMISSION TO ARTISTS, WRITERS AND ACTORS TO GO TO THEIR DARKEST PLACES.
I HAVE ALWAYS BEEN A GENEROUS MUSE TO THOSE WHO DARE SEE THE WORLD THROUGH MY EYES.
BUT TO GO BEYOND FICTION, TO EMBRACE ANGER AND CRUELTY, AND TRY TO USE THEM TO FEEL POWERFUL, A PERSON CAN'T WIND UP AS ANYTHING BUT LOST AND UNBEARABLY SAD.
HA HA! AND THAT'S THE JOKE, OL' SON!

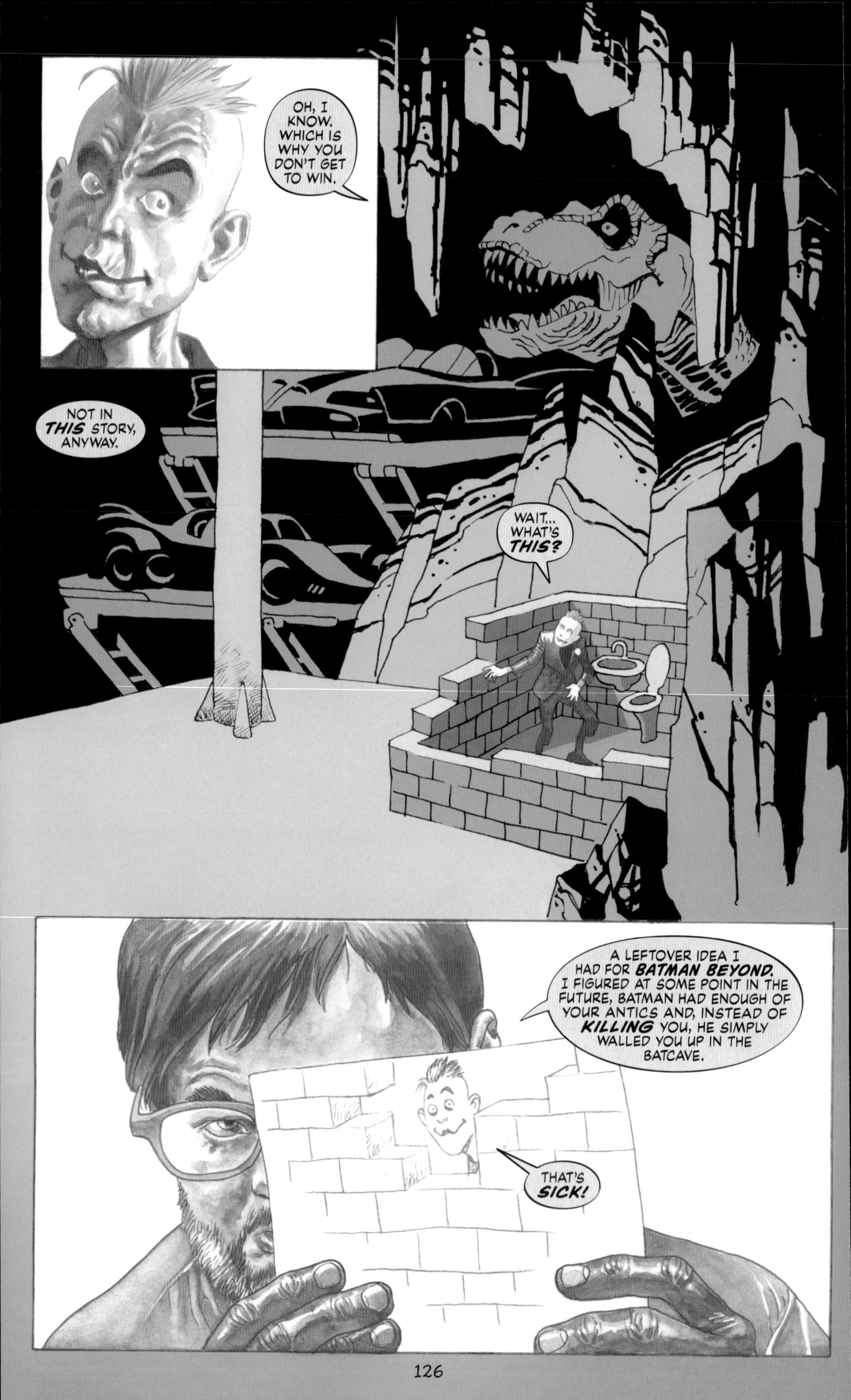
OH, I KNOW. WHICH IS WHY YOU DON'T GET TO WIN.
NOT IN THIS STORY, ANYWAY.
WAIT... WHAT'S THIS?
A LEFTOVER IDEA I HAD FOR BATMAN BEYOND. I FIGURED AT SOME POINT IN THE FUTURE, BATMAN HAD ENOUGH OF YOUR ANTICS AND, INSTEAD OF KILLING YOU, HE SIMPLY WALLED YOU UP IN THE BATCAVE.
THAT'S SICK!

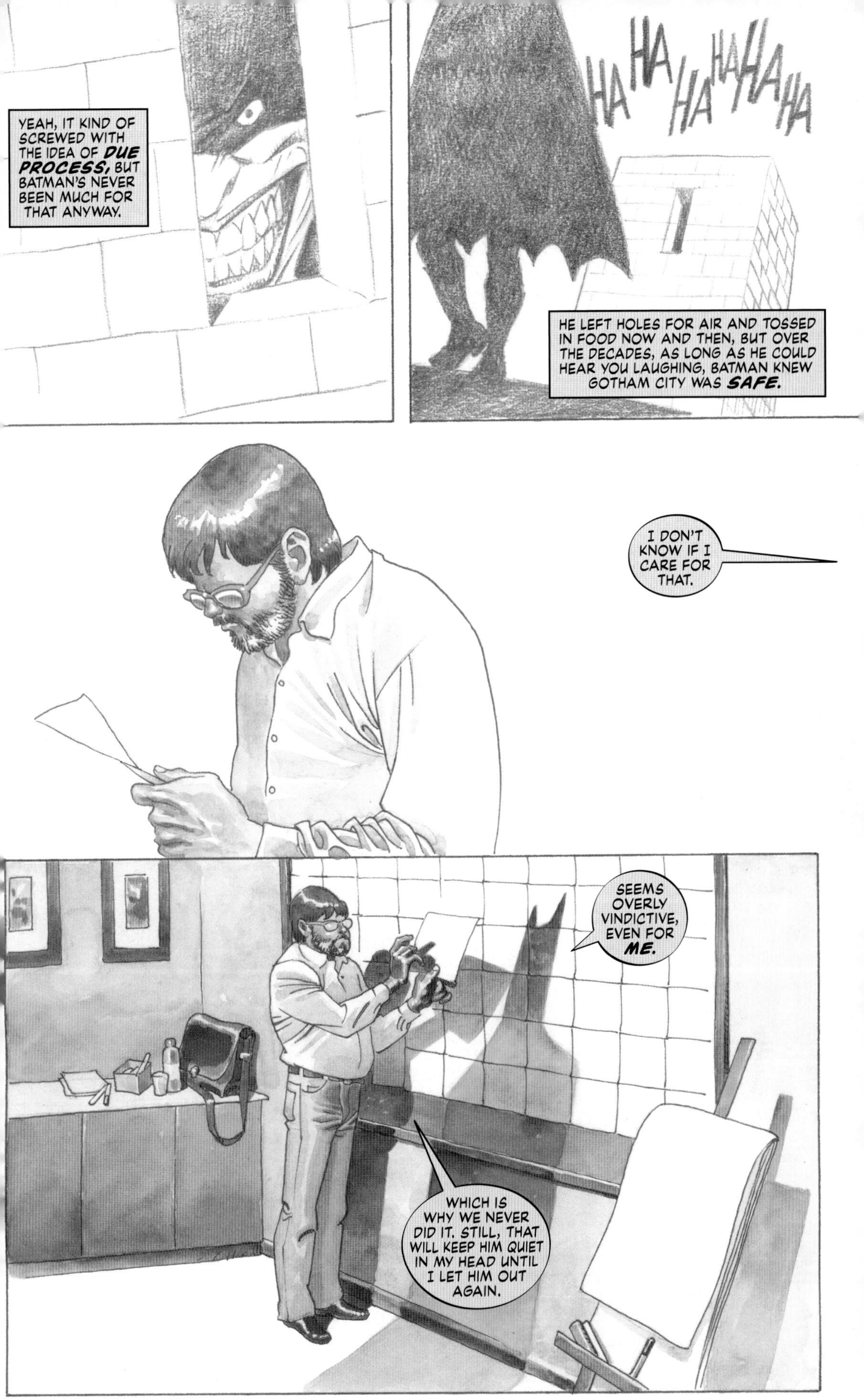

YEAH, IT KIND OF SCREWED WITH THE IDEA OF DUE PROCESS, BUT BATMAN'S NEVER BEEN MUCH FOR THAT ANYWAY.
HAHAHAHAHAHAHA
HE LEFT HOLES FOR AIR AND TOSSED IN FOOD NOW AND THEN, BUT OVER THE DECADES, AS LONG AS HE COULD HEAR YOU LAUGHING, BATMAN KNEW GOTHAM CITY WAS SAFE.
I DON'T KNOW IF I CARE FOR THAT.
SEEMS OVERLY VINDICTIVE, EVEN FOR ME.
WHICH IS WHY WE NEVER DID IT. STILL, THAT WILL KEEP HIM QUIET IN MY HEAD UNTIL I LET HIM OUT AGAIN.

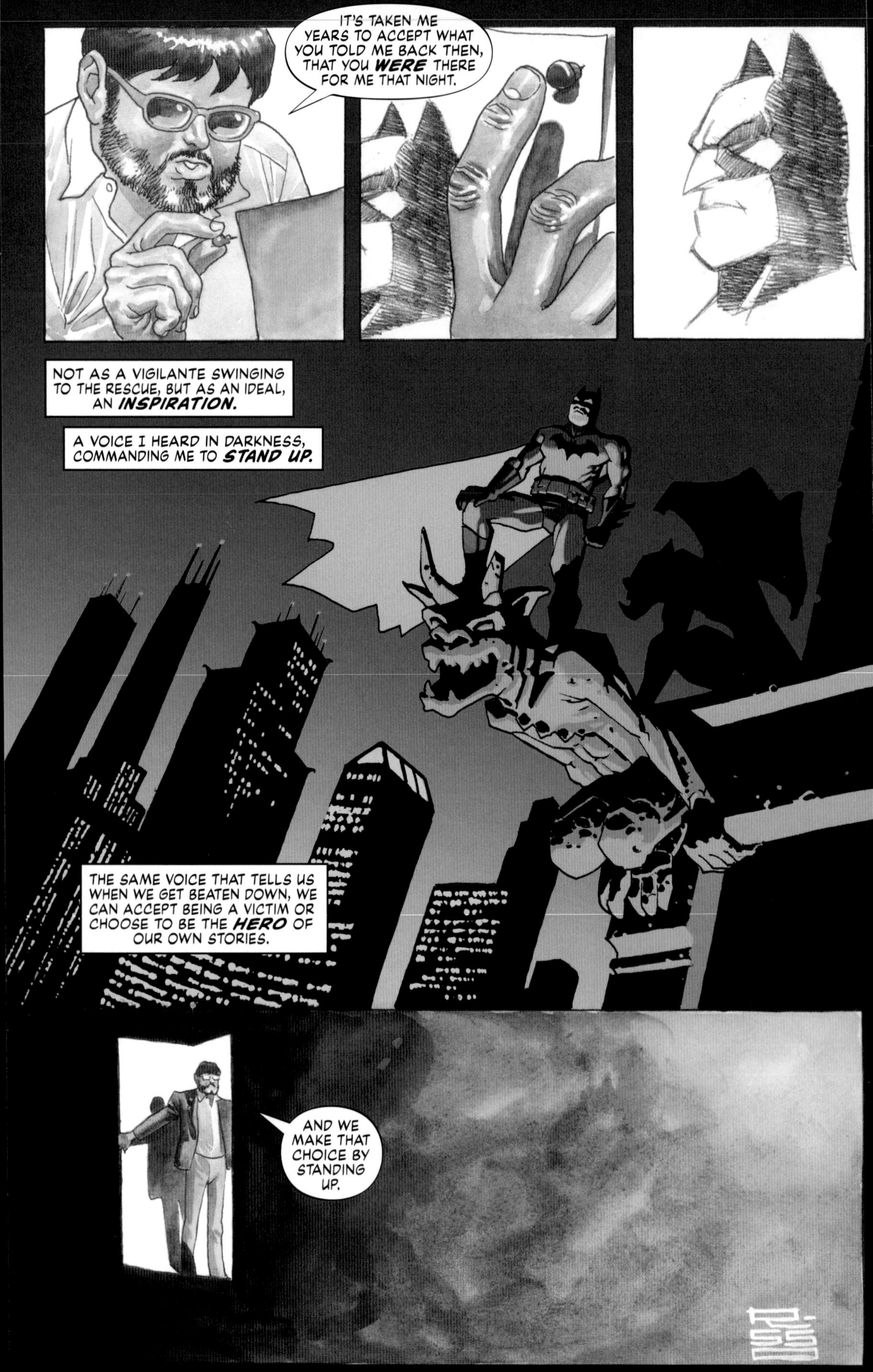
IT'S TAKEN ME YEARS TO ACCEPT WHAT YOU TOLD ME BACK THEN, THAT YOU WERE THERE FOR ME THAT NIGHT.
NOT AS A VIGILANTE SWINGING TO THE RESCUE, BUT AS AN IDEAL, AN INSPIRATION.
A VOICE I HEARD IN DARKNESS, COMMANDING ME TO STAND UP.
THE SAME VOICE THAT TELLS US WHEN WE GET BEATEN DOWN, WE CAN ACCEPT BEING A VICTIM OR CHOOSE TO BE THE HERO OF OUR OWN STORIES.
AND WE MAKE THAT CHOICE BY STANDING UP.

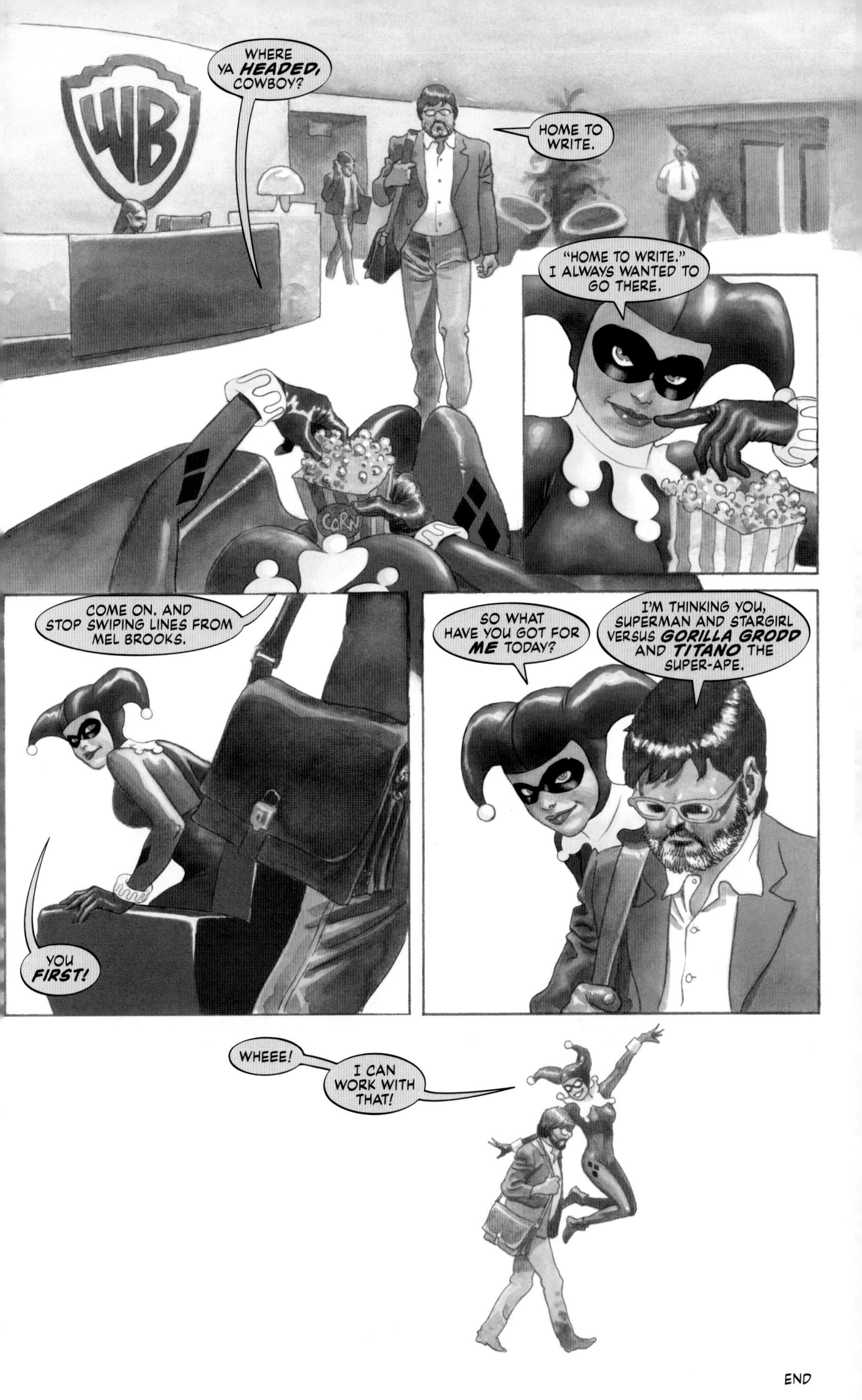

WHERE YA HEADED, COWBOY?
HOME TO WRITE.
"HOME TO WRITE." I ALWAYS WANTED TO GO THERE.
COME ON. AND STOP SWIPING LINES FROM MEL BROOKS.
YOU FIRST!
SO WHAT HAVE YOU GOT FOR ME TODAY?
I'M THINKING YOU, SUPERMAN AND STARGIRL VERSUS GORILLA GRODD AND TITANO THE SUPER-APE.
WHEEE!
I CAN WORK WITH THAT!
END

PAUL DINI writes for television, cartoons, and comic books. He lives in Los Angeles with his wife, Misty Lee, and their Boston terriers, Pixie and the Tank.

EDUARDO RISSO was born in Leones, Argentina, in 1959.

Risso completed his first professional work for the daily paper *La Nación* and the magazines *Eroticon* and *Satiricon*. In 1981, he started working for Columba editions, pencilling the series *El Angel* and *Julio César*. In 1987 and 1988, Risso worked with writer Ricardo Barreiro on the comics *Parque Chas* and *Cain*.

At the same time, Risso was working on the comic *Fulu*, with writer Carlos Trillo, which led to their continued collaboration on several series including *Simon: An American Tale* (Italy and France), *Video Noire* (Italy and France), *Borderline* (Italy), and *Chicanos* (Italy and France).

In 1997, Risso started working on *Alien: Resurrection* at Dark Horse, among other titles. He also drew several short stories for Vertigo and teamed up with Brian Azzarello on the miniseries JONNY DOUBLE, which led to the creation of the multiple Eisner Award-winning series 100 BULLETS. Since then, Risso and Azzarello have continued to work together on hugely successful books including *Batman*, on the critically acclaimed "Broken City" storyline, *Batman: Flashpoint*, and more recently on a Wonder Woman story in *DKIII*.

Risso has also teamed with Brian K. Vaughan on *Wolverine: Logan*, with Glen David Gold for the short story "The Spirit," and with Jimmy Palmiotti and Justin Gray for *Jonah Hex*.

Since 2010, Risso has been the acting president of the Crack Bang Boom International Comics Convention in Rosario, Argentina.

He has won the Eisner, Harvey and Yellow Kid awards for 100 BULLETS as Best Artist, and the Harvey Award for his *Tales of Terror* as the Best American Edition of Foreign Material.

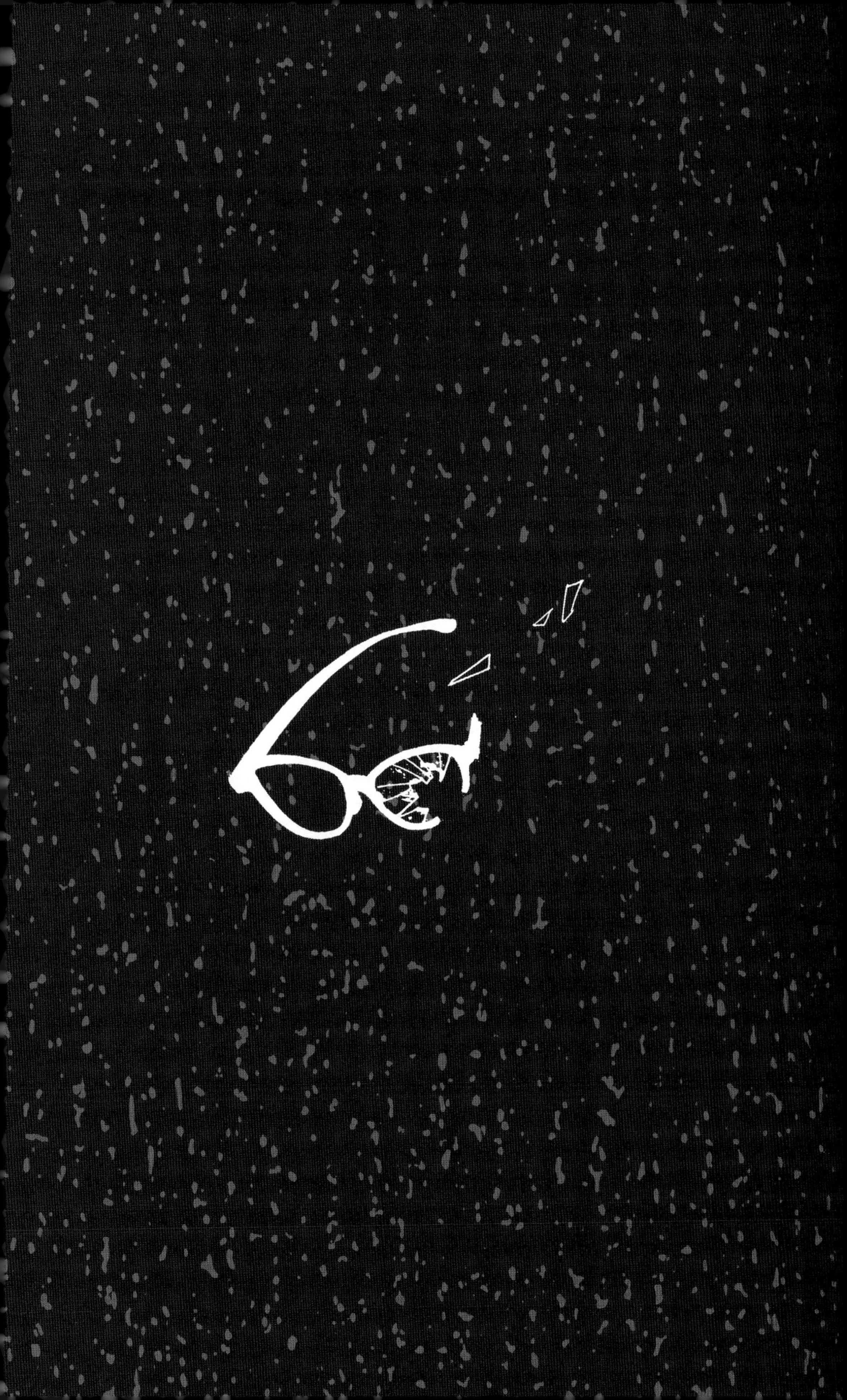

"Chaotic and unabashedly fun."—IGN

"I'm enjoying HARLEY QUINN a great deal;
it's silly, it's funny, it's irreverent."
—COMIC BOOK RESOURCES

HARLEY QUINN
VOLUME 1: HOT IN THE CITY

AMANDA **CONNER**   JIMMY **PALMIOTTI**   CHAD **HARDIN**
STEPHANE **ROUX**   ALEX **SINCLAIR**   PAUL **MOUNTS**

"Chaotic and unabashedly fun."—IGN

*"I'm enjoying HARLEY QUINN a great deal;
it's silly, it's funny, it's irreverent."*
—COMIC BOOK RESOURCES

HARLEY QUINN
VOLUME 1: PRELUDES AND KNOCK-KNOCK JOKES

**HARLEY QUINN VOL. 2:
NIGHT AND DAY**

**with KARL KESEL,
TERRY DODSON,
and PETE WOODS**

**HARLEY QUINN VOL. 3:
VELCOME TO METROPOLIS**

**with KARL KESEL,
TERRY DODSON and
CRAIG ROUSSEAU**

**HARLEY QUINN VOL. 4:
VENGEANCE UNLIMITED**

**with A.J. LIEBERMAN
and MIKE HUDDLESTON**

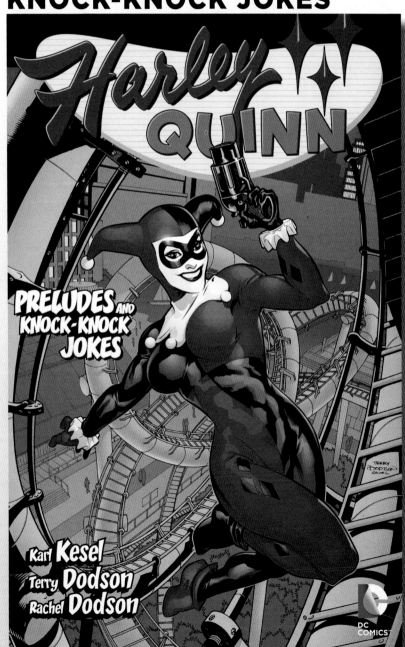

Karl **Kesel**
Terry **Dodson**
Rachel **Dodson**

DC
COMICS™

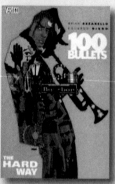